# INSIDERS' GUIDE® TO
# OMAHA & LINCOLN

## HELP US KEEP THIS GUIDE UP TO DATE

We would love to hear from you concerning your experiences with this guide and how you feel it could be improved and kept up to date. Please send your comments and suggestions to:

editorial@GlobePequot.com

Thanks for your input, and happy travels!

# INSIDERS' GUIDE® TO
# OMAHA & LINCOLN

FIRST EDITION

## SARAH BAKER HANSEN

**INSIDERS'** GUIDE

GUILFORD, CONNECTICUT
AN IMPRINT OF GLOBE PEQUOT PRESS

All the information in this guidebook is subject to change. We recommend that you call ahead to obtain current information before traveling.

# INSIDERS' GUIDE ®

Editor: Amy Lyons
Project Editor: Heather Santiago
Layout: Joanna Beyer
Text Design: Sheryl Kober
Maps: Daniel Lloyd © Morris Book Publishing, LLC

ISBN 978-0-7627-6474-7

Printed in the United States of America
10 9 8 7 6 5 4 3 2 1

# CONTENTS

## CONTENTS

To Matthew

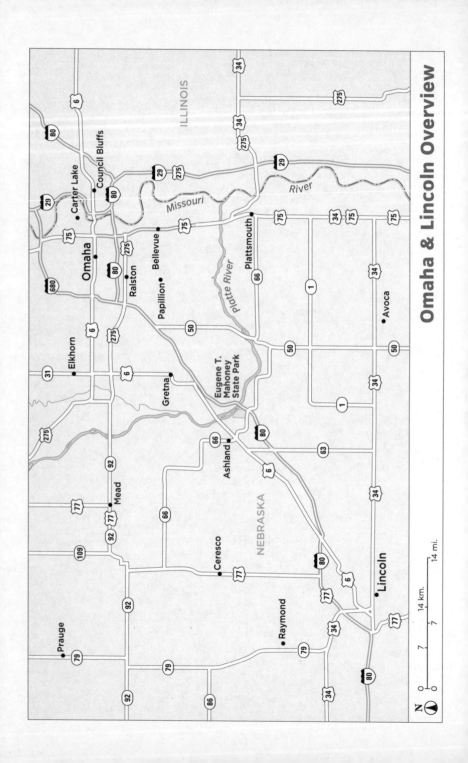

# Omaha & Lincoln Overview

# INTRODUCTION

People from Omaha have the city in their blood. Those born here often leave and find them-selves feeling the yen to come back. The city's gravitational pull on its residents is an open secret, and newcomers quickly feel it too. Omaha's hidden gem of a music scene, its quaint Old Market in the heart of downtown, the low cost and high quality of life, and the vast array of scenic drives beyond the city's borders are strong magnets.

I was born in Omaha, and I live there now. Like many Omahans, I didn't come to appreci-ate the city until I was older. I left and came back, realizing that it wasn't just an OK place to live; it was a great place to live.

I've also called Lincoln home, as a student at the University of Nebraska–Lincoln, the state's flagship school. Now I work in the capital city, commuting back and forth five days a week between Nebraska's two largest metropolitan areas.

When I was offered the chance to write a book about Omaha, I almost couldn't believe it. For three years, I worked as the media relations director for the Nebraska Division of Travel and Tourism, acting as an ambassador for the state both inside and outside its borders. I put thousands of miles on state vehicles, visiting places I'd never even considered visiting, and learning as much as I could about where I was born. The friendly, local experts in tiny towns across Nebraska were my most valuable resource, and with their help I found myself hunting for the highest point in Nebraska, running my fingers over ruts worn from wagons that tra-versed the Oregon Trail, and hanging out with astronomy lovers searching for stars in some of the darkest patches of night sky left in the entire world.

I brought travel writers and media to the state and introduced them to what it had to offer; those trips focused mostly on Omaha and Lincoln. Usually before they left, they told me two things: that they had no idea what Nebraska was like, and that they planned to come back soon.

I also learned a lot about my hometown during those three years. When I told other Nebraskans I lived in Omaha, they almost always asked me questions about it: where to stay, what to do, where to eat. Non-Nebraskans asked me the same questions, and I wanted to have good answers at hand. I became a de-facto Omaha expert.

For me, this book is truly the perfect assignment.

If you haven't ever been to Nebraska—truth is, many haven't—this book is a good place to begin. Nebraskans are known for their honest Midwestern hospitality, and you'll find that in Omaha and Lincoln both. You'll also find a large amount of things to do: good restaurants and great steaks, an adventurous live music scene, a strong local commitment to art and architecture, and some of the country's top tourist attractions.

People come to eastern Nebraska for myriad reasons: to serve at the Air Force Base in Bel-levue; to enroll as a student at the University of Nebraska; or to work in telecommunications or health care, two of the area's largest industries. They hit Omaha in the spring to check out the annual NCAA College World Series, and Lincoln in the fall for a Nebraska Cornhuskers football game. Every summer they descend on Omaha to get some stock tips from Warren Buffett during his annual Berkshire Hathaway Shareholders meeting and convention. (Those "Oracle of Omaha" fans also can't wait to cut into a juicy steak at his favorite locally owned, meaty outpost.)

Whatever the reason you find yourself in Nebraska, you'll be surprised. And I guarantee whether or not you're a permanent transplant or simply a tourist, you'll leave with a bit of the Cornhusker state in your blood, too.

**Part 1**

# WELCOME!

# HOW TO USE THIS BOOK

Welcome to the *Insider's Guide to Omaha & Lincoln!* This book has everything a newcomer will need to learn about visiting—or living in—the two largest cities in eastern Nebraska.

This book aims to provide an insiders' view of things to do, places to go, and general information about the area. What makes this book different from a visitor's guide or tourism brochure is that we are allowed to have opinions. All of the information presented in this book was gathered from personal experience, and the author allowed herself to remain anonymous while doing this research, seeing the city just like you—as a visitor. The end result is a set of travel guidelines that do not pander to certain businesses, but rather present a true-to-life collection of listings that will help you make your decisions about how to best experience both Omaha and Lincoln. Straying from these pages is encouraged. One of the best parts about travel is self-discovery, so use this book as a jumping-off point to explore.

Throughout the book are **Insiders' Tips** (indicated by an **i** ), which give you some tidbits gleaned from locals on things you might not otherwise have known about; sidebars, which condense practical information and basic facts into an easy-to-read list; and **Close-ups** that spotlight things worth spending more time on.

You'll also find listings accompanied by the ✳ symbol—these are our top picks for attractions, restaurants, accommodations, and everything in between that you shouldn't miss while you're in the area. You want the best this region has to offer? Go with our **Insiders' Choice.**

The chapters at the front of the book are helpful for vacation planning. The Getting Here, Getting Around chapter gives a good overview of driving in Nebraska and how the two cities are laid out, and lets you know where things are located.

The History chapter tells the combined story of Lincoln and Omaha's past. The summary of events hits the big points, and will give the newcomer a good idea of what in the past created these two thriving cities as they are now.

The Annual Events & Festivities chapter presents a month-by-month listing of stuff going on in Lincoln and Omaha year-round; the summers are full of outdoor concerts and festivals, while the winter activities celebrate the holidays and the beauty of the season.

Accommodations and Attractions are also helpful for vacationers, or those looking for an adventure in their home state. Eastern Nebraska offers a wealth of things to do, as well as some lovely scenic drives and road trip opportunities.

Chapters about the cities' nightlife, food scenes, and family activities are presented in the form of listings. Restaurants are sorted by cuisine. Don't be afraid to try something not listed here—again, it's about self-discovery. Nebraska is a beef state, and so if you're after a steak, be sure to check out the full array of places where you can feast on the food Nebraska is known for. Nebraska is a foodie's paradise: When it comes to eating, Omaha and Lincoln offer something for every palate. The Kidstuff chapters explore the many family-friendly activities each city offers.

Shopping is a popular pursuit here, and Omaha especially has lots to offer. Omaha and Lincoln are an antiquer's paradise, and we've provided a special section on the hobby for those people to enjoy the thrill of the hunt during their visit.

Speaking of hunting, Nebraska is an outdoorsman's dream. Whether it be harvesting animals, spending time riding a bike down the state's rails to trails systems, or simply enjoying nature, there's a lot to do in the outdoors in Nebraska. Spectator sports in Nebraska become big in the spring and fall, during the annual College World Series and the Nebraska Cornhuskers football team's season. The arts in Nebraska are also a pretty big deal, and Lincoln and Omaha have some cutting-edge, one-of-a-kind galleries, museums, and activities surrounding their two thriving arts communities.

There's lots of places to drive between Omaha and Lincoln, and the cities are so close—just 50 miles apart—that one can make a day trip back and forth to experience the other place. Scenic drives, country experiences, and agritourism—tourism based on the state's agricultural business—are all available in Omaha and Lincoln. Be sure to check out the sections concerning each.

Those who are relocating to Nebraska—welcome! Check out the blue-tabbed pages at the back of the book where you will find the **Living Here** appendix. It offers sections on relocation, retirement, education, health and wellness, and media. It provides quick answers to common questions, and gives a good idea of the lay of the land. If you have kids, you'll want to take a look at the education and child care section, which provides an overview of the city's day care options, school systems, and colleges. The sections on health and wellness will point you toward the hospitals and care centers in Omaha and Lincoln.

This book isn't a phone book. It must be said that businesses come and go as these two cities grow and change, so information can change quickly. Even websites can be wrong if they aren't updated regularly. As such, the information provided here has been kept to generalities rather than specifics, and it is always a good idea to call beforehand to confirm things like hours of operation or entrance fees.

# AREA OVERVIEW

**W**elcome to Omaha, the largest city in Nebraska, and Lincoln, the state's capital city. Eastern Nebraska is the most populous side of the state; most people live in either Omaha or Lincoln, or in a suburb in between the two. Omaha's population, including its suburbs, is close to a half million. Omaha's westward growth continues to make the gap between it and Lincoln smaller, so now only about an hour's drive separates them.

## OVERVIEW

Omaha sits on the banks of the Missouri river. The city's relationship with the river has been long and complicated; only recently did the city begin to redevelop the riverfront area, and it's become a popular spot for recreation, dining, and live music in the summer. Omaha is also a business hub. Five *Fortune* 500 companies call Omaha home: ConAgra, Peter Kiewit Sons, Berkshire Hathaway, Union Pacific, and Mutual of Omaha. More than 30 other Fortune 500 companies have manufacturing plants in the city.

Omaha is also a hub for the insurance industry. Close to 30 insurance companies have their headquarters in Omaha. Other large companies based in Omaha include Omaha Steaks, Oriental Trading Company, Pamida, Valmont Industries, and Godfather's Pizza.

Lincoln, a city of about 250,000, is one of the fastest growing metro areas in the Midwest. Lincoln has more parkland per capita than any other city in the United States, and a great trails network. The Mo Pac trail runs 26 miles along an abandoned railroad corridor and is one of the state's most popular spots for running, biking, and walking.

Eventually, the trail will reach from the center of Lincoln all the way to Omaha. Lincoln is also home to the state's flagship university. The University of Nebraska–Lincoln (UNL) enrolls close to 25,000 students, and its legendary graduates include investor Warren Buffett, comedian Johnny Carson, authors Willa Cather and Mari Sandoz, and many others. UNL is a major research university and just recently became a member of the Big 10 conference.

Both cities continue to experience economic growth. In the late 1990s, Omaha built the Qwest Center Omaha, an arena and convention center and the Holland Performing Arts Center. Gallup company built its Gallup University campus on the Omaha riverfront and First National Bank of Omaha and Union Pacific both built new headquarters in downtown Omaha. Hundreds of old buildings in downtown Omaha were converted into condominiums. The First National Tower is the tallest building between Denver and Minneapolis.

Lincoln is constructing its own arena, in the historic Haymarket district, and the University of Nebraska–Lincoln has plans to construct the Innovation Campus on the state's former fairgrounds; the campus will create a public/private sector hub for research.

Both Omaha and Lincoln are business hubs and growing cities, but, above all, they're full of friendly people and nationally recognized as great places with an affordable, desirable way of life.

## ENVIRONMENT

Omaha and Lincoln have a traditional Midwestern climate and enjoy all four seasons. Warm, humid summers are the norm in eastern Nebraska, and the average high temperature in the mid-80s means things get rather toasty from June until late August. You'll want to be prepared with a big tube of sun block and central air conditioning. Winters are cold and snowy, with average highs in the 30s. Snow accumulation can vary, but the average is around seven inches in January. Winds make blowing snow a concern for travelers. The spring and fall seasons in Omaha and Lincoln are particularly lovely. Watching the wide array of flowering trees burst to life seems to wake everyone from the long slumber of winter. Eastern Nebraskans often have wide smiles the first day in March or April when the snow melts and they can leave their winter coats in the closet. Fall, too, is a Midwestern favorite, and with an average temperature from September to November of 65 degrees, it's a great time to be outside. The fall also brings a tourist favorite: scenic foliage drives. There are lots of them around and between Lincoln and Omaha, and even within the city the drive to and from work or school means you'll be surrounded by leaves in shades of gold, ruby,

rust, and orange. The state's strong agritourism industry means all four seasons bring lots of farm-to-table experiences: farmers' markets in the summer, you-pick-it pumpkin and berry operations in the fall. Winter is the time for cross-country skiing and snow sledding at the outdoor outfitters around and between the two cities.

> **i** Nebraska weather is notoriously temperamental and can change at a moment's notice; it would be wise to check with a local source on the day's conditions before venturing out.

## OMAHA NEIGHBORHOODS

### Downtown

Downtown Omaha has seen a recent revitalization on a number of levels: the Omaha riverfront is bustling with new business and annual festivals, the historic Old Market district continues to be one of the city's most popular tourist attractions and a vast array of condominium development has brought new life to the city's oldest neighborhood. The Old Market is a shopping and eating destination within a historic patch of three square blocks. One-of-a-kind restaurants and locally owned shops, a weekly summer farmers' market, horse-drawn carriage rides, and brick streets make this area a huge draw for locals and visitors both. Downtown living can be pricey for those looking to buy, and many of the condos are owned by young, single people; newly married childless couples; or empty nesters looking for an urban escape. Lots of affordable apartment living options surround the Old Market, though the options in the Market proper aren't as plentiful. The Missouri Riverfront, revitalized in the past 10 years, is

# Vital Statistics for Omaha & Lincoln

**Founded:** Omaha, 1854; Lincoln, 1856

**Area codes:** 402 and 531, 308 for western Nebraska

**Population:** Omaha, 427,872; Lincoln, 281,531

**County:** Omaha is in Douglas and Sarpy Counties, Lincoln is in Lancaster County

**State capital:** Lincoln

**Area cities:** Omaha, Papillion, Bellevue, Gretna, Elkhorn, Lincoln

**Average temperatures:** January: high 32, low 12; August: high 85, low 64

**Annual rainfall:** 30.2 inches

**Average days of sunshine:** 219

**Colleges and universities:** University of Nebraska System, includes campus in Omaha, Lincoln, and Kearney; Creighton University; College of St. Mary; Metro Community College; Southeast Community College; Union College

**Time zone:** Central Standard Time; parts of far western Nebraska are in the Mountain Daylight Time zone

**Major area employers:** Mutual of Omaha, ConAgra Foods, University of Nebraska, Union Pacific, Woodmen of the World, Gallup, Alegent Health Care, Blue Cross Blue Shield of Nebraska, Bryan LGH Medical Center, Cabela's, First Data Resources, First National Bank of Omaha, Info USA, National Research Corporation, Kiewit, Werner Enterprises, West Corporation

**Famous Omahans and Lincolnites:** President Gerald Ford, Warren Buffett (financial phenom), Joba Chamberlain (baseball player), Malcom X (civil rights leader), Marlon Brando (actor), Clayton Anderson (astronaut), Fred Astaire (dancer), Montgomery Clift (actor), Henry Fonda (actor), Nick Nolte (actor)

now home to restaurants; a riverwalk; and the Bob Kerrey Pedestrian Bridge, which spans the river from the Omaha side to Council Bluffs, Iowa.

## Dundee

Located in central Omaha, Dundee is one of the area's largest historic residential districts. Full of mature trees, historic houses, and large parks, Dundee also has a bustling strip of retail development that continues to grow. The west side of the neighborhood is bordered by Memorial Park, a site for live concerts in the summer (an annual Fourth of July event is especially well attended) and a crowded destination for sledding in the winter. Along Underwood Avenue, lots of locally owned restaurants, bars, and shops are a destination for people around the city: the diverse amount of cuisine—including French bistro, American bar food, a popular

**Major airports:** Commercial air travel is available at two airports in Lincoln and Omaha as well as several regional airports across the state.

**Public transportation:** Greyhound has stops in 16 cities across Nebraska. Amtrak stops in both Omaha and Lincoln.

**Military bases:** Offutt Air Force Base

**Driving laws:** Children up to age 6 are required to ride in an approved car seat or booster seat appropriate for the child's size and age. Children 6 to 18 must wear a seat belt. Seat belts are required for adults in the front seat.

**Alcohol laws:** You must be 21 or older to consume alcoholic beverages in Nebraska. Beer and wine can be purchased after 6 a.m. on Sunday and other time during the week. Restaurants may serve liquor on Sunday after noon. Legislation passed in 2010 allows for off-sale liquor and bars to remain open until 2 a.m. in both Lincoln and Omaha. Bar closing times at other locations around the state vary between 1 and 2 a.m.

**Tobacco laws:** Nebraska is a smoke-free state and smoking is banned in all public workplaces, including bars and restaurants.

**Daily newspapers:** *Omaha World-Herald* and *Lincoln Journal Star*

**City sales tax:** 7 percent

**State sales tax:** 5.5 percent, with an exception on food

**Important phone numbers:** 911 emergency, 511 for current road conditions inside Nebraska, (800) 906-9069 from outside Nebraska

**City websites:** www.ci.omaha.ne.us and www.lincoln.ne.gov

**Chambers of commerce:** See the Living Here appendix at the back of the book.

falafel shop, Italian, and coal fire pizza—makes this a great strip for foodies to visit. The University of Nebraska at Omaha is on the southwest side of the neighborhood, and the east side of campus butts up to Memorial Park; during the school year, students are everywhere in the neighborhood. Both UNO students and students from nearby Creighton University rent apartments and converted houses in this area, so the neighborhood is a true generational mix of young people and homeowners who have called the area home for years.

## Benson

Benson is one of the city's hippest new districts, but it hasn't always been this way. The neighborhood, one of Omaha's oldest, used to be its own city, and after being taken over by Omaha proper in the 1917, its small-town main street floundered, and many businesses closed. In the late 1990s, Omaha's independent music scene boomed, and one of its two main clubs—the Waiting Room—opened in Benson in the early 2000s. The club spurred lots of development in the area, and now older businesses—vacuum shops, thrift stores, barber shops—stand next to hip bars, a variety of music venues, street vendors selling ethnic food, and locally owned restaurants. Affordable housing options around the central strip have an eclectic mix of older residents, young couples, and families who recently moved to the area.

## West Omaha

Omaha's booming suburbs quickly spread west of the central part of the city; in the 1970s, the western edge of the city sat around 120th Street; now Omaha's borders span past 200th Street, and the city's aggressive annexation policy recently adopted its farthest west suburb, Elkhorn, NE. Typically, locals consider West Omaha to begin around 72nd Street, but with the rapid westward expansion, the neighborhood could be divided into several sections. Growth on both the north and south sides of the city means that housing and shopping both are booming in West Omaha. New retail developments are home to all the expected chain stores, but some locally owned restaurants and shops dot the landscape, and the persistent traveler will surely uncover some gems. Housing options in West Omaha are vast: Affordable housing and apartment complexes are everywhere; many neighborhoods boast large, upscale homes that come with price tags to match.

## North Omaha

One of Omaha's oldest and most historic neighborhoods, North Omaha today is one of the city's most diverse areas, with African Americans being its primary residents. Loads of Omaha history took place in this neighborhood, and tourist attractions like the birth site of Malcolm X, the Mormon Winter Quarters, and the site of Fort Omaha, now part of the Metro Community College Fort Omaha campus, are some of the area's best historic sites. North Downtown Omaha—a newly revitalized neighborhood between Downtown proper and the beginning of North Omaha proper, around Cuming Street, is full of hip restaurants; home to the city's convention center, Qwest Center Omaha; and home to TD Ameritrade Park, a new baseball stadium that is the home of the NCAA College World Series. Continuous housing development—mostly apartments—and hotels make this up-and-coming area popular with locals, business travelers, and baseball fans. Ethnic food options are vast in North Omaha, and all types of African American cuisine, including soul food, can be found in North Omaha. North Omaha does have higher crime rates than the rest of the city, and travelers would be wise to stay aware of their surroundings while exploring this rich part of Omaha's past.

## Bellevue

Bellevue is the oldest continuous town in Nebraska and was incorporated in 1855. Today, it's the home of the US Strategic Command, which controls the country's nuclear weapon programs. It's home to the 55th Wing, which is the largest wing of the US Air Force's Air Combat Command. Many other important units are stationed at the base, including the Air Force Weather Agency, the Omaha operating location of the Defense Finance Accounting service, and others. Bellevue is a southeast suburb of Omaha, and much of it butts up to the Missouri River. One of Bellevue's most popular tourist attractions is Fontenelle Forest, 1,400 acres of privately owned forestland. The forest has 17 miles of trails, many with lovely views, and is the trailhead for a popular walking trail in the city.

**i** Home to the 55th Wing—known as the Fightin' Fifty-Fifth—Offutt Air Force Base employs more than 10,000 military and federal workers. The 55th Wing conducts aircraft operations from Omaha to bases in Japan, the United Kingdom, Crete, and many other locations around the world. It's the largest wing in Air Combat Command and the second largest in the Air Force.

## Papillion/La Vista

One of the city's fastest growing suburbs, Papillion and La Vista used to be two separate areas but have grown together in the past 10 years. Booming with retail development on the southwest and central sides of Omaha, in Sarpy County, lots of retail strip malls have filled this area and made it a popular big-box and chain store shopping area, as well as a neighborhood chock-full of chain restaurants. La Vista is currently one of Nebraska's fastest growing cities: since 1990, it's platted more than 900 acres of residential subdivisions, 300 acres of commercial space, and 800 acres devoted to business parks. Its Southport Development is home to Omaha's first Cabela's, along with hotels and a large

Embassy Suites Convention Center and Hotel. Companies are also relocating to the area: Paypal, HP Computers, Rotella's Bakery, and Oriental Trading Company all have operations in La Vista.

## Council Bluffs

Council Bluffs sits right across the Missouri River, directly east of Omaha. Council Bluffs has close to 60,000 residents and is a much older city than Omaha; it was incorporated in 1854. Gambling is a big industry in Council Bluffs, and the city is home to Ameristar Casino Hotel Council Bluffs, Harrah's Council Bluffs, and Horseshoe Council Bluffs. Many Omahans regularly travel across the river to play slot machines and table games, eat at buffets and fine dining establishments, and go to concerts at the casino-hotels. Manufacturing is another big industry in Council Bluffs, and Tyson Foods, ConAgra, Grundorf, Omaha Standard, Barton Solvents, American Games, Katelman Foundry, Griffin Pipe, and Red Giant Oil all have operations in the Bluffs. Google also has a server farm in the city.

## BETWEEN LINCOLN & OMAHA

As Omaha's western border continues to fluctuate, the distance between it and Lincoln gets shorter, and more and more development takes place between the two cities. Gretna is one of the fastest growing western suburbs of Omaha, and many people who live here commute to work in Lincoln and drive 30 minutes twice a day between home and work. Affordable tract houses and apartment living are bountiful in Gretna, and the city has its own public school system.

Ashland, Nebraska, about 30 miles west of the Omaha city center, is home to one of

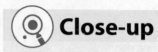

# Close-up

## South Omaha

South Omaha is one of Omaha's thriving neighborhoods. Today's South Omaha is a diverse, lovely place with revitalized streets full of locally owned businesses; bustling shops; delicious restaurants, most focused on authentic Mexican cuisine; and a friendly community that's welcoming and warm. The area that would become this ethnically diverse neighborhood became a city in the late 1880s, when the busy stockyards opened in the area. By 1890, as the stockyards boomed, more than 8,000 people lived in South Omaha. Thousands of immigrants came to the city to work in the stockyards, many from eastern and southern Europe.

Omaha annexed South Omaha in 1915; at that time, it had about 40,000 residents and close to half of those people worked in the meatpacking industry. As the neighborhood grew and matured, the meatpacking industry changed, and in 1999 the stockyards closed. In its wake were many family-owned businesses that continued to support the immigrant population that called South Omaha home.

Today, the only remaining sign of the stockyards is the Livestock Exchange building. Built in 1926, the exchange building is now renovated into apartments and the top floor grand ballroom is a popular spot for weddings and wedding receptions; the tall windows give a magnificent view of the city.

Many who live in South Omaha today are descendants of those original immigrants who came to Omaha to work at the stockyards. Irish, Polish, Czech, Lithuanian, and Italian residents still live there; in recent years, the area has added Sudanese and Hispanic people.

South Omaha is home to a wide array of beautiful, historic churches that show its diverse cultural heritage. Catholic and Orthodox churches of every persuasion fill the area. The recent Hispanic immigrant population took true ownership of the neighborhood, creating family-owned and community-supported businesses along the South Omaha "main street, 24th Street from L to Q Streets. The city took notice of this thriving, welcoming, self-created community. The South Omaha Business Association and the City of Omaha are working together on a major renovation of the South Omaha Main Street. The project includes widening the street to create more parking, replacing stoplights with stop signs to slow down traffic, renovating an existing plaza to make it more welcoming for special events, and giving all the sidewalks a new look.

The neighborhood is already one of the city's most welcoming; this project will sustain that popularity well into the future.

Nebraska's most popular state parks, Eugene T. Mahoney State Park. The park's restaurant and lodge are open year round, and its attractions include housekeeping cabins, lodge rooms, camping, horseback rides, nature trails, sports fields, an indoor theater and water park, miniature golf, and a driving range. Ashland is also home to the Strategic Air and Space Museum, which focuses on the history of the Bellevue-based Strategic Air Command. Ashland is popular for people who want the convenience of living near Omaha and Lincoln but want to maintain the aura of small-town life. The town's main street features a cluster of shops and restaurants, and lots of large, modern houses blend with smaller, affordable housing options to make this one of the area's most popular "in-between" neighborhoods.

## LINCOLN NEIGHBORHOODS

### College View

The College View neighborhood surrounds Lincoln's Union College campus. Originally, the neighborhood was a separate village of its own, and many of those old buildings still stand just west of the edge of campus. Coffee shops, restaurants, and retail businesses thrive in this charming neighborhood. Union College is a four-year private university owned and operated by the Seventh Day Adventist Church.

**i** The Nebraska Division of Travel and Tourism is headquartered in downtown Lincoln, and its annual publication—the *Nebraska Travel Guide*—offers lots of ideas for Nebraska travelers. Its website, www.visitnebraska .gov, is also chock-full of helpful hints, lodging options, attractions, and much more.

### Downtown

Lincoln's central business and entertainment district is in its thriving downtown. It's an eclectic mix of restaurants, both fine and casual dining; bars (especially along the O Street corridor); retail establishments; and office space. It plays host to lots of students who live and study on the adjacent University of Nebraska–Lincoln campus. The historic Haymarket district is in the heart of downtown, and is one of the oldest parts of the city. Historic warehouses have been converted into business, galleries, and restaurants, and in the summer it plays host to a thriving, bustling weekend farmers' market. A handful of old buildings have been converted into apartment and condominium living. Locally owned businesses, coffee shops, and restaurants, as well as unique bars, wine shops, and antiques stores make the area a popular destination for tourists and locals alike. A popular First Friday art walk takes place in downtown Lincoln each month; hundreds of people gather to take in the art and enjoy wine and snacks.

### Language

English is the predominant language spoken in both Lincoln and Omaha, though both cities have a vast and diverse population of immigrants. Omaha has a thriving Mexican community in South Omaha, and Spanish speaking residents live in many parts of the city. Nebraska is also a big resettlement spot for refugees, and Lincoln alone has resettled more than 5,500 people since the early 1980s. Both cities have a large population of Chinese, Thai, and Vietnamese citizens. Lincoln has also become a home for refugees from Afghanistan, Vietnam, Bosnia, Mexico, Russia, Ukraine, Tajikistan, Iraq, Sudan, and China. These refugees and immigrants are bringing new life and diverse culture to Nebraska's urban communities. Asian markets, Latino-owned businesses, and a variety of ethnic restaurants are thriving. Lutheran Family Services of Nebraska is a huge force in helping immigrants and refugees resettle in Nebraska. It operates New American centers, refugee assistance programs, and immigration services; learn more at http://lfsneb.org.

# Visitor Information

## Omaha Convention and Visitors Bureau
1001 Farnam St., Omaha
(402) 444-4660, (866) 937-6624
www.visitomaha.com

You can request free information about Omaha, including a welcome packet and an official visitor's guide, from the Omaha Convention and Visitors Bureau. The office is conveniently located just outside of Omaha's Old Market and has a wealth of information on-site, as well as friendly volunteers happy to answer questions. The CVB also has an on-site coffee shop. Eppley Airfield also has a visitor's desk in the main lobby, and it is staffed during regular business hours with a helpful volunteer and visitor information guides.

## Lincoln Convention and Visitors Bureau
1135 M St., Ste. 300, Lincoln
(800) 423-8212
http://lincoln.org

The Lincoln Convention and Visitors Bureau will send free information and a welcome packet, too. The office is located in downtown Lincoln, and has a satellite location in the Lincoln Haymarket where tourists and recently relocated residents can pick up a wealth of free information.

## Nebraska Division of Travel and Tourism
Nebraska Department of Economic Development
301 Centennial Mall South
PO Box 94666, Lincoln, NE 68509
www.visitnebraska.gov
(888) 444-1867 to request information

The Nebraska Division of Travel and Tourism puts out a free statewide travel guide each year. The comprehensive guide covers the whole state and includes lodging, things to do, attractions, and events. The guide is available online as a downloadable PDF or can be ordered via the state's website, by calling the toll-free number listed above, or by mail.

## Time Zone
Nebraska operates in two time zones: Eastern Nebraska is in the Central Standard Time Zone and the edge of western Nebraska is in the Mountain Standard Time Zone. Lincoln and Omaha both observe Daylight Savings Time. It begins on the second Saturday in March at 2 a.m. and reverts to standard time on the first Sunday in November at 2 a.m. Nebraskans set their clocks one hour forward in March and one hour back in November.

## Safety
Omaha and Lincoln are both safe cities. In its early years, Omaha was a bustling frontier town, rife with gambling and prostitution. In the mid-1900s, Omaha was a center for betting and unemployment, as the railroad and meatpacking industries changed. Since

then, crime has been reduced in the city of Omaha, and in recent years has been lower statistically than crime in cities of similar size, according to the FBI.

In 2006, the FBI ranked Omaha for homicides as 46th out of the 72 cities in the United States of more than 250,000 residents, making it safe for most of the people who live here. Lincoln, too, has a record of safety. In 2009, the city's Police Department reported a 4 percent fall in crime from 2008, marking the lowest number of crimes since 1985.

# GETTING HERE, GETTING AROUND

Transportation has always been important to Omaha: The Omaha riverfront was the starting point for the First Transcontinental Railroad. Union Pacific has been headquartered here since it began in 1867. In 1872 the company opened the first bridge across the Missouri River to Omaha, and the historic Overland Route continues to run through Omaha today. Eppley Airfield started operating in 1940, though air travel didn't become popular in Omaha until the 1960s. Today, Omaha's airport handles about 400 flights a week and handled more than 4.4 million passengers in 2007. Omaha is the primary gateway to the state for out-of-state travelers. Omaha's Eppley Airfield is the state's largest airport, and plays host to a wide variety of commercial airlines as well as some private jet services. Shuttle buses, car services, and vans all offer options to get passengers to destinations around Omaha and to Lincoln.

Lincoln has a small but busy airport that cooperates with Eppley on transporting travelers between the two destinations.

The two metro areas are about an hour apart by car, and the quick 50-mile drive means that professionals often commute between the two destinations on a daily basis for work. The easiest way to get back and forth between Lincoln and Omaha is via I-80; the drive is a straight shot southwest and takes drivers over the Platte River and past a number of tourist attractions, including Mahoney State Park, Quarry Oaks Golf Course, and the Strategic Air and Space Museum.

The drive between Omaha and Lincoln is primarily flat—mostly farmland—and is a pretty spot-on picture of what most people think Nebraska looks like. While it's true eastern Nebraska is primarily flat, once you continue west on I-80 and head a bit north, the state's landscape changes drastically and is made of steep bluffs and buttes and rolling grasslands known as the Sandhills. Sunsets in Nebraska are breathtaking, and if you find yourself driving at dusk or dawn, you'll be stunned by the beauty of the prairie sky.

## OVERVIEW

Lincoln and Omaha are driving destinations. The two cities—both in the heart of the Midwest—are close to the eastern edge of the state and on its most populous end, meaning that most people traveling in and out of Nebraska enter and exit through one of the two.

# BY PLANE

## EPPLEY AIRFIELD
4501 Abbott Dr.
(402) 661-8017
www.flyoma.com

Nine commercial airlines and a few passenger charter airlines serve Omaha's Eppley Airfield. Abbreviated as OMA, the airport is simple to find and easy to navigate. Just outside of downtown Omaha, Eppley is the state's largest airport. If you're coming to the airport from West Omaha, plan on a 20-minute trip each way, depending on traffic. Eppley offers free wireless Internet in the terminal.

Eppley has one simple terminal and two concourses—A and B—inside. TAC Air and Elliot Air terminals, which play host to charter flights, are outside the main terminal. OMA offers non-stop service to Memphis, Las Vegas, Houston, Dallas, Salt Lake City, Denver, Phoenix, Milwaukee, Minneapolis/St. Paul, St. Louis, Atlanta, Washington DC, New York, Detroit, Los Angeles, Cincinnati, Chicago, San Diego, and seasonal non-stop service to Florida. International service is available, though not on flights originating in Omaha.

**i** Omaha and Lincoln's airports are far from the hustle and bustle of most major airports, and though travelers should still arrive with plenty of time before their flight, the air travel experience is usually calm and pleasant and runs without a hitch.

## LINCOLN AIRPORT
(402) 458-2480
www.lincolnairport.com

The Lincoln Airport is smaller, and two commercial airlines operate here: Delta/Northwest and United Express. Located in the northeast corner of the city, the airport offers 7 shuttle buses from Lincoln to other Nebraska communities. Both Duncan Aviation and Silverhawk Aviation operate private and charter flights in and outside of Lincoln. A food court and lounge, wireless Internet, and a number of major rental car companies are all on-site.

## Commercial Airlines

**AIRTRAN (VIA SKYWEST)**
(800) 247-8726
www.airtran.com

**AMERICAN AIRLINES**
(800) 433-7300
www.aa.com

**CONTINENTAL AIRLINES**
(800) 525-0280
www.continental.com

**DELTA AIR LINES**
(800) 221-1212
www.delta.com

**FRONTIER/MIDWEST**
(800) 432-1359
www.frontierairlines.com

**SOUTHWEST AIRLINES**
(800) 435-9792
www.southwest.com

**UNITED AIRLINES**
(800) 864-8331
www.united.com

**US AIRWAYS**
(800) 428-4322
www.usairways.com

## Regional/Commuter Airlines

**DUNCAN AVIATION**
(402) 475-2611
www.duncanaviation.com

**SILVERHAWK AVIATION**
(402) 475-8600
www.silverhawkaviation.com

## FROM THE AIRPORT TO THE CITY

### Car Rentals

Omaha and Lincoln are driving towns, and especially if a traveler will go between the two metros, a car is the easiest way to get around. Many of the area's major attractions are several miles apart, and, again, driving is easiest. Car rental desks are located in the baggage claim areas of both Eppley and the Lincoln Airport.

**ALAMO**
(800) 462-5266
www.alamo.com

**AVIS**
(800) 331-1212
www.avis.com

**BUDGET**
(800) 527-0700
www.budget.com

**DOLLAR (OMAHA ONLY)**
(800) 800-3665
www.dollar.com

**ENTERPRISE**
(800) 261-7331
www.enterprise.com

**HERTZ**
(800) 654-3131
www.hertz.com

**NATIONAL**
(800) 227-7368
www.nationalcar.com

**THRIFTY (OMAHA ONLY)**
(800) 847-4389
www.thrifty.com

### Van Service

There are a number of shuttle options that operate in both Omaha and Lincoln and between the two cities. Shuttle companies provide ground transport to a number of destinations, and courtesy shuttles run between the terminal and the long-term parking lots on a regular daily schedule. A number of local hotels offer courtesy shuttles to and from lodging and the airport, and a few even operate shuttles to take guests to tourist attractions in the neighborhood surrounding the hotel.

**A&B SHUTTLE**
(877) 359-6624
www.citywideride.com
A&B offers bus and limousine service from Omaha, Lincoln, and Sarpy County. Airport shuttle reservations are required 24 hours in advance and the service takes reservations during regular business hours Monday through Saturday by phone or fax. They also have an online reservation system. A&B does provide limited service on holidays; call for availability. Price for a ride generally runs between $16 and $42, and A&B charges flat rates depending on zones. Price is determined also by the number of passengers and the time of day. The service charges a fee for cancellation on all confirmed reservations; the fee changes depending on how close to the departure time the reservation is cancelled.

**BLACK TIE LIMOUSINE & SHUTTLE SERVICE**
(800) 938-2608
www.blacktieiowa.com

Black Tie Limousine and Shuttle caters to business travelers, and will shuttle professionals to and from the Omaha, Sioux City, and Sioux Falls airports and between multiple business locations, if necessary. The family-owned business has been operating for more than 15 years.

## DASHABOUT ROADRUNNER SHUTTLE
### (800) 720-3274
### www.dashaboutshuttle.com

The DashAbout shuttle offers rural transportation in Colorado, Nebraska, Wyoming, and Kansas. It operates metro airport shuttles in both Omaha and Lincoln and has "town taxis" in Sidney and Columbus (both in Nebraska). Reservations are required and can be made Mon through Fri from 9 a.m. to 5 p.m. by calling the number above. Vans run on three different routes through Nebraska. The first runs from North Platte, Ogallala, Big Springs, Chappell, and Sindney with flag stops. The second route runs from McCook, Trenton, Benkelman, and Haigler with flag stops. The third runs from Imperial to Denver, Colorado. Reservations are required 24 hours in advance and cancellations are required 48 hours in advance to get a full refund.

## I-80 EPPLEY EXPRESS
### (800) 888-9793
### www.eppleyexpress.com

Eppley Express offers shuttle service between a number of Nebraska destinations, including Omaha, Lincoln, Kearney, Grand Island, and York. The service offers vans and a variety of motorcoaches in different sizes. A full list of departure locations and times is available on the website, and fares range from $39 to $60, depending on the distance. Eppley Express also offers same-day to and from a location to an airport as a package

deal. Service from the Kearney to the Grand Island/Hastings area and from York or Lincoln to Omaha is available as a package. Call to schedule a departure time and receive a custom rate. Eppley motorcoaches are available to charter group tours through Nebraska or elsewhere in the United States. The motorcoach fleet features reclining seats, individual reading lights, TVs, and VCRs. Call for rates and further information.

## OMALINK
### (402) 475-5465, (877) 473-5465
### www.omalink.com

OmaLink provides transportation between Omaha and Lincoln from a number of locations: airports; hotels and motels; college campuses; and custom pickup points, such as a home or office location (there is no additional charge for being picked up at an office).

The vans are a ubiquitous site along I-80 and, though reservations are recommended, the vans will also take walk-up passengers for a ride. In Omaha, passengers can get on a van at the Eppley Airfield Ground Transportation area, on the center of the main level near terminal door three; in downtown Omaha; or anywhere else in the city for an additional charge. In Lincoln, the vans can be boarded at any Lincoln hotel, college, university, or the airport. Drivers will assist passengers with baggage, and tipping is recommended. Military and seniors receive $5 off the ticket price and a solider returning home from a tour of duty receives free shuttle service. OmaLink also provides corporate and group discounts, private charters, and special conference rates.

Rates for a one-way trip between Omaha and Lincoln are $49.95 for one passenger; $74.90 for two. Round-trip rides are $79.95 for one and $114.90 for two.

OmaLink also offers a few other special services: They will courier a package between Lincoln and Omaha, provide a ride from Omaha for a Nebraska Cornhuskers football game, take people to doctor or hospital appointments, and stop at any one of the interstate exits between Lincoln and Omaha to drop off or pick up passengers.

Cancellations made more than 24 hours before the departure time get a full refund; those made less than one day in advance will get a $20 surcharge. No-show passengers are charged the full rate for the trip.

## Taxis

**CAPITAL CAB (LINCOLN)**
**(402) 477-6074**

**YELLOW CAB (LINCOLN)**
**(402) 477-4111**

**OMAHA TAXI DISPATCH**
**(402) 333-TAXI (8294)**
**www.happycab.com**
Omaha Taxi Dispatch operates four cab companies: Happy, Yellow, Checker, and Cornhusker; and it is the city's largest transportation authority. Cabs can be hailed for standard rates or hired by the hour for a special rate. Base fare is $1.95 with an additional 30 cents per mile and 30 cents per 43 seconds of a traffic delay. Out of town rates are $2.25 per mile, and a cab for a group rented per hour is $22. For seniors, the rates above the base fare are 15 cents.

## BY CAR

It's practically impossible to get lost in Omaha. The city's streets are on a grid, and the freeway system makes a loop around almost the entire city, with the exception of the northeastern-most corner. Interstates 80, 680, and 480 form a loop around the city, and the North Freeway continues that loop around the north side of Omaha, though it ends at 30th Street and one must head south down 30th Street until reconnecting to the interstate near downtown Omaha. Those headed to the airport can take either the North Freeway or I-680; those headed downtown or to the Old Market will probably want to take I-680 east. I-680 is on the west side of Omaha; I-80 on the south side of town leads drivers east and west around the city; I-480 takes drivers north and south toward and from downtown and North Omaha.

I-80 leads thousands of drivers per day from Omaha to Lincoln and vice versa. I-180 leads travelers south from I-80 into downtown Lincoln, a number of exits before the downtown exit lead drivers to 84th, 56th, and 27th Streets, respectively.

Lincoln doesn't have an in-town freeway system, though Cornhusker Highway and Highway 2 lead drivers from the north and south parts of the city to downtown.

Omaha's grid of streets have a strict system: east-west streets have names, and north-south streets are numbered; there are almost no exceptions to this general rule. The main through-town east-west street in Omaha is Dodge Street, which west of 72nd Street becomes West Dodge Road. Other major east-west streets are Pacific Street; Center Street (which becomes West Center Road west of 72nd Street); and Blondo, Maple, and Fort Streets. Major north-south streets include 13th, 60th, 72nd, 120th, 132nd, and 144th Streets and Saddle Creek Road, and into the west suburbs: 156th, 168th, and 204th Streets.

In Lincoln, the main east-west thoroughfare is O Street. In Lincoln, the system is the same: east-west streets are named, while north-south streets are numbered.

## BY BUS

### OMAHA METRO BUS SYSTEM
(402) 341-0800, (402) 341-0807 (TDD)
www.ometro.com

Metro bus system is the main mode of public transportation in Omaha, and the bus system—recently re-branded, with newly designed buses and exteriors—gives about 3.7 million rides a year. Metro bus passes are available at a number of grocery stores around the Omaha area, and a rider can purchase individual rides on the bus ($1.25) or a prepaid card for a set number of rides at a discounted price. Discounts are offered to students and seniors and children; those under age 5 ride free. Omaha Metro has a number of "park and ride" lots around the city where people can park their vehicle and take a bus across town. All Metro buses have bike racks, and riders can bring their bike free of charge. A transfer on the Metro bus is 5 cents, and must be purchased when the rider pays the fare.

### STARTRAN
Schedule Info: (402) 476-1234
www.lincoln.ne.gov/city/pworks/startran

In Lincoln, the StarTran bus is the city-owned bus transport option and is popular for both students and commuters. Per-ride fare is $1.75 and a 20-ride pass costs $33. Discounts are offered to seniors, and children under age 4 ride free. Transfers are free on the StarTran bus, and passengers should have exact change ready when boarding the bus as drivers are not allowed to give change or handle or deposit fares. If a rider does not have change, he or she will get a change card, which can be used on a future trip. Star-Tran also offers the HandiVan service, created for individuals who can't ride the regular city bus. Riders must pre-register for this service and it's free for eligible riders. Riders can bring a passenger along for $3.50.

## WALKING & CYCLING

Omaha and Lincoln both have walkable downtown areas, though the rest of the two cities is mainly traversed by drivers in their cars. Many of the main attractions in this book are located in the respective downtown areas of the two cities, and it's possible to take public transportation to each area and explore on foot from there. Visitors who choose a lodging option in the central business districts can plan on walking just about everywhere if they decide to stay in the area. Lincoln and Omaha are becoming more bike friendly: Both downtown Omaha and Lincoln now have clearly marked bike lanes for commuter riders, and bikes are for rent in downtown Omaha so tourists can ride around the downtown area instead of walk. Traffic is generally heavy, so bikers should be extra careful.

**i** Lincoln has more than 100 miles of hard surface and crushed rock trails, and the trails don't go unused! The city's runners, walkers, bikers, and hikers keep these trails busy; be sure to respect other exercisers when using the system.

Recreational biking is a growing hobby in Omaha and Lincoln, and the trails system in both cities is usually busy with bikers. For more information on recreational biking, visit either www.omahatrails.com or www.gptn.org.

# HISTORY

Omaha's history is indivisible with the Missouri River and the cattle that once roamed its legendary stockyards. It's got a lawless history, with exciting tales of gambling, prostitution and other illicit activity. It grew out of the desire of some land grabbers and, over the years, became a city with a steady economy, a solid reputation, and an affordable cost of living.

Lincoln became Nebraska's capital before it was barely even a city; it grew on the banks of a salt creek a few miles away from an Oregon Trail trading post. When the railroads came to town, they followed the path of those salt creeks, which led to traveling tributaries of transportation. Today it's the home to the state's flagship school, the University of Nebraska–Lincoln; a thriving network of outdoor trails; and the state's singular, beautiful state capitol building.

## OVERVIEW

As you read this book, you'll notice that many parts of the culture—food, popular attractions—have ties to the history of Omaha and Lincoln. History is a deep part of the culture here, and Omaha and Lincoln are connected to the rest of the state of Nebraska in profound historical ways.

In the following pages, you will find only the highlights of Omaha and Lincoln's history. It's such a lengthy story that volumes could be written about it (and probably have been!). I've attempted to capture some of the important parts of a much longer story. As you explore the cities on your own, you'll experience the history—and the unique cities it's created—for yourself.

## EARLIEST HISTORY

Native Americans, including the people of the Omaha and Ponca Tribes, first settled the

land where Omaha sits in the 17th century. The word "Omaha" means "dwellers on the bluff."

In 1804, the Lewis and Clark expedition traveled over the river where Omaha would be constructed. Between July 30 and August 3, 1804, Meriwether Lewis and William Clark, along with their traveling party, met with tribal leaders at the Council Bluff, about 20 miles north of where Omaha is today. Americans built a number of fur trading posts about 20 miles south of the Council Bluff; one of these posts later became Bellevue.

Fifty years after Lewis and Clark landed, the founders of Omaha came across the river from Council Bluffs, where they'd ended up settling on their westward journey toward California. William D. Brown saw there was money to be made by ferrying these settlers across the river, and started doing as much around 1852. He made the first claim to the land in 1853—while Indians were still living there—and after that, many other prospectors began to lay claim to their own pieces of land on the west side of the Missouri. Through a series of treaties, the Native Americans ceded the lands they lived on to the US government, and, in 1854, Omaha became a city.

**i** The 1879 trial of Standing Bear vs. Crook took place in Omaha. Chief Standing Bear made a speech during the trial, saying, "God made me, and I am a man." The trial led to the ruling that "an Indian is a person" under the law and the case garnered national attention and allowed many Ponca people to return to the Niobrara River valley, their home.

## MORMON WINTER QUARTERS

The Mormon people stopped in Omaha during the winter of 1846 and 1847 during their travels west, and their harrowing journey is captured in the Winter Quarters memorial. About 2,500 Mormons were ousted from their former settlement in Illinois and were on a journey to find a new settlement. They decided to stay on the banks of the Missouri for the winter and resume their westward journey come spring.

They built sod houses and cabins on the frozen ground and built large fires. The cold that winter was bitter and the Mormons, who left Illinois in a hurry, didn't have proper supplies. They traded with Indians to get goods, but even with that, many of the settlers became ill and died of diseases like scurvy, tuberculosis, malaria, fevers, and chills. Close to 400 Mormons died that winter.

Today, the LDS Church has a memorial to those who died at Winter Quarters; the memorial is open to the public. Brigham Young also supervised the construction of the Florence Mill, which still stands today. The settlers used the mill to grind corn, wheat, and rye; today it has been renovated into a public space and art gallery.

## THE CAPITOL BATTLE

John W. Prey was the first notable settler in Lancaster County. He convinced a party to leave its original settlement in Council Bluffs, Iowa, and continue westward to Salt Creek, where there were fewer people and abundant timber. Prey surveyed the area and began building a house. By 1859, others followed Prey to the area. At the time, it was considered the edge of the "Great American Desert," and settlers didn't believe many people would want to live west of the part of Lancaster County they'd settled.

Omaha was Nebraska's first capital, and Nebraska's first state capitol was built on the same hill where settlers established the city during a Fourth of July picnic. Omaha remained the capital until 1867, when Nebraska became a state.

Most of the state's population at the time lived south of the Platte River, closer to Lincoln. These people had to travel to Omaha—a harrowing trip—to do business, and so voted to have the capital moved to Lincoln. Omaha and Lincoln long battled over which city would be the capital; eventually, the state capital was relocated to Lincoln because it was in the center of Nebraska at the time and also because of the population. Lincoln officially became a city on July 29, 1867.

## RAILROADS & PROSPECTORS

Omaha's economy was boom and bust during the early years. In the mid-1850s, money was made in real estate, and the city's population grew rapidly. Lots of buildings were constructed that year. Settlers and prospectors moving west to find gold in the 1860s often stopped in the city. By 1860, about 4,000 people lived in Omaha. The jobbing and wholesaling district brought new jobs to the city. That same year, the first telegraph line came to Omaha, connecting it to St. Louis and the rest of the United States. In 1863, ground broke for the first Transcontinental Railroad, and Union Pacific came to town. Congress approved Union Pacific to start building westward railroads two years later and construction began out of Omaha starting in 1866. The city grew a lot around this time: Construction of schools, growth in manufacturing, and opening of churches happened everywhere.

## LINCOLN'S GROWTH

Steam engines began running to Lincoln in 1870, and the state's land office moved to the city the same year. Lincoln became a popular starting point for immigrants. Cheap land was advertised everywhere; immigrants arrived by boxcar and wagon to the city. In 1867, the city of Lincoln had about 30 residents; three years later the population had skyrocketed to 2,500.

The University of Nebraska was founded in 1869, and the campus covered a four-block area. Its first building, University Hall, was built of wood and sun-dried bricks in the Franco-Italian style of architecture. The university built its second building in 1886, and construction began on the university library

in 1890, which is still on campus today and is known as Architecture Hall. It's one of the most beautiful buildings on campus. In 1873, the university constructed the agriculture-centric East Campus. The first University of Nebraska campus in Omaha opened in 1902, when the Medical Center became part of the system. By 1909, nearly 4,000 students received their education at the University of Nebraska.

**i** The 1898 Trans-Mississippi and International Exposition held in Omaha drew more than two million people to the city. The world's fair explored the development of the west, and included 21 classical buildings that featured products from around the world and a 2,000-foot lagoon in the center of the temporary structures.

## THE OMAHA STOCKYARDS

Omaha's Union Stockyards began in 1883. Within the stockyard's first 20 years of operating, four of the five major meatpacking businesses were located in the city. The Union Stockyards first provided a feeding station for animals on their way to the East Coast. The first stock exchange was a small on-site barn; the second, more substantial building rose in 1885 and included apartments for traders and convention space. In 1900, the stockyards added new pens, a sheep barn that held 100,000, and a huge horse and mule barn that spanned two blocks. By 1910, 20,000 animals arrived at the stockyards each day from farms and ranches in 20 states. Union Pacific Railroad delivered livestock to market, and tens of thousands of animals arrived at the yards each day to be slaughtered. Among the four big meatpacking companies of its day, the stockyards in Omaha slaughtered more than one million cattle, pigs, and sheep each year, and more than 5,000 people worked there. The stockyards acted as the backbone of Omaha's economy for more than 100 years.

## CULTURAL CHANGES, CIVIL UNREST

Thousands of immigrants moved to the city to work in the stockyards, resulting in a number of diverse neighborhoods across the city. South Omaha was home to Irish immigrants and Bohemians. North Omaha became home to African Americans, Jewish, and Eastern European people. Upper class white residents built elegant mansions in central Omaha; many of these grand homes still exist today in the city's Gold Coast neighborhood. These residents also formed Bemis Park, Field Club, and Midtown Omaha.

The early 19th century was filled with gambling, drinking, and prostitution in the city's "sporting district." Violence was rampant, and the city had its fair share of labor issues.

Omaha has a long history of civil unrest. The city's population exploded in the early 1900s, and labor strikes, racial tension, and ethnic strife ran rampant. The first chapter of the National Association for the Advancement of Colored People west of the Mississippi started in Omaha in 1912. Mob riots and hangings became a sad regularity.

North Omaha's vibrant culture hit its peak between the 1920s and the 1950s. Musicians and national bands performed at neighborhood clubs, and popular entertainers of the day toured to the city. The neighborhood birthed lots of creative people, including Jewish feminist author Tillie Olsen, novelist Wallace Thurman, trumpeter and big band leader Lloyd Hunter, and jazz singer Anna Mae Winburn.

## LINCOLN GROWTH

Lincoln annexed surrounding towns to push its population above 80,000 by 1930. Groundwork for the state's third state capitol building—the one still standing today—began in 1922. Designed by famous architect Bertram Goodhue, the structure is full of symbolism. Goodhue designed the capitol to be a skyscraper, and hired sculptors to decorate it and one to create a golden sculpture of a sower to decorate its top. In 1934, Nebraska dissolved its two-house legislature and moved its government to a unicameral system; today it's the only state to operate on a unicameral system.

**i** Enron began in Omaha in 1932 as the Northern Natural Gas Company. In the late 1980s, Enron CEO Kenneth Lay moved the company's headquarters to Houston.

## THE DECLINE OF THE STOCKYARDS

In the 1950s, Omaha overtook Chicago as the country's largest meatpacking and livestock market, a claim it held until 1973. The unions saw the industry through the civil rights movement, and in the late 1950s and 1960s, about half of Omaha's workers were involved in the industry. In the 1960s, business at the stockyards began to change and the market took a downturn. The meatpacking industry began to move slaughterhouses to rural areas, and started to hire non-union workers. More than 10,000 Omaha workers lost their jobs, which led to abject poverty. In the 1960s, three major race riots destroyed North Omaha's business district; recovery has been slow since.

In the late 1980s, the stockyard facilities started to fall into disrepair, and in the 1990s, the city of Omaha bought 50 acres of the land for an office park and condemned the rest save for the Livestock Exchange Building, which was preserved. Today's stockyards are a mixed use development, with Metropolitan Community College's South Omaha Campus, a mixed use Livestock Exchange Building that includes apartments and commercial space, and a new home for the South Omaha Library.

## THE UNIVERSITY GROWS

The University of Nebraska grew quickly in the 1920s. Many buildings rose on campus during this period, including Memorial Stadium and the Nebraska Coliseum. The World War II area brought even more development, including the student union, Love Memorial Library, and Mueller Tower, whose chimes still ring today.

Enrollment skyrocketed in the 1950s, and transformed the campus. In 1969, the University of Nebraska became an umbrella name for three campuses: the University of Nebraska–Lincoln, the University of Nebraska at Omaha, and the University of Nebraska Medical Center, also in Omaha. Two years later, it took on the University of Nebraska at Kearney.

## MILITARY & BUSINESS

As the city came out of the 1930s and the Great Depression, Offutt Air Force Base grew just south of the city, in Bellevue. The Glen L. Martin Company opened there in the 1940s and built, among other planes, the *Enola Gay* and *Bockscar* used during World War II. The Strategic Air Command moved to Offutt in 1948 and brought with it jobs and a much needed economic boost.

Throughout the 1950s and 1960s, Omaha began to be the insurance center it is today. More than 40 insurance companies, including Woodmen of the World and Mutual of Omaha, opened in the city during that decade. In 1969, the Woodmen Tower became Omaha's tallest building and first skyscraper.

**i** In 1945, the *Enola Gay* was one of two B-29 Superfortresses manufactured in Bellevue at a factory that's now Offutt Air Force Base. That same year, a Japanese fire balloon exploded over midtown's Dundee neighborhood. The Japanese launched more than 9,000 such explosive balloons during WWII.

## MODERN DEVELOPMENT

Omaha and Lincoln have experienced lots of growth since 1970.

The University of Nebraska–Lincoln continues to expand. Large-scale research facilities like the Beadle Center for Biomaterials Research, the Ken Morrison Life Sciences Research Center, and the International Quilt Study Center place it at the forefront of its game. New residence halls, major expansions to Memorial Stadium, and the Student Union are also part of the building boom.

Lincoln's economy relies on industries including banking, information technology, education, insurance, and transportation. One of its largest employers is Bryan LGH Medical Center, which has more than 20,000 employees.

The historic Haymarket district has been redeveloped into a thriving business area. The city of Lincoln recently approved a plan to construct its own arena in the Haymarket. The construction project will create more than 8,000 jobs and more than 1,000 permanent jobs once the structure is done. The arena will be the new home of the University of Nebraska basketball team, and the city hopes to draw big-name music groups into Lincoln.

West Omaha has become a bustling suburb, full of large homes and lots of people. North and South Omaha have continued to be cultural hotbeds with diverse populations and singular businesses. Downtown and the city's riverfront have seen vast renovation.

In 1989, Omaha felled Jobber's Canyon, a warehouse district in downtown Omaha, to construct a park and campus for the ConAgra Foods campus. The destruction of the 24 buildings represents the largest National Register historic district ever lost. Several of the nearby buildings to what once was Jobber's Canyon have since been redeveloped into condominiums. At the turn of the 21st century, Omaha got a new tallest building: One First National Center towered over the Woodmen Tower beginning in 2002. The city began to redevelop its north downtown area, and built the arena and convention center, Qwest Center Omaha. TD Ameritrade Park, a new ballpark, opened in 2011.

Construction is also changing the face of midtown Omaha. Mutual of Omaha renovated its campus along with Turner Park into the Midtown Crossing complex, which has become a hotbed for nightlife, restaurants, and condo living. The site of the former Ak-Sar-Ben horse racing complex is also being redeveloped into the mixed use Aksarben Village. Blue Cross Blue Shield of Nebraska built a new headquarters in the complex.

The city's riverfront area is an attraction once again, especially with the Bob Kerrey Pedestrian Bridge, a walking and biking bridge that spans the river from east to west. Omaha's riverfront has become a space for condo living, dining, and live outdoor music festivals in the summer. Council Bluffs is in the beginning stages of developing its own riverfront, which will eventually create activities on both sides of the bridge.

# ANNUAL EVENTS & FESTIVITIES

As the seasons change in Nebraska, so do the annual events that go on in Lincoln or Omaha. More often than not, the events on this list have something to do with the season. Fall activities are centered on the stunning fall foliage, eating food that comes with the annual harvest, or Oktoberfest. Winter events often are holiday-centric or tied in with cold weather outdoor activities. In the spring, people simply want to get outside, and athletic and ethnic festivals are popular this time of year. Summer certainly has the most diverse offerings, with live music festivals, food and drink, fireworks, sports, and arts ruling the season.

The diverse festivals listed in this chapter are, to be sure, a sampling of a much larger festival circuit that spans the state of Nebraska; some of the best, well-attended festivals take place outside of the metro areas of Lincoln and Omaha, and those looking for a true small-town festival experience would be well served to take a Nebraska road trip and experience some of these singular events first-hand.

## JANUARY

### CATHEDRAL FLOWER FESTIVAL
St. Cecila's Cathedral
100 N. 62nd St., Omaha
(402) 568-3100

Flowers are the perfect antidote to Nebraska's winter weather, and the annual Cathedral Flower Festival is the best in the city. Each year at the end of January, the festival takes place in Omaha's historic St. Cecilia Cathedral—worth visiting without the festival for its own special beauty—and draws more than 15,000 visitors. Local florists transform thousands of varietals of flowers into works of art that decorate the cathedral space; special events are often scheduled during the run of the show.

## APRIL

### EASTER EXTRAVAGANZA
Lauritzen Gardens
100 Bancroft St., Omaha
(402) 346-4002

Lauritzen Gardens knows how to run an Easter egg hunt, and it's not your run-of-the-mill backyard search. The Easter Bunny arrives first thing in the morning—the cafe on-site is open so parents can grab a coffee—and craft activities fill the morning before the hunt begins. The two-hour main event is divided into three age groups so everyone gets a fair shot. Lauritzen's Children's Garden is overflowing with hidden treasure, and kids will have a ball seeking it out.

# MAY

## CINCO DE MAYO

**Historic S. 24th Street, Omaha**
**www.cincodemayoomaha.com**
South Omaha comes alive on Cinco De Mayo, and the community's vibrant Mexican residents have been celebrating with a parade, food, and live music for more than 20 years. The festivities span a number of days and include a parade and all day fiesta that includes lots of bands, carnival rides, a stage devoted to kids' entertainment, vendors, and loads of delicious authentic Mexican cuisine. The final day of the celebration includes a fun run/walk and more live entertainment.

## LINCOLN CZECH FEST

**4901 S. 56th St., Lincoln**
**www.lincolnczechs.org**
One day a year, Lincolnites become more Czech than Nebraskan. During the annual Lincoln Czech Fest, thousands of people gather for kolache and other baked goods, sauerkraut, hot dumplings, and sausage. The free festival's main stage has a slew of acts that fill the day: accordion music, dancers, and the crème de la crème: live polka music. Throughout the day "Czech Royalty" is crowned, with the big moment being the crowning of the Lincoln Czech Queen. Don't miss it for all the pomp and circumstance you can take while munching a kolache.

## ✳LINCOLN NATIONAL GUARD MARATHON AND HALF MARATHON

**Starting line on the University of Nebraska–Lincoln Campus**
**www.lincolnrun.org/marathon.htm**
One of the most popular athletic events in Nebraska, the Lincoln Marathon and Half Marathon is truly exhilarating for its participants. The half-marathon course winds through Lincoln, and cheering fans encouraging the 10,000 runners on make the jog oh-so-much easier—and fun, to boot. The event sells out every year without fail, so participants should register early to be guaranteed a spot in the race. The certified run is a Boston Marathon qualifier. The night before the run, all race participants can chow down in a free pastathon held on the UNL campus.

# JUNE

## TASTE OF OMAHA

**Omaha Riverfront**
**www.showofficeonline.com/tastehomepage.html**
Taste of Omaha is foodie heaven for the city of Omaha. Many of the city's top chefs, best restaurants, and well-known food companies take to the Omaha riverfront and cook outdoors for thousands of pleased eaters. Live music accompanies the food, and five stages are scattered around the festival; music is playing almost non-stop and all the stage shows are free. The array of food served at the event runs the gamut: Nebraska beef takes center stage next to pizza; ribs; and ethnic food, like Mexican, Italian, Greek, Asian, and Polish.

## TOUR DE NEBRASKA BICYCLE RIDE

**Begins and ends outside of Lincoln**
**www.tourdenebraska.com**
Since the mid-1980s, happy bikers have been pedaling across rural Nebraska as part of the Tour De Nebraska. The ride, a five-day tour that begins and ends in a town near Lincoln that varies each year, lets riders leave things like cell phones, computers, and answering

machines behind. The organizers plan the route and arrange for food and campsites. The ride usually fills up by late March and is limited to 200 cyclists. The route sticks to paved roads and riders get a map of each day's travels. Cyclists are encouraged to train by riding three to four days a week for at least 20 miles in preparation for the trip.

## ❉SUMMER ARTS FESTIVAL
**10th to 15th Streets on Farnam Street, Downtown Omaha**
**www.summerarts.org**

What started out as a small artist festival has turned into a big one. A world music pavilion, young artist exhibition, children's stage and play area, local artists' market, and lots of food are some of the highlights. More than 100 juried artists from around the country show their wares in the streets; artists come to Omaha from 27 states. Artwork runs the gamut and includes jewelry, functional pottery, 2D work of all kinds, photography, fiber art, and woodworking. The Omaha ArtSeen gives participants the chance to interact with local artists doing live, on-site demonstrations of things like clay throwing, lamp work, and woodworking. Poetry readings, live music, and the Taste Fest food pavilion round out the artsy offerings.

## BANK OF THE WEST CELEBRATES INDEPENDENCE AT MEMORIAL PARK
**60th and Dodge Streets, Omaha**
**www.bankofthewest.com**

A Fourth of July specialty, the Bank of the West Concert in Omaha's Memorial Park is one of the most popular summertime events. The free show always features some big name bands: In 2010 it was Styx, Foreigner, and Kansas. The free event

draws thousands of people to the park to dance, relax, and celebrate the holiday. Concert goers are encouraged to give a donation while at the event that supports an Omaha-based charitable organization. Parking is limited at the event, and carpooling is strongly advised. The park opens at 5 a.m. the day of the concert and people arrive early to claim the best spots. Alcohol isn't allowed, though food is and a select amount of vendors sell food during the show. A grandiose fireworks show closes the night. In the event of bad weather, the show is not rescheduled.

## JULY

### RAILROAD DAYS
**Downtown Omaha and Council Bluffs, Iowa**
**www.omaharailroaddays.com**

Five of Omaha's and neighboring Council Bluffs' biggest attractions get together once a year to celebrate the area's railroad-centric past. Lauritzen Gardens, the Durham Museum, the Union Pacific Railroad Museum, the Historic General Dodge House, and the RailsWest Railroad Museum join forces for the multi-pronged event. Families can buy a $10 pass that provides admission to all five locations as well as transportation between the venues for the weekend-long event. Each venue offers a wide array of events and exhibits focused on trains and railroads that vary from year to year; visit the website for a full schedule of events and an exhibition listing.

### MEADOWLARK MUSIC FESTIVAL
**Sheldon Museum of Art, 12th and R Streets on the UNL campus**
**http://meadowlarkmusicfestival.com**

The state's only music festival focused on classical music, Meadowlark Music Festival takes place in the green space outside the beautiful Sheldon Museum of Art on the UNL campus. A UNL professor started the event 10 years ago, and its first-rate chamber performers continue to draw crowds to the city. A subsidized ticket program allows everyone to attend Meadowlark's regular concerts, and the musicians perform in schools and community centers around Lincoln. Each year Meadowlark collaborates with a visual artist to produce a piece of art inspired by the event; the work is displayed at a variety of venues and then becomes a part of the permanent collection of the Museum of Nebraska Art, located in Kearney.

## ✳MAHA MUSIC FESTIVAL
**Downtown Omaha riverfront**
**http://mahamusicfestival.com**
The most up-and-coming music festival in Nebraska has to be the MAHA music festival. Though only a few years old, in 2010 the festival drew big name acts such as Spoon, The Faint, Superchunk, Ben Kewller, and the Old 97s. Local Omaha acts joined the roster and the event draws a stellar turnout of people of all ages. The concert is general admission and many people arrive long before the music begins to secure a good seat; the music begins at 12:30 p.m. and continues until 11 p.m. No outside food or drink is allowed, but an array of vendors—many from locally owned restaurants—sell food and beverages, including alcohol, on-site.

## AUGUST

### CAPITAL CITY RIBFEST
**Downtown Lincoln**
**www.pershingcenter.com/ribfest**

The scent of roasting barbeque wafts through the humid streets of downtown Lincoln (and through the air of most of downtown's office buildings) during Capital City Ribfest. A popular lunchtime destination on Friday, and popular all day during its weekend run, the event draws pit bosses from around the country to serve up a wide variety of BBQ recipes. Food includes 'que from Australia, Texas, and Southern, Memphis, and Southwestern-style ribs and sandwiches. Live music that includes rock, folk, bluegrass, and country permeates the event during the entire weekend. During Thursday and Friday over the lunch hour, visitors can get free Ribfest admission by donating a can of food.

### DEFENDERS OF FREEDOM AIR SHOW
**Offutt Air Force Base, Bellevue**
**www.offuttairshow.com**
One of the most exciting displays of aeronautics (even for those who aren't into planes) is what makes the annual Defenders of Freedom Air Show so much fun. The US Air Force Thunderbirds along with a wide variety of demo teams and planes fly during this daylong event, which also features a lot of planes displayed on the ground for visitors to look at up-close. The show doesn't ever have a set schedule, so visitors are encouraged to arrive when they can, relax, and enjoy the display. The event is free, and families can bring their own drinks and food, though coolers are not permitted. Because the event takes place on a military base, visitors should be prepared for bags and other items to be searched for security reasons.

# SEPTEMBER

## INTERNATIONAL FORT OMAHA INTERTRIBAL POWWOW

**Metro Community College Fort Omaha Campus**
**www.mccneb.edu/intercultural**

Held on the same grounds where Ponca Chief Standing Bear was held prisoner, the annual Fort Omaha Intertribal Powwow holds special meaning. A celebration of the state's Native American past, the powwow features traditional dance, music, art, storytelling, and food from Nebraska's four tribes: the Northern Ponca, Omaha, Santee Sioux, and Winnebago. Thousands of people attend the yearly event that draws close to 400 artists of all ilk to participate. The powwow is different each year, but always opens and closes with prayer in English and native languages. The music and dance along with the delicious native cuisine makes attending the powwow well worth the time.

## RIVER CITY RODEO

**Qwest Center Omaha**
**455 N. 10th St., Omaha**
**www.rivercityrodeo.com**

The second largest rodeo in the world doesn't come to Omaha without fanfare. AkSarBen's River City Rodeo has all the things one would expect: top cowboys who compete for a spot to come to Omaha, fast-paced action, and cash prizes. But it also has a livestock show, concerts, a BBQ contest, a parade, and trail rides. The family-centric event teaches how farms work and gives children a chance to touch, see and—let's be honest—smell farm animals up close. Concerts include big-name performers: The recent roster included Sawyer Brown and Jack Ingram.

# OCTOBER

## OKTOBERFEST

**German-American Society**
**3717 S. 120 St., Omaha**
**http://germanamericansociety.org**

Oktoberfest is a big deal in Omaha. The traditional German celebration of the harvest is centered at one location—the city's German-American Society—but satellite celebrations take place all over the city in the fall. Many restaurants celebrate with German food on the menu—sauerkraut, kielbasa, boiled cabbage and carrots, rye bread, and lots of beer are usually included. The German American Society's celebration includes live music, dancing, food, and spirits—food usually includes a roasted whole hog. Other venues around Omaha to look for Oktoberfest celebrations include midtown's Gerda's German Restaurant and Bakery; the Crescent Moon Ale House; Huber Haus; and WheatFields restaurant, which has numerous locations around town.

## *VALA'S PUMPKIN PATCH FALL FESTIVAL

**12102 S. 180th St., Gretna**
**http://valaspumpkinpatch.com**

Vala's Pumpkin Patch is one of Omaha's most popular seasonal attractions, and its annual Fall Festival is packed with activity. Just some of the stuff that goes on every day, seven days a week: pig races, live music, pumpkin chuckin' cannon show (yes, this is what you think it is), hayrack and train rides, peddle car rides, pony rides, haunted houses, storytelling, and a 3-acre corn maze that gets redesigned each year. Many attractions come free with admission, and the variety of haunted houses are appropriate for all ages—some are tame, while others are actually spooky; the best one is housed in the original 100-year-old barn that stands on the property.

## *OMAHA NORTH HILLS POTTERY TOUR
**Four locations North of Omaha**
**http://omahanorthhillspotterytour.com**
A scenic drive and artistic event in one, the Omaha North Hills Pottery Tour leads drivers on one of the area's best fall drives—through Omaha's North Hills—with stops at four pottery studios that feature the work of a growing list of artists each year. Florence Mill, Dennison Pottery, Too Far North, and Big Table Studios are the four studio stops; the drive begins in Omaha proper but quickly changes into countryside with beautiful fall foliage and small, quaint towns along the way. The weekend-long event is a great way to fill a Saturday or Sunday afternoon.

## NOVEMBER

### *HOLIDAY LIGHTS FESTIVAL
**Downtown Omaha**
**http://holidaylightsfestival.org**
The Omaha Holiday Lights Festival kicks off Thanksgiving night when the city's mayor flips the switch, illuminating more than one million lights decorating the downtown Gene Leahy Mall. But that flip is just the beginning of a two-month-long holiday celebration that ends on New Year's Eve with a dramatic fireworks show. The tradition began in the year 2000, and it's grown each year—more people attend and the list of events continues to grow. Every Saturday evening carolers walk through the mall and perform among the lights. At the beginning of December, a Family Day allows people to visit a number of downtown Omaha attractions for free, and all the participating locations have activities and events on-site. The annual Dickens in the Market performance is also part of the festival, and for one day performers in period clothing will inhabit a Charles Dickens–inspired village and interact with shoppers and diners in the Old Market area. The New Year's Eve fireworks show is one of the largest displays in the area, and usually more than 30,000 people convene in downtown Omaha to see the show. Visit the website for the most current list of participating organizations and a full event schedule.

## DECEMBER

### CHRISTMAS AT UNION STATION
**Durham Museum**
**http://durhammuseum.org**
The main event at Christmas at Union Station really isn't an event, it's a giant pine tree. It's the biggest indoor Christmas tree in Omaha—in the region, even—and the lighting ceremony, slated yearly for the day after Thanksgiving—draws thousands. Food, music, and a visit from Santa are the main draws for the one-day event, and the Christmas tree display continues through the end of the year. A number of other special events—including more visits from Santa, an Ethnic Holiday Festival, a concert series, an exhibition about Christmas trees, and a holiday miniature display—complete the yearly celebration.

## Part 2

# OMAHA

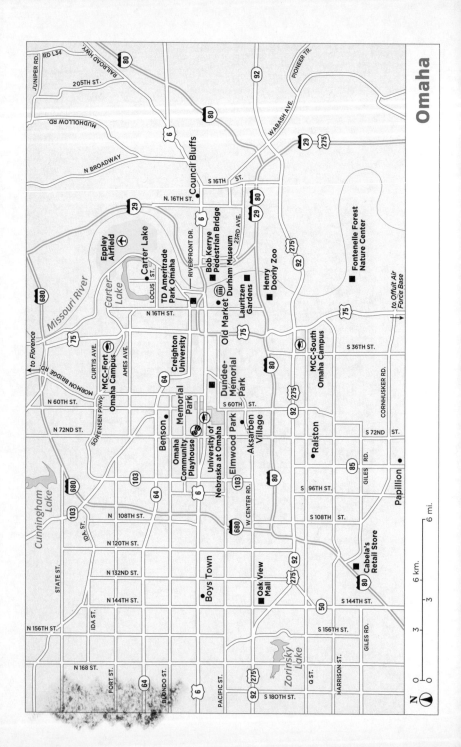

# Omaha

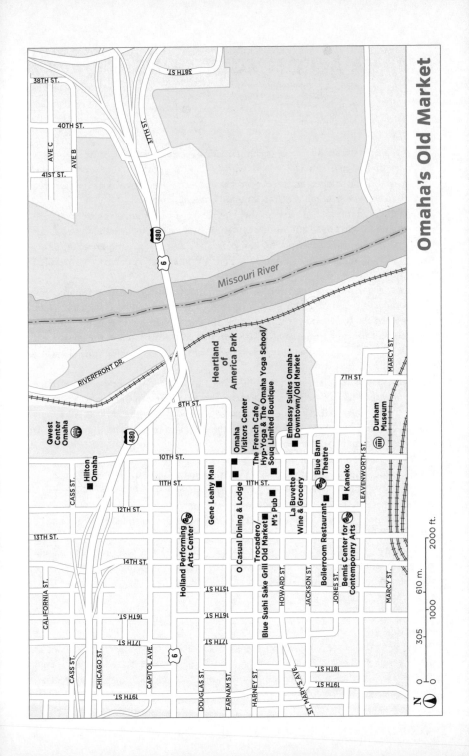

# Omaha's Old Market

38TH ST.

40TH ST.

AVE C

AVE B

41ST ST.

38TH ST.

37TH ST.

480

6

Missouri River

RIVERFRONT DR.

Heartland of America Park

8TH ST.

480

Qwest Center Omaha

Hilton Omaha

CASS ST.

10TH ST.

11TH ST.

12TH ST.

13TH ST.

14TH ST.

Holland Performing Arts Center

Gene Leahy Mall

O Casual Dining & Lodge

Trocadero/ Blue Sushi Sake Grill Old Market

Omaha Visitors Center

The French Cafe/ Hyp-Yoga & The Omaha Yoga School/ Souq Limited Boutique

11TH ST.

M's Pub

La Buvette Wine & Grocery

Embassy Suites Omaha - Downtown/Old Market

Blue Barn Theatre

Kaneko

Boilerroom Restaurant

Bemis Center for Contemporary Arts

LEAVENWORTH ST.

7TH ST.

Durham Museum

MARCY ST.

CALIFORNIA ST.

CASS ST.

CHICAGO ST.

CAPITOL AVE.

6

19TH ST.

17TH ST.

16TH ST.

15TH ST.

DOUGLAS ST.

FARNAM ST.

HARNEY ST.

ST. MARY'S AVE.

HOWARD ST.

JACKSON ST.

JONES ST.

MARCY ST.

18TH ST.

19TH ST.

N

0    305    610 m.

0    1000    2000 ft.

# OMAHA ACCOMMODATIONS

Omaha offers a wide array of accommodations for visitors. Lots of hotels—most part of national chains—offer a wide variety of options. High-end options, middle-of-the-line rooms, and economy choices are all available in every Omaha neighborhood and near many attractions and business centers.

For those who prefer to travel in the comforts of a recreational vehicle, there are lots of RV parks that offer a multitude of amenities: parks for kids, swimming pools, hot tubs, and community gatherings for campers. The Parks & Recreation chapter offers further lodging options for campers as well as RV travelers; state parks are detailed there.

The traveler who prefers a unique accommodation will find that in Omaha, too. The city offers a boutique hotel in a historic downtown building with excellent proximity to the Old Market (see map on p. 35) and the Orpheum Theater. Omaha's one bed-and-breakfast offers a popular getaway for locals looking for a weekend "staycation" and is a popular option for newlyweds or those looking for a romantic retreat.

The business traveler will find many hotels located conveniently close to office parks in west Omaha, Papillion, and La Vista. Those traveling to Omaha for a convention will find many lodging options around downtown's Qwest Center Omaha. And best of all, things like wireless Internet, 24-hour business centers, and top-notch concierge services have become the norm.

Many Omaha hotels offer free shuttle service to and from their facilities to the Omaha airport; some also offer service to businesses and restaurants located around the hotel. The Getting Here, Getting Around chapter goes into full detail about transportation options to and from hotels to airports, as well as to and from Omaha and Lincoln for professionals who have business in Omaha or Lincoln and need a way to get back and forth.

Lodging in Omaha is relatively inexpensive, and travelers will find many of the hotels listed in this section on major discount websites; it's worth doing a bit of price comparison before booking.

## Price Code

The following price code has been included to give you a rough idea of what one regular double occupancy room or overnight stay will cost at each of the following places.

When choosing a hotel, it is important to bear in mind that costs can vary greatly from high season to low, so you may be pleasantly surprised to find a lower price when you actually go to make the reservation. Additionally, many of the hotels and accommodations here offer special rates, packages, and sales, so be sure to check around before you book.

| | |
|---|---|
| $ | . . . . . . . . . . . . . . . . Less than $70 |
| $$ | . . . . . . . . . . . . . . . . $70 to $100 |
| $$$ | . . . . . . . . . . . . . . $100 to $200 |
| $$$$ | . . . . . . . . . . More than $200 |

## *Quick Index by Cost*

**$$$**

**CoCo Key Water Resort,** Central, 41

**The Cornerstone Mansion Bed-&-Breakfast,** 44

**Courtyard by Marriott Aksarban Village,** Central, 41

**Courtyard by Marriott Omaha,** Downtown, 37

**Courtyard Omaha La Vista,** La Vista, 43

**Doubletree by HIlton,** Downtown, 38

**Element Omaha Midtown Crossing,** Midtown, 41

**Embassy Suites Downtown/Old Market,** Downtown, 38

**Embassy Suites Omaha—La Vista Hotel & Conference Center,** La Vista, 44

**Fairfield Inn & Suites,** North Downtown, 39

**Hampton Inn & Suites Downtown,** North Downtown, 39

**Hampton Inn & Suites Southwest,** La Vista, 44

**Hampton Inn—Lakeside,** West Omaha, 42

**Hilton Omaha,** Downtown, 38

**Holiday Inn Downtown Omaha,** North Downtown, 40

**Holiday Inn Express Hotel and Suites,** West Omaha, 43

**Homewood Suites by Hilton,** North Downtown, 40

**The Magnolia,** Downtown, 39

**Omaha Marriott,** West Omaha, 43

**Staybridge Suites,** Central, 42

**$$**

**Regency Lodge Omaha,** West Omaha, 43

**$**

**Sleep Inn and Suites at the Airport,** Airport, 40

**West Omaha KOA,** West Omaha, 42

## DOWNTOWN

### COURTYARD BY MARRIOTT OMAHA $$$
101 S. 10th St.
(402) 346-2200
www.marriott.com/omacy

Located just outside of the Old Market area and conveniently in between the market and the neighboring Qwest Center Omaha and TD Ameritrade Park, the Courtyard by Marriott's 167 rooms and

14 suites are popular, especially during sporting events like the newly-arrived College World Series. On-site parking is available for both daily and hourly rates, and a shuttle runs to and from the nearby Eppley Airfeld on a regular schedule; guests must reserve a ride in advance. The nicely appointed suites and guest rooms include all the basics that we've come to expect from hotels: coffee, tea, water, Internet service, and a minifridge. Cribs

and rollaway beds are available upon request. The hotel has a fitness center, indoor pool, and whirlpool. In-hotel restaurant choices are slim, though with the adjacent Old Market, most guests probably don't mind. The Courtyard Cafe in the restaurant offers a popular breakfast buffet that includes hot and cold items.

### DOUBLETREE BY HILTON $$$
**1616 Dodge St.**
**(402) 346-7600**
**www.doubletree1.hilton.com**
One of the area's older hotels, the downtown Doubletree is popular for business travelers working with one of the many companies located in downtown Omaha. The Doubletree is on the north end of 16th Street and is a bit farther of a walk to the Old Market area, though definitely doable. The hotel is located across the street from both the First National Bank of Omaha and the Union Pacific Headquarters; the hotel's "pay to park only once" means that business travelers can park in the hotel garage just once and walk to their destinations. The hotel's lobby and many of its guest rooms were recently remodeled, lending a modern feel to the property. The hotel has an on-site swimming pool, fitness center, and Starbucks coffee shop. The 19th floor Executive Meeting Center provides 30,000 square feet of flexible meeting space popular for business conventions as well as special events. Signatures Restaurant serves breakfast, lunch, and dinner, though diners would be advised to check out some of the area's unique local dining.

### ✳EMBASSY SUITES DOWNTOWN/ OLD MARKET $$$
**555 S. 10th St.**
**(402) 346-9000**
**www.omaha.embassysuites.com**
At the foot of the Old Market, the Embassy Suites is not just one of downtown's nicest hotels, it's as close as one can get to the popular historic district. Like all the hotels in the chain, the hotel has a tall central atrium surrounded with rooms featuring a private bedroom and separate living area. The executive and presidential suites are larger than one can imagine, and the presidential suite—popular for wedding parties—is the size of a small apartment, with a full kitchen, dining room, sitting area, and two bathrooms. The hotel's complimentary cooked-to-order breakfast that includes omelets, waffles, and other egg dishes, as well as a vast array of cold items on a buffet, is popular with guests and visitors not staying in the hotel. The hotel also has a complimentary manager's reception every evening, with free cocktails and snacks. Embassy offers a complimentary shuttle to and from Eppley Airfield.

> **i** The revitalization of North Downtown Omaha—including the construction of TD Ameritrade Stadium—led to a wide variety of new lodging options in the area. Close to the airport, the historic Old Market district, and downtown businesses, this is one of the city's most popular areas to stay.

### HILTON OMAHA $$$
**1001 Cass St.**
**(402) 998-3400**
**www.omaha.hilton.com**
Easily the city's poshest hotel, Hilton Omaha opened in 2004 and is the state's only

hotel earning a AAA Four Diamond ranking. The modern lobby features artwork by a number of local Omaha artists, and Omaha ceramicist Jun Kaneko has a group of his famous "Dango" sculptures outside the hotel's entrance. The decor throughout the hotel is warm yet modern, and it's connected to the adjacent Qwest Center Omaha via a glass skybridge. The hotel's 450 guest rooms feature all the amenities. The hotel is currently undergoing a $35 milllion expansion project that will add 150 guest rooms, a second 7,000 square foot ballroom and 100 new parking spaces. Twelve luxury suites include a presidential suite and executive suites, all located on the executive level of the hotel, which has its own private lounge that serves complimentary non-alcoholic beverages, free continental breakfast, and snacks throughout the day and in the evening. Executive suite guests also get turn-down service each evening. The hotel restaurant and bar, the Liberty Tavern, serves meals all day long and has a popular outdoor patio on 10th Street that features a large enclosed fireplace that's used on a seasonal basis. The hotel has an on-site fitness center, pool, and spa that offers massages and facials. More than 30,000 square feet of meeting space include a 10,000-square-foot ballroom that is popular for conventions and private events alike. The hotel has free 24-hour-a-day shuttle service back and forth from Eppley Airfield.

**THE MAGNOLIA**               $$$
**1615 Howard St.**
**(402) 342-2222**
**www.magnoliahotelomaha.com**
One of Omaha's only boutique hotels, the Magnolia is designed with a modern take on an original 1920's Italian sculpture in the

building. Marble floors, travertine walls, and Roman columns are juxtaposed with elegant modern chandeliers and furniture. Guest rooms and suites lend views of the Omaha skyline and the hotel's courtyard. The newly renovated rooms are decorated in chocolate brown and turquoise and equipped with high-speed Internet, large work spaces, Nintendo, and in-room Starbucks, along with all the other expected amenities. Six thousand square feet of meeting space accommodate special events, meetings, and many weddings. The hotel offers a reception with free beer and wine each night, free airport transportation, and a complimentary bedtime cookies and milk buffet.

## NORTH DOWNTOWN

**FAIRFIELD INN & SUITES**               $$$
**1501 Nicholas St.**
**(402) 280-1516**
**www.marriott.com/omafd**
With a hip color palette of orange, vivid green, and royal blue, north downtown's Fairfield Inn and Suites' 83 rooms and 30 suites are both hip and affordable. The color palette continues through the lobby, breakfast room (where food is served daily), and pool and fitness center. Outside the pool, a sundeck welcomes guests to wind down after a long day. Free on-site parking is a plus. The hotel doesn't have any on-site restaurants, though a self-service kiosk called The Market offers sandwiches, frozen meals, and dry snacks for those who need to eat on the go.

**HAMPTON INN & SUITES**
   **DOWNTOWN**               $$$
**1212 Cuming St.**
**(402) 345-5500**
**www.omahadowntownsuites**
**.hamptoninn.com**

Hampton Inn (which is right next door to Homewood Suites) is the closest hotel to the new TD Ameritrade Stadium, and will likely be the lodging choice of lots of baseball fans. The hotel's 139 guest rooms and suites are decorated in a warm palette of browns and gold, and the hip lobby seating area and the rooms offer free high-speed Internet. Suites include a kitchen with a mini-fridge, microwave, and sink. A free breakfast buffet is served daily and can be taken to go. The Suite Shop is stocked with travel items, snacks, and microwaveable meals. There isn't a restaurant on-site, but dining options around the area make that just fine. Free shuttle service to and from the airport is available all the time.

### HOLIDAY INN DOWNTOWN
### OMAHA $$$
**1420 Cuming St.**
**(402) 341-0124**
**www.holidayinndowntownomaha.com**
The new north downtown Omaha Holiday Inn is the first in the state that meets the hotel chain's new standards. The hotel has two popular amenities: a water park and the Union Pizzeria and Sports Bar. The 114 guest rooms all have either a single king bed with a pullout sofa or two king beds; none of the rooms have queen or double beds. The hotel offers free shuttle service to the airport and to the Old Market, the Henry Doorly Zoo, and other downtown Omaha attractions. The 10,000-square-foot water park includes a three-story body slide and a play structure with a dump bucket, oversize hot tub, and swimming pool. The waterpark is only open to hotel guests, and is free. The hotel also has a state-of-the-art fitness center and wireless Internet.

### HOMEWOOD SUITES BY HILTON $$$
**1314 Cuming St.**
**(402) 345-5100**
**www.omahadowntown**
**.homewoodsuites.com**
Located right off Cuming Street across from the new TD Ameritrade Stadium and the Hampton Inn, the Homewood Suites is set up for the longer-term guest. Each of the 123 one- or two-bedroom suites has a separate living and sleeping area with a full-size kitchen that includes a large refrigerator, microwave, two-burner stove, and dishwasher. Two televisions and free Internet, as well as two voicemail-equipped phones, make each room as close as it can be to being like home. The hotel serves free breakfast seven days a week and on Monday through Thursday evenings serves a light dinner and beverages. For business clients, the hotel also offers audiovisual equipment available for rent, free printing services, and fax and photocopying centers. Long-term guests can also use the free shuttle service within a 5-mile radius of the hotel, on-site laundry rooms, and complimentary grocery shopping service.

## AIRPORT

### SLEEP INN AND SUITES AT THE
### AIRPORT $
**2525 Abbott Dr.**
**(800) 688-2525**
**www.sleepinn.com/hotel/ne019**
Omaha's airport is close to downtown, so lodging options abound, but one of the closest hotels to Eppley is the Sleep Inn and Suites. An affordable option, the hotel has simple guest rooms with basic decoration and the usual in-room amenities. Suites include a separate sitting area and bedroom,

and the hotel has free breakfast daily and a public computer free for guests to use. The hotel is also one of the only ones in the area that's pet friendly.

## MIDTOWN

### ELEMENT OMAHA MIDTOWN CROSSING                $$$
3253 Dodge St.
(402) 614-8080
www.starwoodhotels.com

Westin's first property in Omaha, the Element Omaha Midtown Crossing, opened in late 2010. The hotel is part of Westin's new line of hotels in urban areas (in this case, Omaha's thriving new Midtown Crossing development) with a focus on being environmentally friendly. The hotel's airy, contemporary decorating in shades of brown, white, and green is carried through the lobby, breakfast bar, and 132 guest rooms. Element's state-of-the-art fitness center and healthy food options at the Rise breakfast bar and Restore Gourmet pantry (for eating on the go) encourage healthy living. Open, airy public spaces are popular for business travelers for meetings and working, as well as socializing after the workday is done. Guest rooms have fully equipped kitchens and the chain's signature Heavenly Bed. The hotel doesn't have an on-site restaurant, but loads of choices in Midtown Crossing and many more just a short jaunt away make this OK for travelers. The hotel has one large conference room and is fully equipped with audiovisual equipment and other technology, including free wireless, to cater to a more intimate business meeting.

## CENTRAL

### COCO KEY WATER RESORT                $$$
At the Holiday Inn Omaha Convention Center
3321 S. 72nd St.
(402) 393-3950
www.cocokeywaterresort.com/locations/omaha

A great place for families, the Holiday Inn Omaha Convention Center's main draw is certainly the CoCo Key Water Resort, which is also the city's only indoor water park that's open year-round. Part of a national chain of waterparks, CoCo Key Omaha features an Olympic-size, beach entry pool, poolside cabanas, slides for kids of all ages, a huge dump bucket, a fast paced river ride, an indoor/outdoor spa (for guests 16 and older), and an interactive game room with arcade and video games. The park is available to hotel guests but also offers day passes to those not staying at the hotel. Passes are available online or at the door and day pass guests must bring their own towels. The hotel itself, attached to the waterpark, caters to families but also corporate travelers, with a fitness center, business center, and free wireless Internet throughout the hotel. An on-site restaurant, Tradewinds Restaurant and Lounge, is open for three meals a day and also provides room service throughout the hotel. A Scooter's Coffee House in the hotel serves coffee, espresso drinks, tea, and pastries.

### COURTYARD BY MARRIOTT AKSARBEN VILLAGE                $$$
1625 S. 67th St.
(402) 951-4300
www.marriott.com/omawt

This new hotel in the Aksarben Crossing development, an up and coming spot for dining and nightlife, offers all the comforts of other Courtyard by Marriott locations but adds a location right in the center of Omaha. The 130 guest rooms and four suites are decorated in warm hues of red and brown with hints of lime green, and the scheme is reflected in the lobby and breakfast area. Rooms have a mini fridge and a pull out sofa bed. The on-site restaurant, Bistro, serves breakfast and dinner in a casual, urban setting. The hotel caters to its business traveler with a series of "media pods" in the public spaces of the hotel, which offer semi-private booth seating; free wireless Internet; power outlets for computers, phones, and other devices; and a flat screen television with a personal remote control.

## STAYBRIDGE SUITES $$$
**7825 Davenport St.**
**(402) 933-8901**
**www.staybridge.com/omahane**

Opened in 2011, Omaha's first Staybridge Suites brings a high-end extended-stay facility to central Omaha. The hotel features 65 deluxe studio rooms and 37 one- and two-bedroom suites. Set up for the business traveler, the rooms are equipped with large desks, ergonomic seating, speaker phones, and personal voice mail. Other amenities include fully equipped kitchens in each room, free laundry facilities, a workout room, free daily breakfast, a library with free books and games for guest use, and a 24-hour free business center. An on-site convenience store carries snacks, sundries, beverages, and meals that can be prepared in a hotel room. The lobby area features the hotel's signature "Just Like Home Theater" with a 60-inch plasma television, surround sound, and comfortable seating.

# WEST OMAHA
## WEST OMAHA KOA $-$$$
**14601 US 6**
**(402) 332-3010**
**www.koa.com**

Close to lots of local attractions, the West Omaha KOA is equipped for 80-foot full hook-up pull-throughs and 50 amp service. Tent sites and cabins are also available, and the cabins, cottages, and lodges are all heated, air conditioned, and furnished. Rates depend on the season. Amenities include a playground, a minigolf course, a swimming pool, a shuffleboard court, horseshoes, banana bikes, badminton and basketball courts, and sand volleyball. The on-site Kornhusker Kafe serves breakfast, and pizza delivery is available. An on-site dog park lets owners exercise their pets. Seasonal weekend activities include hayrack rides, ice cream socials, and themed breakfasts.

## HAMPTON INN—LAKESIDE $$$
**17606 Arbor Plaza**
**(402) 330-9500**
**www.omahawestlakeside.hamptoninn .com**

The 110-room Hampton Inn at Lakeside in West Omaha is popular with business travelers and tourists alike. It has free high-speed Internet and a lap desk made especially for a laptop computer in every room and a staff eager to suggest restaurants and activities to guests. Rooms are simply appointed in hues of tan, green, and burgundy, and the hotel offers a number of special services for guests, including free beverages and breakfasts; valet service; and a number of business services, including audiovisual equipment rentals, free printing, and meeting spaces.

## HOLIDAY INN EXPRESS HOTEL
### AND SUITES $$$
17677 Wright St.
(402) 333-5566
www.hiexpress.com/omahawest

This newer Holiday Inn Express offers the basics any hotel guest expects at an affordable rate. Located off a main street in West Omaha, it's convenient for business travelers working in that part of town as well as families visiting relatives who live in the suburbs of Omaha. The hotel is pet friendly (something rather rare in Omaha hotels) and serves free breakfast daily.

## OMAHA MARRIOTT $$$
10220 Regency Circle
(402) 339-9000
www.omahamarriott.com

The 300 rooms and suites at the Omaha Marriott are well appointed in warm hues, and the full-service hotel caters to the business guest with ample room for meetings and conventions. The hotel has 14 meeting rooms, totaling 12,000 square feet, and 2 concierge levels with special services, including a private lounge. Much of the meeting space has been recently remodeled. The on-site restaurant, the Omaha Chophouse, has a decidedly old-school flavor, with a menu featuring a variety of cuts from locally owned Omaha Steaks alongside a variety of soups, salad, and seafood entrees. The restaurant is open year-round and serves lunch, breakfast, and dinner daily.

## REGENCY LODGE OMAHA $$
909 S. 107th Ave.
(402) 397-8000
www.regencylodge.com

An urban oasis, the Regency Lodge truly is like a mountain resort in the middle of Omaha. Surrounded by gardens and lushly appointed inside with fireplaces, sleigh beds, and full kitchens in many of the rooms, the Regency Lodge is a popular venue for special events and weddings. Wednesday, Thursday, and Friday, the lodge plays host to the city's only piano bar, from 5:30 to 8:30 p.m. The hotel offers a number of special package deals; the romance package includes lodging, a bottle of champagne, and chocolate-covered strawberries. Family-focused packages include lodging and trips to either the Omaha Children's Museum or the Henry Doorly Zoo. Package prices vary depending on what type of room is booked. Full details are available on the website.

# LA VISTA

### COURTYARD OMAHA LA VISTA $$$
12560 Westport Pkwy.
(402) 339-4900
www.marriott.com/hotels/travel/
omalv-courtyard-omaha-lavista/

Located on the other side of the Embassy Suites (below) and the La Vista Conference Center, the Courtyard Omaha La Vista offers a second lodging option for those doing business or attending a convention on the outskirts of the city. The hotel's 235 rooms and 11 suites are decorated in warm autumnal hues and some feature a separate seating area and bedroom. A public fire pit and modern outdoor seating area provide a space for relaxation and fun for guests, and the hotel lobby is home to the "Go Board," a touch screen that guests can use to find driving directions, get a weather update, or find a spot to eat dinner. Before guests leave, they can print out airline boarding passes for free in the lobby.

### *EMBASSY SUITES OMAHA—LA VISTA HOTEL & CONFERENCE CENTER   $$$

**12520 Westport Pkwy.**
**(402) 331-7400**
**http://embassysuites1.hilton.com**

West Omaha's answer to the downtown Embassy Suites, this new location also doubles as a popular convention center. La Vista is 20 minutes from downtown Omaha and 40 minutes from Lincoln. The business traveler will find many large companies nearby—Omaha Steaks, PayPal, and Werner Enterprises included—and the hotel does much to cater to professional clients. The Embassy BusinessLink center has computer stations that have Internet access and other office tools, and Internet access is free in the hotel atrium and in the adjacent Caffeina Marketplace Cafe. The La Vista Nines is a contemporary restaurant located on-site; the menu includes a mix of American fare and is available for lunch and dinner. Embassy's 257 suites all have a separate living room and bedroom, two televisions, a wet bar, microwave, refrigerator, and Internet access. Each evening the hotel has free food and drinks as part of the evening manager's reception, and free breakfast is served in the morning.

### HAMPTON INN & SUITES SOUTHWEST   $$$

**12331 Southport Pkwy.**
**(402) 895-2900**
**www.omahalavistasuites.hampton inn.com**

Located near the Embassy Suites La Vista, the Hampton Inn and Suites Southwest has 120 nicely appointed guest rooms that have all the usual amenities. It's in the Southport development, a multiuse retail and office park, near Cabela's, a popular Nebraska-based outdoor store. The hotel offers business services and free Internet for its corporate clients, and has a free breakfast each morning.

## BED-&-BREAKFAST

### THE CORNERSTONE MANSION   $$–$$$

**140 N. 39th St., Omaha**
**(402) 558-7600**
**www.cornerstonemansion.com**

Omaha's only B&B, the Cornerstone Mansion is located in the city's historic Gold Coast neighborhood. The B&B is in the Offutt House, owned by prominent Omaha couple Charles and Bertha Offutt. They built the more than 10,000-square-foot manse in 1894. (Offutt Air Force base, in Bellevue, is named after their son Jarvis.) The house is listed on the National Register of Historic Places and has undergone lots of renovations since it became a B&B in the mid-1980s. The hotel has updated electrical, new finishing, updated plumbing, and all the comforts the modern traveler requires. The house has seven guest rooms, each with its own private bath; four of the rooms are multi-room suites. All rooms include free wireless Internet, telephones, and televisions; some rooms have fireplaces, sun porches, decks, and claw-foot tubs. Other singular amenities include a large library with a mahogany and onyx fireplace, a more than 100-year-old Weber Box Grand Piano, a formal parlor, and a gazebo-filled garden. Breakfast is served in the formal dining room, and the B&B serves a continental breakfast on weekdays and a full, gourmet breakfast on Saturday and Sunday.

# OMAHA RESTAURANTS

Omaha is a town of people who like to eat out. Almost any type of food—and lots of it fine—is available somewhere in the city. Nebraska is a state steeped in agriculture, and this bounty translates to the tables of thousands of Omaha restaurants. The wide variety of cuisine represented in this chapter offers food at every price level, every level of dining—fine to casual—and all around, the restaurants on this list offer great food.

Omaha's culinary offerings have grown immensely in the past five years, with restaurants like The Boiler Room, Grey Plume, and others opening their doors to captive audiences who love to eat.

There's a special spotlight on something quintessentially Omaha: the old-school steak house. If you've been to one, you know what it's about, and, if not, get thee to a steak house when you arrive in the city. At least one was featured in a major motion picture, another is a favorite of the Oracle of Omaha. Beef is at the heart of what these places do, and, though it's secondary, the atmosphere at all of them is memorable and fun.

## OVERVIEW

The restaurants in this chapter are presented by type of cuisine and in alphabetical order. The styles of cuisine are loosely categorized; some are rather difficult to categorize. A price code has been incorporated so you can find what you're looking for.

Omaha has a strict smoking ban and smoking is not allowed in any workplaces, restaurants, or bars. No restaurants have smoking sections, but some have opened their patios or gardens to smokers.

There are thousands of restaurants in Omaha, and this is just a small sampling of the types of cuisine and places diners can get it. Everyone has his or her own favorites when it comes to restaurants and food; many of the listings here are my favorites. You are encouraged to use this guide as

a jumping-off point and explore the city's foodie offerings for yourself.

### Price Code

The following price code has been included to give you a rough idea of what an average dinner of entrees for two will cost excluding cocktails, wine, appetizers, dessert, tax, and tip. Omaha has a wide array of restaurants, including very reasonable and ultra-fine dining, and every price point in between. Unless otherwise noted, all restaurants accept major credit cards.

| | |
|---|---|
| $ | Less than $10 |
| $$ | $10 to $30 |
| $$$ | $30 to $50 |
| $$$$ | More than $50 |

**Nicola's Italian Wine & Faire,** Italian, $$–$$$, 72

**O Dining and Lounge,** Asian, $$–$$$, 58

**Omaha Prime,** Steakhouse, $$$, 51

**Orsi's Italian Bakery & Pizzeria,** Pizza, $$, 78

**Pasta Amore e Fantasia,** Italian, $$$, 72

**Peru, Mucho Gusto,** Ethnic, $$, 64

**Petrow's,** American, $–$$, 54

**Piccolo Pete's,** Steakhouse, $$, 51

**Pitch Pizzeria,** Pizza, $$–$$$, 78

**Pizza King,** Pizza, $$, 79

**Pudgy's Pizzeria,** Pizza, $$, 79

**Rice Bowl Chinese Restaurant,** $–$$, 59

**Roja Mexican Grill,** Mexican & Tapas, $$, 76

**Runza,** American, $, 54

**Ryan's Bistro,** Fine Dining, $$$, 69

**Sakura Bana,** Asian, · $$–$$$, 59

**Sgt. Peffer's Cafe Italian,** Italian, $–$$, 73

**Shucks Fish House & Oyster Bar,** American, $$–$$$, 55

**Soup Revolution,** American, $, 55

**Spaghetti Works,** Italian, $$, 73

**Spezia,** Italian, $$$, 73

**Stella's Hamburgers,** American, $–$$, 55

**Surfside Club,** American, $–$$, 55

**Sushi Japan Yakiniku Boy,** Asian, $$, 59

**The Taj Kabob and Curry,** Ethnic, $$, 64

**Ted & Wally's Ice Cream Shop,** Sweets, $, 80

**13th Street Coffee Shop,** Coffee Shops, $, 61

**Three Happiness Express,** Asian, $–$$, 60

**Twisted Cork Bistro,** American, $$–$$$, 56

**Upstream Brewing Co.,** American, $$–$$$, 56

**Urban Wine Company,** Fine Dining, $$–$$$, 70

**V. Mertz Restaurant,** Fine Dining, $$$$, 70

**Valentino's,** Pizza, $, 79

**Vincenzo's,** Italian, $$–$$$, 73

**Vivace,** Italian, $$–$$$, 74

**Worker's Take-Out,** American, $, 56

**Zio's New York Style Pizzeria,** Pizza, $–$$, 80

**Zum Biergarten,** Ethnic, $$, 64

**Zurlo's Bistro Italiano,** Italian, $$$, 74

# AMERICAN

### AMARILLO BARBECUE $$
**303 Fort Crook Rd. North, Bellevue**
**(402) 291-7495**

Good barbeque happens in Bellevue, and Amarillo is one of the city's most popular spots. Smoky, spicy sauce and meaty meats are the focus at Amarillo, and sides like jalapeno corn bread and smoky baked beans are also great. Amarillo has been perfecting its smoking technique—and its sauce recipes—for years; it also makes delicious smoked sausage and smoked chickens. Amarillo built its popularity on baby back ribs, and they're the signature item on the menu: Smoky, saucy, and tender, they will please any BBQ fan. Amarillo is simple in its country style decor; the focus here is on the food.

### AMATO'S CAFE & CATERING $$
**6405 Center St.**
**(402) 558-5010**

Sammy Amato started selling his signature sausage and pepper sandwiches out of a county fair booth (as told on the Food Network's *Diners, Drive-Ins and Dives*) and now he runs a popular diner out of midtown Omaha. He's making those sandwiches the same way he always has: a hoagie bun toasted with garlic, handmade sausage (that he makes every day), and a sauce made of peppers and house-made marinara. His signature chicken fried steak sandwich is also doused in the pepper-marinara mix, topped with cheese and double breaded before it's cooked. The inside of Amato's isn't anything fancy—simple diner chairs and red tables—but its hearty, homemade food is the star anyway. Amato's famous ricotta pancakes are another staple, and Sammy makes the cheese, based on his mother's recipe, every day, and puts it in pancake batter along with a handful of fresh blueberries, then cooks it on a hot griddle. If you really want to go for it, top your pancake with a fried egg and enjoy.

**BIG MAMA'S KITCHEN**          **$$–$$$**
**3223 N. 45th St., Turning Point Campus**
**(402) 445-MAMA (6262)**
**www.bigmamaskitchen.com**
Home cooking done right. Big Mama's Kitchen owner Patricia "Big Mama" Barron has been cooking her traditional American cuisine for more than 30 years. Barron ran a catering business out of her kitchen before opening the full-service restaurant in North Omaha in 2008. The restaurant is in a former cafeteria space, and some of that school day charm is still visible in the large space, full of big tables and a corner kitchen. Soul food is at the heart of what Big Mama's Kitchen makes, and the menu includes dishes like fried catfish and greens, chitterlings, feather bones, hot wings, loose meat sandwiches, and Cuban sandwiches, among many other items. Big Mama's serves breakfast, lunch, and dinner, and the breakfast menu includes lots of home cooking: a house recipe breakfast casserole, thick cut bacon, eggs, hash

browns, and biscuits. At Big Mama's you simply must put the diet aside to enjoy the delicious flavors of a home-cooked meal.

**BRONCO'S**                              **$**
**4540 Leavenworth St.**
**(402) 551-7477**
**www.broncoburgers.com**
An Omaha standard for more than 50 years, Bronco's is a fast-food restaurant but it's an old-school one: The burgers and fries are made by hand every day, and things like a pork tenderloin, two- or three-piece chicken dinners, and a frankfurter are on the menu. All the hamburgers are available in single patties or double, and the Big Bronco Burger (a larger version of the original), a chicken sandwich, and a fish sandwich are available deluxe or plain. Bronco's two locations are similar—mostly set up for takeout, each location has a few booths and a drive-through with an open kitchen so you can watch your food being prepared. Bronco's is the only locally owned, non-chain fast-food restaurant in the city, and the food stands out as clearly being of the fast-food genre, but created and cooked by hand. Bronco's second location is at 1123 S. 120th St. (402-334-7477).

**CRESCENT MOON**                  **$–$$**
**3578 Farnam St.**
**(402) 345-1708**
**http://beercornerusa.com**
Known mostly for its vast variety of brews, Crescent Moon also has a solid menu of bar food. A few singular appetizers—fried pickle chips, fried cheese curds, and breaded green pepper rings—are definitely worth a try, especially with a frosty mug in hand. The Moon Wings are another popular choice, and this author knows at least one group of

men who go there on a weekly basis solely for "wing night" when the spicy bites go on special for 40 cents each. The all-you-can-eat deal includes inferno wings or chipotle wings and the special isn't good for to-go orders. The restaurant has daily lunch specials and various happy hour deals depending on the night; check its website for further details and prices.

## CUNNINGHAM'S BISTRO $$$
**2101 N. 120th St.**
**(402) 933-8780**

Tucked in a West Omaha strip mall, Cunningham's Bistro (formerly known as Brunettes Bistro) has a dark, cozy atmosphere and is split into two halves: one an intimate restaurant, the other, a sportier bar. The bar used to be separate, but the owners decided to merge the two and put them under one name. The menu is served on both sides, though the restaurant doesn't have television sets, and the bar does. The menu is a hybrid of bar food (fried pickles) and classier, bistro menu items (bruschetta.) Sandwiches, fish and chips, and burgers sit next to fancier items like a ribeye steak served with maytag smashed potatoes and seasonal vegetables, shrimp and lobster ravioli, and bacon-wrapped scallops. The bar side has regular specials—a recent example being five beers for $5—and its regularly updated Facebook page has an array of food and drink discounts.

## DINKER'S BAR $-$$
**2368 S. 29th St.**
**(402) 342-9742**
**www.dinkersbar.com**

A familiar crowd eats the delicious burgers at Dinker's; it's the kind of place where generational followings are the norm. In business in

the same location since 1965, it's always been a joint for a cold beer and a good burger. The order-at-the-grill setup invites diners to come right up and make their choice: the restaurant has daily lunch specials like chicken fried steak, pot roast sandwich, hot pork cutlet, tuna and noodles—you get the idea. Dinker's makes its burgers daily by hand, using an ice cream scoop and a hand press. The burgers are cooked to order and served as a single, a double, or a massive triple, which equates to close to a pound of beef. Burgers can be prepared just about any way, and options include a patty melt, jalapeno burger, spicy buffalo burger, Husker burger (bacon, cheese, and barbeque sauce), and a Bluejay burger (swiss cheese, bacon, and bleu cheese dressing). Diners can top any burger on the menu with a fried egg. The restaurant recently added some outdoor seating, which is popular in nice weather.

## DUNDEE DELL $$
**5007 Underwood Ave.**
**(402) 553-9501**
**www.dundeedell.com**

A popular neighborhood bar and casual eatery, the Dundee Dell has been around for what seems like forever. Decorated in traditional dive bar decor of big booths, rickety tables, lots of beer signs, and random memorabilia, the Dell, as it's affectionately known, also serves a mean bag of fish and chips. A huge beer list arranged by price on a separate menu means even the most discerning drinker will find something to love, and those who order a glass of wine can expect a healthy pour for a more than reasonable price. The fish and chips are served with some delicious fried sliced potatoes, and diners can choose to dunk the lot in tartar sauce, ketchup, or vinegar (the last

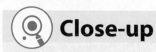

# Close-up

## Steaks in Omaha!

Omaha—in case you didn't know it already—is a beef town. Though the stockyards are long gone, the industry remains, as do the restaurants who serve the beef raised right here in Nebraska. Omaha Steaks is today one of the city's most well-known and respected companies, and its beef is served at many of the restaurants mentioned below. The company started in 1917 and has been known as **Omaha Steaks** since 1966. It operates through a mail order website (www.omahasteaks.com) and through more than 80 stores in 28 states.

Omahans love their meat, and they also love their locally owned and operated steak houses. There's something for everyone here when it comes to style. Some of the steakhouses are new, while others have been around for what seems like forever (and have menus and decor to match). But that vintage style and focus on product—great steaks—is what's kept so many of them around for so long.

**Gorat's Steak House** (4917 Center St., Omaha, 402-551-3733, $$) is at the top of the old-school heap. It's Warren Buffet's favorite steak house, and sometimes, you'll see him eating dinner there. Sometimes, he's even with his pal Bill Gates. But even without a Warren sighting, Gorat's is reliably the same: lots of rooms with lots of tables, a menu that never changes, and a lounge with regular performing acts that are entertaining in the most vintage sense of the word. The petite filet is simply great; Gorat's cooks 'em hot so err toward rare if you like a medium rare steak. During the annual Berkshire Hathaway Shareholders meeting, crowds descend on the restaurant, which is booked weeks in advance. If you're headed to Omaha for the meeting, consider calling ahead. Way ahead.

**Johnny's Cafe** (4702 South 27th St., Omaha, 402-731-4774, $$) was where Jack Nicholson took his steaks in the movie *About Schmidt;* the restaurant looks just like it did in the movie. It's near where the stockyards used to be, and its vibe is decidedly 1960s: mirrors, lots of red, and a huge bar and dining area. The steaks are solid, each table gets an on-the-house appetizer, and the atmosphere is one of a kind.

**Cascio's** (1620 South 10th St., Omaha, 402-345-8313, www.casciossteakhouse .com, $$) is another great old-school stop. The bar is a quiet hangout and the service is good. The steaks and spaghetti, especially, are delicious. The restaurant is dark and divided into a number of rooms. It's been in business since 1946.

The ✳**Drover** (2121 S. 73rd St., Omaha, 402-391-7440, www.droverrestaurant .com, $$$) has an excellent salad bar, is a bar that's a fun local hangout for mixed

is definitely the best). The rest of the menu features bar food at its finest, and the Dell also makes a mean patty melt. The Dell has regular monthly beer tastings on the third Sunday of the month at 4 p.m. and the third Wednesday at 7 p.m. Scotch tastings take place the first Sunday of every month at 4 p.m. and the first Wednesday at 7 p.m. It also

plays host to the periodic wine tasting or other special events; check the website for the most recent details.

**11-WORTH CAFE**                                                     $
**2419 Leavenworth St.**
**(402) 346-6924**
**http://11worthcafe.com**

crowds, and offers a mean selection of fresh, flavorful seafood. The vibe can be surprisingly romantic, and the bar serves some stiff drinks that even the Duke himself would probably love. The Whiskey Steak is the main event on the Drover's menu. For more than 40 years, Whiskey Steak has been the restaurant's signature item. The meat is marinated in a combination of secret ingredients, including whiskey, for 15 minutes, beginning when a diner places his or her order. Then the hunk of certified Angus beef is grilled to order over an open flame while being basted with the special marinade. The finished flavor is truly unique.

**Brother Sebastian's Steak House** (1350 S. 119th St., Omaha, 402-330-0300, www.brothersebastians.com, $$$) has been around for more than 30 years and is a theme restaurant designed to look like a monastery with robed waitstaff, small dark rooms, and the soft sounds of chants taking over for music. It's not everyone's style, but it has a great, old-school menu and vintage prices to go along with it. A long list of steaks—practically every cut—includes the signature Filet Sebastian, which is a 12-ounce center cut tenderloin grilled to order and served with sautéed mushrooms and hollandaise sauce.

**Eli Caniglia's Venice Inn** (6920 Pacific St., Omaha, 402-556-3111, www.canigliasveniceinn.com, $$) and **Piccolo Pete's** (2202 South 20th St., Omaha, 402-342-9038, $$) were featured in a steak battle on the Food Network's show *Food Wars*. (Spoiler alert: Caniglia's won.) Caniglia's Venice Inn has been around for more than 50 years and is decidedly old-school. It also specializes in Sicilian and Italian dinners. Though Caniglia's Venice Inn won the television challenge, Piccolo's has always had a closer place in this writer's heart. It's been around since 1933 and has one of the most memorable neon signs in the city out front: a festive man playing a piccolo. Piccolo's is a huge, open space with lots of tables and lots of arched mirrors and chandeliers. It's *mostaccoli* and meatballs is fantastic, the steaks are big and juicy, and the beef stroganoff is a must try if you're into that sort of decidedly old-school menu item. (And one assumes you wouldn't be here if you weren't.)

Omaha also has more modern takes on the steak house. **Omaha Prime** (415 South 11th St., Omaha, 402-341-7040, www.omaha-prime.com, $$$) is the Old Market's answer to steak and is a hugely popular business lunch and dinner spot, as well as a popular place for a special occasion. It doesn't have the same old-school vibe as the older steakhouses do, but it's decidedly manly and meat is clearly the order of the day. It's one of the few restaurants in the country to serve only USDA Prime Grade beef.

A diner in the truest sense, the 11-Worth Cafe looks like it's transported into today from the 1950s. The outdoor neon sign, the retro booths, and the soda fountain meet a decidedly retro menu, featuring signature items like chicken fried steak, breakfasts that come slathered in the 11-Worth's homemade country sausage gravy, and the All American Grilled Steak Hoagie, where sautéed top sirloin is cooked with onion and served on a grilled hoagie with American cheese. If you join the 11-Worth's VIP club, you get 15 percent off your order Monday through Thursday. Members of the club also receive coupons in the mail, and a select few printable coupons are available online.

The cafe also offers its signature gravy to go in reheatable pouches in quart size and half gallon size. Customers can also buy biscuits to go in packages of six.

## GOLDBERGS II $-$$
**5008 Dodge St.**
**(402) 556-2006**
**www.goldbergsindundee.com**

With the slogan "Burgers, Beers & Bloody Marys," diners know what they're in for when they go to midtown's Goldbergs II. (The "II" in the name separates the midtown Goldberg's from another similar outfit in West Omaha.) Outside of its wide variety of cooked-to-order burgers (including a delicious patty melt), Goldberg's offers 14 varieties of bread pudding; flavors vary daily and diners can buy a single serving or a whole pan to take home. Homemade sandwiches and entrees, soup, salad, and traditional American appetizers round out the menu. Goldberg's II is a casual restaurant; it has the feel of a bar but is still appropriate for families and can easily accommodate large groups. The decor is simple: lots of wood booths and tables and a popular outdoor seating area that faces the busy Dodge Street corridor.

> **i** Johnny's Cafe is featured in the Alexander Payne–directed film *About Schmidt*. Warren Schmidt, played by Jack Nicholson, has his retirement dinner at the restaurant.

## HARTLAND BBQ $$
**5402 NW Radial Hwy.**
**(402) 397-5765**
**www.hartlandbar-b-que.com**

Voted the best barbeque in the city a number of times, Hartland has a meaty, smoky menu. Hartland is a hole in the wall in Omaha's Benson neighborhood, and its decor is simple, with tables, chairs, and an order-at-the-counter style setup. Daily specials include three slow smoked baby back ribs served with two sides and cornbread for $7.99 or the diner's choice of a smoked sausage, chopped pork, or chopped chicken sandwich served with a soda and chips for $5.50. Hartland sells meat by the pound, including slow-smoked Angus brisket, hardwood-smoked pork, and sometimes cold-smoked pork ribs to go. It also sells slow smoked chicken and half and full racks of baby back ribs. Homemade sides include baked beans, creamy cucumbers, green beans, potato salad, or coleslaw. It's simple, good, home-cooked barbeque at a reasonable price.

## JACKSON STREET TAVERN $$$
**1125 Jackson St.**
**(402) 991-5637**
**www.jacksonstreettavern.com**

Jackson Street Tavern is one of the newest restaurants to open in Omaha's Old Market and has a menu with an interesting blend of tapas and American dishes. The Tavern lives up to its name, with bulky dark wood tables, a long wood bar, and television sets high on the walls. The front section of the restaurant has pull-up garage doors, making it a fun place to sit in warmer weather. Located on bustling Jackson Street, a seat in the front offers some good people watching. The restaurant serves lunch and dinner and has a special late night menu featuring tapas specials and drinks at reduced prices; that menu goes into effect at 11 p.m. and lasts until 2 a.m. A regular happy hour runs daily from 4 to 6 p.m. Creative sandwiches, salads, and entrees decorate Jackson Street's menu. The *Cavatelli di mare* is a popular pasta dish featuring sea scallops, gulf shrimp, and Maine lobster meat finished with roasted garlic cream sauce. Sandwiches are named after different cities, and the Omaha Hilltop sandwich features roasted turkey, applewood smoked bacon, hard boiled eggs, shredded lettuce, tomato, and thousand island dressing on marble rye. The tapas aren't anything singular but taste good when 11 p.m. rolls around. Try the roasted garlic hummus pita strips or the chicken satay with cucumbers and peanut sauce.

### JAMS BAR & GRILL                    $$
### 7814 Dodge St.
### (402) 399-8300
### www.jamseats.com

A popular after-work hangout and lunch hour escape for West and Central Omaha professionals, Jams is also a happening spot for dinner on the weekends. The restaurant has a funky vibe, with a huge mural of people covering one wall and a bar that stretches the length of the other wall; patrons sit at booths and tables in the center. Some of the most popular dishes include the Midtown Meatloaf, served with mashed potatoes and broccoli; the crab cakes, which come alone or part of a salad; and the chicken enchilada, served with verde sauce, jack cheese, salsa, and southwestern sour cream. If you have room for dessert at the end, be sure to check out the tray; the homemade selections always prove delicious.

### LISA'S RADIAL CAFE               $-$$
### 817 N. 40th St.
### (402) 551-2176

The perfect spot for a Saturday or Sunday morning greasy spoon breakfast, Lisa's Radial Cafe serves diner food at its finest. The front room of Lisa's includes an old-fashioned soda shop counter where diners sip hot coffee and read the paper while they wait for a table. The walls are covered with kitsch: think photos of Marilyn Monroe covered with twinkling lights, Mickey Mouse and Elvis posters, and anything else that falls into the category of "Americana." Prices at Lisa's are cheap and service is fast: Your cup of coffee will never go empty here. The stuffed French toast and banana pancakes are both great, and if you like gravy some menu items include a sea of it. The egg and cheese sandwich is another yummy breakfast pick. The Radial Raft is probably the menu item that best describes what diners find at Lisa's: It includes a layer of hash browns topped with homemade biscuits all floating on a plate of sausage gravy topped with two over-easy eggs.

### LOUIE M'S BURGER LUST            $-$$
### 1718 Vinton St.
### (402) 449-9112
### www.louiemsburgerlust.com

Louie M's Burger Lust is a South Omaha staple. The diner started serving doughnuts and juice in 1980 and slowly grew into the full service, burger-centric restaurant it is today. The restaurant has a memorable atmosphere, with brick walls, neon signs, arched doorways, and plenty of vintage charisma. A long list of hamburgers predictably makes up the bulk of the menu. With (or without) just about any ingredient, the burgers are fully customizable. A taco burger, Cajun burger, mozzarella and black olive burger, Italian burger, and the egg-n-burger are just a few of the notable sandwiches. French fries, served with or without chili and cheese, and onion rings are the preferable sides. Other menu items include an old-fashioned Coney dog, a classic Reuben, and an Italian sausage sandwich. Louie M's serves a daily lunch special priced at $7.99; check the website for the full listing.

## NEBRASKA BREWING COMPANY    $$
**7474 Towne Center Pkwy., Papillion**
**(402) 934-7100**
Nebraska Brewing Company is West Omaha's answer to a locally owned burger joint with good beer. True to form, lots of the menu items feature the restaurant's housemade brew. Chicken strips feature a batter spiked with ale, mussels are steamed in brew, and the gourmet macaroni and cheese is flavored with the house's Infinite Wit. Most of the food on the menu is pretty standard pub fare: burgers and sandwiches, soup, salad, and a few higher-end entrees like steak medallions and lobster pasta alfredo. Nebraska Brewing Company distributes its beers to restaurants around the area and does have a tasting platter available—for the indecisive, sample a serving of six small glasses for $8. The atmosphere is rustic and casual, with a double level dining room and a large patio that's great in nice weather.

## PETROW'S    $–$$
**5914 Center St.**
**(402) 551-0552**
**www.petrows.com**
An old-school soda shop and restaurant, Petrow's serves diner food, pie, breakfast, and some seriously good malts and milkshakes. A full breakfast menu has everything a diner could dream of: steak and eggs, waffles and pancakes, egg dishes of all kinds, omelets, potato casseroles, and homemade cinnamon and pecan rolls from the bakery. The restaurant is decorated like

a 1950s soda shop, with big booths and tables, an old-fashioned soda shop counter, and television sets in a back room, which is great for larger parties. Family and senior citizen friendly, Petrow's draws a mixed crowd during all hours of the day. The lunch and dinner menu continues down the same track as the breakfast menu: hearty diner classics with a retro twist. Burgers, sandwiches, French dips, hot beef sandwiches, chili, and pork tenderloins. Shakes and malts come in a wide variety of flavors. Petrow's serves beer and wine; a full list is available at the restaurant.

## RUNZA    $
**Numerous locations in Omaha and Lincoln**
**www.runza.com**
When you get to Nebraska, you're for sure going to hear one word pretty soon after your arrival, and that word is "Runza." Runza is two things: a chain of fast-food restaurants based in the state, and a sandwich. Runza, of course, serves Runzas. The first one, created in 1949, is pretty much the same today: It's a thick pocket of homemade bread dough stuffed full of ground beef, onions, cabbage, and a secret blend of spices, then baked and served hot. Runzas are really popular in Nebraska—so much that Nebraskans who live elsewhere or those who had a Runza during a visit and had a later craving can order them frozen shipped to their home and bake them at their leisure. Today, Runzas come in the original form and as a Cheese Runza, a Swiss Mushroom Runza, a Cheeseburger Runza, a Barbeque Bacon Runza, and a BLT Runza. The restaurant also sells great, handmade burgers and tasty fries and onion rings, which are available combined as

"Frings." Runza restaurants are all decorated the same: a forest green, gold, and wood scheme with booths, tables, and a Nebraska-made menu.

## SHUCKS FISH HOUSE & OYSTER BAR                  $$–$$$
**1218 S. 119th St. (inside Absolutely Fresh Seafood)**
**(402) 827-4376**
**http://absolutelyfresh.com**

Shucks Fish House & Oyster Bar serves delicious, fresh seafood prepared simply with an emphasis on flavor. The calamari is a great starter: It's perfectly chewy and crispy, with a light breading. The majority of the menu is focused on fish and seafood, though a few pub standards are in the mix for those not in the mood for crustaceans. Shucks has a casual atmosphere: Rolls of paper towels and jugs of sauce sit on the tables. The restaurants are part bar, part restaurant and usually packed. House-made seafood soups and stews, fish platters available in a variety of combinations, and a delicious ahi tuna "steak" sandwich are all tasty options. Louisiana Po' Boys are here, too, as are New Orleans–inspired spiced fish and house-made barbeque. Shucks has another location at 16901 Wright Plaza (402-763-1860).

## SOUP REVOLUTION                  $
**Truck location varies, but usually in downtown Omaha**
**(402) 881-7593**
**www.soup-revolution.com**

Omaha's first foray into roving food trucks comes with Soup Revolution. The soup is prepared beforehand in a commercial kitchen, and then loaded onto a white van with a blue and grey star logo on the side. The soup van has proven quite popular with downtown Omaha professionals, and there's often a line over the noon hour. Chef Sara Demars Cerasoli posts the menu for the day on Facebook and Twitter. Soup Revolution also has a partnership with Dundee's eCreamery, and serves soup for lunch at their 50th and Underwood store each Tuesday. The soup will vary seasonally, and some of the fall 2010 offerings included chicken tortilla, wild mushroom and red rice, chorizo and black bean, red lentil and pot roast stew, and curried chicken and coconut milk.

## STELLA'S HAMBURGERS                  $–$$
**106 Galvin Rd. South, Bellevue**
**(402) 291-6088**

The slogan at Stella's is "Food doesn't have to be fancy to be good," and that's the truth at this Bellevue burger joint that has been in business since 1936. The restaurant is a serious neighborhood joint with a surf style interior decor design. The simple menu serves an array of sandwiches and burgers, which are the main event. The burgers come in singles or doubles, and there's a wide array of burger enhancements: cheese, jalapenos, a fried egg, onion, bacon, ranch, and even peanut butter (locals say it's rather tasty). Sides include tasty onion rings and authentic diner french fries. Food at Stella's is served on a napkin, and diners get a toothpick to take a stab at the fries.

## SURFSIDE CLUB                  $–$$
**14445 N. River Dr.**
**(402) 451-9642**

Surfside is a summertime staple in Omaha. There's barely a menu—diners choose from fried chicken or fried catfish—and decide whether they want to eat inside or outside, and it's an easy choice when it's warm. The outside seating area is sparse (as is the inside of the greasy spoon) and lends a panoramic view of the Missouri River. A note of caution: Passengers on boats passing by are prone to lewd gestures, so either take it with good humor, or don't go to the Surfside—it's been happening for years and probably won't stop any time soon. The catfish is grilled tender, the chicken is hot and juicy, and the beers and cocktails are icily refreshing on a hot summer day. Surfside is a once-a-year type joint, but it's a tradition for many locals.

## TWISTED CORK BISTRO          $$–$$$
10730 Pacific St., #110
(402) 932-1300
twistedcorkbistro.com

A tiny bistro with just a few seats, Twisted Cork Bistro serves both lunch and dinner to an enthusiastic following. The restaurant emphasizes locally sourced, boldly flavored food and handcrafted wine. The owners hail from Seattle, so many of their favorite products from the Northwest are worked into dishes that otherwise use Midwestern ingredients. It's so serious about using local food that it lists its providers on its website. The menu is fresh and tasty, and seafood (that aforementioned Northwestern bent) has a strong presence among burgers, chowder, and salads. An interesting wine list features bottles from Oregon and Washington, among other places. Finally, for the adventurous, consider the five-course tasting menu. For $37 (add wine for an additional $20), diners can enjoy a five-course meal of specially selected items.

## UPSTREAM BREWING CO.          $$–$$$
514 S. 11th St. (Old Market location)
(402) 344-0200
www.upstreambrewing.com

Tasty, reasonably priced pub food and a list of house-made beers make the Upstream's two locally owned locations popular stops on opposite ends of the city. The two-level Old Market location has an open bar and lots of seating on the main floor and a roof deck and pool tables above. The laid-back atmosphere of the West Omaha location has similar decor and an equally welcoming vibe. Hundreds of playing cards stuck to the ceiling in the downtown location catch many a diner's eye; see it happen in person when magician Joe Cole performs every Wednesday at 7 p.m. The downtown location has lots of happy hour specials on an evening and late night basis, as well as a weekly Sunday brunch. On Monday nights at the West Omaha location, kids eat free off their designated menu. Upstream's signature burgers, excellent mashed potatoes and french fries, and popular thin crust pizza are menu staples; vegetarians (and even meat eaters) will want to check out their homemade black bean burger that comes with a side of southwestern sauce that's simply great. Appetizers to sample include the spinach artichoke dip served with homemade beer bread and a great beer cheese soup. The west Omaha location is at 17070 Wright Plaza (402-778-0100).

## WORKER'S TAKE-OUT          $
1620 Dodge St.
(402) 991-6131
www.workerstakeout.com

A simple sandwich shop serving hot and cold sandwiches, Worker's Take-Out has a serious following among young Omaha. The restaurant shut down in its original midtown location and recently relocated to share a downtown space with a locally owned coffee house chain. Worker's signature sandwich is a pressed Cuban, but the menu offers lots of options, including some brand new ones that came with the new location. Worker's is now serving a Greek chicken sandwich, salsa verde and chips, homemade red and deviled egg potato salad, and in-house created roast beef. Worker's posts daily specials via its Facebook page and Twitter account; follow both to stay in the know.

## ASIAN

**BLUE SUSHI SAKE & GRILL** $$$
**14450 Eagle Run Dr. (West Omaha location)**
**(402) 445-2583**
**www.bluesushisakegrill.com**
Blue Sushi Sake & Grill has cool restaurants on each side of Omaha. The downtown location has the added bonus of the Sake Bombers Lounge, which offers an all-day happy hour including half-price sushi rolls on Sunday along with a funky, fun atmosphere. Blue has some simply great rolls— the Crunchy Blue, a spicy crab and cilantro interior, crispy panko crust, and eel sauce garnish, is one of the house favorites. The atmosphere at both locations of Blue are hip: giant aquariums, shelves full of bottles of vodka slowly infusing with creative flavors, large video screens showing looped surf videos, and glowing blue lights just about everywhere. All three Omaha locations have a daily happy hour every night and a reverse happy hour on weekends. The daily special runs from 4:30 to 6 p.m. and

includes $2 beers, $5 martinis, half-price appetizers, and $4 sushi. The same deal runs on Friday and Saturday from 10:30 p.m. to midnight. Other locations are at 416 S. 12th St. (Old Market location; 402-408-5566) and 16939 Wright Plaza (Baby Blue location; 402-547-5959).

**CHINA ROAD** $$
**4006 Twin Creek Dr., Bellevue**
**(402) 291-8855**
**www.yourchinaroad.net**
China Road is one of the more popular Americanized Chinese restaurants in Omaha. It has a subtly Asian-meets-American-strip-mall decor (and location) and a giant menu, featuring pork, beef, chicken, seafood, vegetarian items, and house specialties. Sizzling pots are served with food simmering in a clay pot, and some more authentic dishes adorn the menu: *Jampong* is a combination of shrimp, scallop, crab meat, scallions, celery, carrots, napa cabbage, and onion in a spicy noodle soup. The house special sizzling salmon is a baked hunk of fish served with snow peas, water chestnuts, carrots, bamboo shoots, scallions, mushrooms, and pineapple. The traditional Chinese favorites are here: broccoli beef, mu shoo pork, cashew chicken, sweet and sour dishes, and appetizers like crab Rangoon and egg rolls. For a take-out meal or weeknight dinner, China Road is a solid Chinese choice.

**HIRO** $$$
**3655 N. 129th St. (West Omaha location)**
**(402) 933-0091**
**www.hiro88.com**
Hiro has two locations in Omaha, one in West Omaha and one just outside of the Old Market (**Hiro 88,** 1308 Jackson St.;

402-933-5168). Though the two restaurants have similar menus, the vibe at each one is distinctly different. The West Omaha location is more formal and quieter, with a great long bar and singular enclosed entryway. The downtown location is much funkier, with a bigger, separate bar decorated with a giant statue of Buddah, louder music, and generally just more flash. The downtown decor is contemporary and stark; the crowd is decidedly younger. Hiro 88 has one of Omaha's largest selections of sake, available by the bottle or glass, and also has a sake flight for the adventurous. Sake bottle service at Hiro 88 is a posh option, and comes with a reserved seating area and a round of complimentary mixers for the sake. Hiro 88 has happy hour drink and food specials Mon through Fri from 3 to 6 p.m. and 10 p.m. to close, and again on Sat during the late night hours. The reverse happy hour includes half-price sushi.

**J. C. MANDARIN**          $$
**842 N. 98th St.**
**(402) 393-7988**
**www.jc-mandarin.com**
J. C. Mandarin is a step up from most locally owned Chinese restaurants: It's got a classy, Asian-inspired décor, and both locations are popular with the surrounding office parks for quick, efficient, and tasty business lunches. A daily lunch special at both locations includes fried rice, steamed rice, soup, and the meal of choice; carry-out lunches include the same rice choices and a crab Rangoon. J. C. Mandarin has a huge—if not somewhat intimidating—menu, with loads of appetizers; soup; and entrees featuring meat, seafood, and vegetables. Notables include sizzling rice soup; and Amazing Chicken that includes the meat sautéed

with snow peas, water chestnuts, baby corn, broccoli, and mushrooms in the savory "amazing" sauce; JC Delicacy, which is beef, chicken, and shrimp cooked in hot sauce with vegetables; and crispy honey chicken. Parties of two or more with agreeable palettes can try a family dinner that includes soup, appetizers, and a choice of entree. The second location is at 2859 S. 168th St. (402-333-1991).

**✳NEW GOLD MOUNTAIN**          $–$$
**15505 Ruggles St.**
**(402) 496-1688**
**www.newgoldmountain.com**
New Gold Mountain serves the most authentic Chinese food in the city. Hidden away in a non-descript strip mall, the restaurant is well worth the drive from wherever you live in Omaha. The interior looks like most other strip-mall Chinese restaurants, but the food truly sets New Gold Mountain apart. It serves a delicious dim sum and has two menus: one traditional, authentic Chinese and a second "Americanized" Chinese; if you want the real experience, ask for the traditional menu. (A selection of Vietnamese items is available too; they're listed on a board on the wall.) The food at New Gold Mountain is fresh and tasty, and when you order dim sum the small plates come out one by one, in no particular order. Don't be afraid to ask one of the servers for advice, or to try something new—everything is great at New Gold Mountain.

**O DINING AND LOUNGE**          $$–$$$
**1015 Farnam St.**
**(402) 502-7888**
**www.odining.com/dining**
With a hip, Asian-inspired decor and a menu full of excellent, Asian fusion dishes, O Dining

and Lounge is one of downtown Omaha's most popular eateries. The food is a blend of French, Chinese, Korean, Japanese, Vietnamese, and American food; and, though that seems quite the melting pot, O pulls it together into a menu that has wide variety and many standout dishes. O serves more than 40 wines by the glass and also has a select list of reserve wines; Asian beers are here alongside other domestics and imports. The decor could also be described as Asian fusion: black lacquer tables and chairs meet more modern prints and paintings on the wall, and a quiet bar tucked on the second floor has a great view of the Gene Leahy Mall. Service is friendly and helpful. One of the most popular items on the menu is the Rice Bowl Medley: It's a sort of healthy version of fried rice that's mixed to order tableside. A number of creative vegetarian dishes dot the menu—veggies stir fried with mock duck included. Almost anything can be customized to the diner's liking; don't hesitate to ask if you prefer tofu to beef or chicken.

### RICE BOWL CHINESE RESTAURANT $-$$
**505 N. Saddle Creek Rd.**
**(402) 558-1222**

The Rice Bowl is truly a hole in the wall. It's located in a tiny white building on the corner of two busy streets, and its parking lot isn't much bigger than the restaurant itself. Though it doesn't look like much and the atmosphere is pretty non-descript, the food inside is served fast, hot, and cheap, and it's a popular midtown spot for Americanized Chinese takeout. A few popular dishes include peanut butter chicken, which is simply breaded white meat cooked in a tasty, tangy peanut butter sauce and topped with green onions; Yum Yum Chicken, white

meat in a spicy garlic sauce; and standbys like broccoli beef and egg foo young. Most of the larger, family-sized dishes at the Rice Bowl come in cheaper or just at $10, making this an economic choice for takeout or a fast lunch or dinner.

### SAKURA BANA $$-$$$
**7425 W. Dodge Rd.**
**(402) 391-5047**
**www.sushiomaha.com**

Sakura Bana is the Old Market's original sushi bar. It's been there for years and serves reasonably priced, tasty, authentic sushi, sashimi, and bento boxes. Its prices are really what diners like about Sakura Bana; most Omaha sushi restaurants are fancier than Sakura, with themed drinks and rolls and fancier interiors. Sakura takes somewhat of a bare bones approach, with an open sushi bar, simple tables and chairs, and efficient service. Sakura has followed suit of many Omaha restaurants with a special menu and happy hour: Mon through Fri between 11 a.m. and 2 p.m. and again from 5 to 7 p.m., a selection of sushi and rolls on the "Dream Menu" are $2.99 each. The special runs on Sat and Sun from 5 to 7 p.m. The Dream Menu includes a number of signature house rolls made with singular ingredients: The caterpillar roll has shrimp tempura, avocado, cucumber, cream cheese, and eel sauce.

### SUSHI JAPAN YAKINIKU BOY $$
**14134 W. Center Rd.**
**(402) 778-0840**
**www.omaha-sushi.com**

A super popular West Omaha sushi bar, Sushi Japan seats guests at traditional tables but also at its active sushi bar; and for small parties, bar seats are definitely the place to be. Different sides of the restaurant have different menus, and some cooked dishes are available only at the Yaniniku tables that have grills installed. Sushi Japan offers all varieties of Japanese food, including noodle bowls, tempura, udon, and soba noodle dishes and a wide variety of sashimi, maki, and sushi rolls. The atmosphere is clean and refreshing, decorated in pale wood and light hues, and on weekend evenings, Sushi Japan does a brisk trade. On New Year's Eve, the restaurant has a special buffet that features celebratory Japanese food.

## THREE HAPPINESS EXPRESS     $–$$
**5107 Leavenworth St.**
**(402) 558-8899**

Three Happiness is a great little Chinese place in the heart of midtown. The dining room is clean and simple and service is fast and friendly. It's a hugely popular neighborhood take-out place, and for good reason: The food is great. Americanized Chinese is the name of the game here. Each order comes with the diner's choice of soup and an egg roll or crab Rangoon. Portion sizes are large enough to easily share. Some of the menu items that garner rave reviews include the hot and sour soup, the General's Chicken, the Yum Yum Chicken, the twice baked pork, and the peanut butter chicken, which comes in a huge portion. (Vegetarians will also appreciate the option to get peanut butter tofu, which is rich and delicious when mixed with rice.) Three Happiness is a solid choice for well-priced Chinese food to stay or go.

## COFFEE SHOPS

**AROMA'S**     $
**1033 Jones St.**
**(402) 614-7009**

Located in the bottom of the Old Market Lofts, Aroma's is a quiet coffee shop that's a popular place for students to do homework and study and for professionals to have off-site meetings. Aroma's has a patio out front that's popular in nice weather, and the interior is decorated with local art hanging on the brick walls, a fireplace, and lots of tables and chairs, as well as tons of electrical outlets, to make work and studying easier than ever. A couch toward the back of the shop is a popular gathering place for book clubs and other groups. Aroma's offers a daily selection of coffee and tea, and a refill on a cup of coffee to stay is free. Scones, cookies, and muffins are available to nosh on, and the attached bakery next door sells sweet treats during daytime hours.

## ✳BLUE LINE COFFEE     $
**4924 Underwood Ave.**
**(402) 502-6707**
**www.bluelinecoffee.com**

One of Omaha's most popular locally owned coffee shops, Blue Line has two locations, one in North Downtown and another in Dundee. Blue Line brews locally created Cultiva coffee, and the downtown location serves lunch and dinner along with beer, wine, and cocktails. Both are located in some of the most urban areas of the city, so foot traffic and a regular flow of customers in and out the door is constant; both locations do brisk business in the morning. Free wireless Internet and music that's there but not too loud make both Blue Lines popular for remote office work or studying. Both too are popular for after-dinner drinks or coffee: The Dundee location is adjacent to lots of restaurants, and the downtown location is near Slowdown and Filmstreams. The interior of both stores is similar: quirky coffee shop meets local restaurant. The second location is at 749 N. 14th St. (402-932-3917).

### 13TH STREET COFFEE SHOP $
### 519 S. 13th St.
### (402) 345-2883

Right on the edge of the Old Market, 13th Street Coffee Shop is one of the area's longest running locally owned hangouts. Live music and poetry readings happen here regularly, and the menu includes all the classic coffee drinks, pastries, sandwiches, and authentic Italian gelato available by the scoop. The two-level shop is also a popular place for studying and reading, and the friendly baristas make the drinks quickly and efficiently. The vibe here is purely local—local musicians play, local poets read, and local art adorns the walls.

## ETHNIC

### AMSTERDAM FALAFEL
### AND KABOB $–$$
### 620 N. 50th St.
### (402) 504-3223
### www.eatafk.com

Amsterdam Falafel is a small, locally owned joint in Dundee that serves, hands down, the best falafel in Omaha. Everything on the tiny menu is made fresh to order, and bicycle delivery is available within a limited area. Amsterdam aims to be a fresh local eatery that serves late into the night: It's open until 2 a.m. Thurs, Fri, and Sat. The falafel sandwich includes two large patties of falafel in a tasty pita that can be topped with a fresh vegetable slaw, hummus, and three sauces: garlic, herb, and/or spicy. The lamb kabob includes thinly sliced meat, vegetables, and

garlic sauce or spicy sauce and is served in toasted bread. The curry fries are a delicious, spicy side item—perfect for sharing and served stabbed with a tiny fork. Amsterdam has predictably funky decor: big colored dome chandeliers; a hand-painted mural on one wall; and a mix of indoor, outdoor, and counter seating.

### BANGKOK CUISINE $–$$
### 1905 Farnam St.
### (402) 346-5874

With a great lunch buffet and some excellent pad thai, downtown Omaha's Bangkok Cuisine is a popular lunch spot and also a great place for takeout. Bangkok Cuisine isn't winning too many points as far as decor: old carpet and non-descript tables meet sort of funky wall art and a big television set. Though it's not the best place for a romantic evening, it works well for the lunch hour (and often has a line) and the takeout is fast, hot, and cheap. The pad thai can be prepared with a customized level of spiciness as well as with the diner's choice of pork, chicken, tofu, beef, or seafood (which is $1 more). Most of the entrees cost less than $8.

### BOHEMIAN CAFE $$
### 1406 S. 13th St.
### (402) 342-9838
### www.bohemiancafe.net

Operating just south of downtown Omaha since 1924, the Bohemian Cafe serves authentic European food. It's one of the area's most noticeable restaurants: Its glowing, red neon sign out front and colorful mosaic tiles instantly signify it as something special. The waitstaff, clothed in traditional Czech outfits, is knowledgeable and friendly, and can describe any of the menu items that diners might have never tasted. Inside, the restaurant is just as colorful as the exterior and continues the play on the neighborhood's Czech heritage. Though it may sound strange, the liver dumpling soup is actually delicious—its warm brown both surrounds a central dumpling, once cut it breaks into small, savory bites. The Bohemian Cafe has a whole variety of daily specials each week; a full list is available on its website or on the cafe's menu. The restaurant's feature dinners include many old-school, traditional recipes: *jaeger schnitzel,* which is veal steaks in wine sauce with mushrooms; *svickova,* Czech-style sauerbraten; roast pork loin; Czech goulash; breaded sweetbreads; polish sausage; and plum dumplings, which are served a la carte and take about 30 minutes to prepare. The attached Bohemian Girl Cocktail Lounge is known for its wide selection of big chilled mugs of draft beer and imported Czech bottled beers.

## DHABA INDIAN CUISINE $$
**2012 N. 117th Ave.**
**(402) 505-6950**
**www.dhabaomaha.com**
Located in a West Omaha strip mall, Dhaba delivers some seriously good Indian food at a reasonable price. In India, a *dhaba* is a place along the road for weary travelers to stop and refresh along the way. Dhaba in Omaha does have a refreshing decor, with many small tables, lots of windows, and a few large booths down one wall, butting up to a bar. Dhaba has a lunch buffet on weekdays, and offers lunch and dinner service daily, as well as carry-out. The Thali specials are one of the most enjoyable culinary experiences at Dhaba. The large tray of food has a number of small compartments and together creates an array of singular flavors; it also gives those new to Indian food the chance to try many things at once. Dhaba serves a vegetarian and meat Thali, both at a reasonable price.

## EL BASHA $-$$
**7503 Pacific St.**
**(402) 934-6266**
A simple Lebanese and Mediterranean menu and the option to smoke a hookah make El Basha a popular midtown Omaha hangout and eatery. The *shawarma* is one of the most popular menu items and comes either chicken or beef. The meat is served with tahini sauce, grilled tomatoes, and onion on fresh bread or pita. Traditional Mediterranean items like gyro sandwiches, hummus, falafel, and kebab are also on the menu. Outdoor seating during nice weather and more than reasonable prices make El Basha a popular stop for foodies.

## FLAVORS $$
**1901 Farnam St.**
**(402) 933-4140**
**www.omahaflavors.com**
Well-priced Indian is what Flavor's does best. Its lunchtime buffet—really popular with downtown professionals—offers a daily rotating array of Indian dishes. The buffet always includes vegetarian options, soup, and naan. The restaurant is small and neat, with simple decor and a friendly, knowledgeable waitstaff. Appetizers and desserts on the house are the norm at Flavors. The regular menu includes one with meat and a separate one for meatless entrees. The restaurant has an appropriate name—"flavor" is the key.

## GREEK ISLANDS $$
3821 Center St.
(402) 346-1528
www.greekislandsomaha.com/
restaurant

Omaha's Greek Islands has been serving authentic Greek cuisine for more than 25 years and is still one of the city's most popular Greek restaurants. Simply decorated with white tables and mirrors, the walls at Greek Islands are covered with murals of the country depicting both ancient and modern scenes. Diners will find all the Greek food they're familiar with: mousaka, souvlaki, pastichio, and gyros. Much of the traditional Greek food has been given a twist: pastichio is available in a vegetarian version, and gyros come with chicken or just vegetables instead of the traditional lamb (though they have that, too). Save room for dessert: Baklava ice cream is delicious.

## JAIPUR $$$
10922 Elm St.
(402) 392-7331
www.jaipurbrewhouse.com

Tasty Indian food and hand-crafted beers are what the Jaipur does best. The West Omaha staple is one of the only fine dining establishments in the city that specializes in Indian cuisine. The Jaipur is casual enough for a business lunch but also dark and romantic enough for a dinner date; the decor is simple but elegant. The menu offers all the standards of Indian cuisine: tandoori cooked items, mulligatawny soup, and delicious naan served with a crave-worthy green dipping sauce. The menu includes meat and fish, but also vegetarian items, many focused around soft Indian cheese. The Jaipur brews a number of beers in-house and

their specialty Jalapeno Ale is a local favorite and the best seller on the menu.

## MAI THAI $$
14618 W. Center Rd.
(402) 333-0506

A popular West Omaha Thai restaurant with a Vietnamese bent, Mai Thai is an unassuming restaurant hidden in a strip mall. The restaurant is tiny and the decor is simple and colorful; the reasonable prices and tasty grub are what keep patrons coming back for more. The menu includes the owner's family recipes as well as house recipes created especially for the restaurant. Diners can choose their level of spicy (one is mild, five is spicy) on every dish on the menu, making for a customized experience. The vast menu serves some familiar items (pad thai, fried rice, sweet and sour chicken) but is mostly original. The seafood Hor Mok is a red curry steamed and served inside a whole coconut. Tropical Bird Nest is a combination of seafood served over a crispy "nest" of noodles. The Chicken Mango—a dish many rave about—is sweet and savory but simple, featuring stir-fried chicken, red peppers, carrots, onions, cashews, and a fresh mango sauce. The chef recently added Vietnamese pho to the menu and a huge bowl runs only $8.

## MOTHER INDIA $$
3572 Leavenworth St.
(402) 763-2880

Fast, competitively priced Indian cuisine is what continues to make Mother India one of Omaha's most popular stops for Indian food. It's a small hole in the wall right off a busy street and has a decidedly urban feel. Most of the staff is Indian, as are the cooks, so the cuisine is authentic, spicy, and delicious. A small board on the wall displays a regularly rotating schedule of specials; and in warmer weather, lots of diners enjoy the restaurant's small patio (which takes up part of a larger parking lot) that is creatively decorated with colorful umbrellas and clean tables and chairs. Mother India serves lunch and dinner to stay or to go, and is usually crowded. The appetizers are just so-so, but the main dishes are great: sizable, spicy, and full of flavor. Chicken Tikka Korma, the house curry, and a variety of special dishes—vegetarian and meat—will please just about everyone.

### PERU, MUCHO GUSTO                    $$
**7755 L St.**
**(402) 932-0049**
Peru Mucho Gusto isn't a restaurant one goes to for atmosphere. Here's it's all about the imported Peruvian cuisine. The restaurant, located in a strip mall, is sparsely, simply furnished. Most of the food served at Peru Mucho Gusto is locally produced, but, when necessary, the owners fly in seafood and spices direct from Peru. Most diners will likely be unfamiliar with Peruvian cuisine, and the friendly waitstaff is happy to describe dishes and make recommendations. Yucca Frita and garlic sauce are a good way to start the meal; the authentic sauce is the Peruvian equivalent to ketchup. The popular ceviche comes in a huge portion that includes fish marinated in lime juice and Peruvian chilies with a side of white and sweet potatoes, onions, and corn. The restaurant has live music on Friday and Saturday nights.

### THE TAJ KABOB AND CURRY            $$
**668 N. 114th St. (Old Mill District)**
**(402) 933-1445**
Reasonably priced Indian food is the name of the game at The Taj, which is wildly popular with locals. Chicken Tikka Masala is

the dish of the house, and the spicy, meaty, saucy dish is probably the most ordered item. Located in a strip mall, the restaurant doesn't look like much from the outside and has a simple decor once you get inside, but the food is great, the prices are low, and the delivery is efficient. Vegetarians will find much to love here as the list of meatless entries is long and flavorful. A wide variety of soups and naan all cost less than $3 and most appetizers are around $6. The Taj does not serve alcohol.

### ZUM BIERGARTEN                      $$
**513 N. Fort Crook Rd., Bellevue**
**(402) 733-1900**
Zum Biergarten is the place Omahans go when they're in the mod for some schnitzel, craving some homemade bratwurst, or really in the mood for sauerkraut. The German-focused menu includes all the ethnic food one could want (and probably more than that). Potato pancakes, roast pork, German potato salad, Bavarian chicken, dumplings: It's all there. Even the made-from-scratch dessert menu has a Deutsch bent. The name, which means "To the beer garden," is also apropos: The restaurant serves wine, eight brands of German beer, and German liquor like Jagermeister and Rumple Minze. The restaurant is simply decorated in shades of burgundy and doesn't have the kitsch factor of some themed restaurants. Though colder weather might seem like the opportune time to visit, the restaurant wants to be all-seasons, and tops meals with lighter sauce and a side of light, pickled vegetables that seem more appropriate for summer than winter. The weekend lunch special is called the Tour of Germany and includes a platter of food: It may include things like a pork cutlet, a breaded schnitzel,

a salad, homemade potatoes, and a number of other side dishes.

## FINE DINING

### *THE BOILER ROOM $$$$
**1110 Jones St.**
**(402) 916-9274**

There isn't another Omaha restaurant that even comes close to the Boiler Room. Let's start with the singular atmosphere: The two-level restaurant is located in what used to be the actual boiler room of the old Bemis Bag Company Building, dating from 1887. After the bag company left the building in 1983, the space sat empty for more than 20 years before Mark and Vera Mercer and Chef Paul Kulik opened the Boiler Room in 2009. The beautifully done renovation left the best of the vintage building: warm brick walls and concrete floors. Simple tables and chairs and modern metal railings and stairs create edgy contrast. The dining room is on the second level and overlooks the sunken bar and kitchen area. Vera Mercer's original artwork covers the walls; her large-scale images of food are a modern take on the still life, and Mark Mercer's small abstract clay sculptures decorate the bar area. The bar is a busy downstairs hub (see the Nightlife chapter for more on the bar's craft cocktails). An adjacent wine cellar has a vast selection. The menu changes weekly—sometimes even more often—and the food is both locally produced and seasonally appropriate. It's hard to capture with words how singular the food is at the Boiler Room. Portions are small and diners are encouraged to sample a choice from each course presented on the menu. Chef Kulik creates food with a focus on unique flavors; fresh, local ingredients; and artistic presentation. Whole roasted fish, locally produced steak and pork, and seasonally appropriate vegetables are the staples of the menu; the delight comes with the preparation, helpful, well-educated staff, and memorable presentation.

### *DARIO'S BRASSERIE $$–$$$
**4920 Underwood Ave.**
**(402) 933-0799**
**www.dariosbrasserie.com**

A French bistro transplanted into the heart of Dundee, Dario's Brasserie is a warm, welcoming restaurant that's popular with the neighborhood locals and the rest of the city, too. Owner Dario Schicke moved to Omaha from Sarajevo via New York City and opened the restaurant in 2006. The restaurant serves delicious, simple food—think homemade soups, quiche, crepes—and has an extensive, excellent selection of fine Belgian beers. Lighting is warm inside Dario's, and simple wood tables with mismatched vintage chairs sit next to a long red booth. The restaurant serves brunch, lunch, and dinner and the menu changes seasonally. The connecting thread through all the menus is simple, hearty French food. Crepes filled with fruit and cheese, both sweet and savory, are a can't-miss item. The Belgium Pommes Frites are a delicious appetizer served in a cone with ketchup and horseradish. Order them even if you think you don't want any. The 36 Hour Sous Vide Boneless Beef Short Ribs are served alone at dinner time and as a sandwich at lunch. A satisfying cheese plate is big enough to eat as a meal, and is especially good when enjoyed with a glass of wine or a beer.

## *DIXIE QUICK'S MAGNOLIA ROOM $$
1915 Leavenworth St.
(402) 346-3549
www.dixiequicks.com

Hands down, Dixie Quick's Magnolia Room is the best brunch spot in the city of Omaha. Chef Rene Orduna and his partner Rob Gilmer run a welcoming, eclectic art gallery meets funky restaurant with personality to spare. Recent expansions to the space have added an additional gallery space / dining room and a third space devoted solely to the RNG Gallery and its exhibitions. The long restaurant is all connected by one busy, central hallway. After being featured on the Food Network's *Diners, Drive-Ins and Dives,* business at Dixie Quick's exploded; these days, it's wise to call ahead for a brunch (or dinner) reservation. Don't leave a message, the answering machine says, make your reservation with a human. No matter the hour, patrons order off a huge chalkboard on the main dining room wall. Everything on the menu, brunch or dinner, is simply delicious and lovingly prepared. The menu varies slightly from day to day, and on a busy morning, things sometimes sell out. Especially popular items include the eggs Benedict and eggs Blackstone, which is just like Benedict but with tomato and bacon instead of ham; an amazing breakfast quesadilla; the Dixie scramble; and oatmeal and ice cream, which Chef Orduna's mom prepared for him one childhood day when she ran out of sweetener for his usual morning oatmeal. (It's really, really good.) The dinner menu continues the Tex Mex meats home-style southern cooking tradition. The fried chicken is predictably to die for; also great are the char-broiled pork loin, the selection of spicy pastas, and the chicken Pernod. Go to Dixie Quick's when you're in Omaha. You'll love it.

## FLATIRON CAFE $$$$
1722 Saint Marys Ave.
(402) 344-3040
www.theflatironcafe.com

One of the city's finest dining establishments (and also one of the most romantic), the Flatiron Cafe is located in the city's flatiron building, originally built in 1912 as a hotel. The triangular shaped building has a wedge-shaped dining room and a bar and tables that are arranged to fit in the unique space. Windows make most of the dining room's walls, lending a lovely view toward the Old Market and the city skyline; inside, white tablecloths and dramatic flower arrangements set the mood. The hand-written dinner menu changes regularly, with a seasonal focus—a recent menu featured a lobster and chive stuffed crepe, crunchy tiger prawns with lemon remoulade, and fresh mozzarella and Boursin stuffed wontons. Entrees include beef, seafood, and other meat that is beautifully prepared and artfully served.

## FRENCH CAFE $$$$
1017 Howard St.
(402) 341-3547
www.frenchcafe.com

One of the Old Market's original restaurants—and still one of its most romantic and charismatic—the French Cafe has been a city standard for more than 40 years. Classically designed, with lots of dark wood, glass, vintage chandeliers, and a stunning wall of black-and-white photography of a French outdoor market, the decor has the type of old-school fanciness that somehow remains modern. In recent years, the restaurant has gone through quite a few menu changes and kitchen changes, but it seems to have stabilized again, finding renewed success with a mix of classics that it's always retained—delicious French onion soup, Caesar salad prepared tableside, and five versions of steamed mussels—among newer dishes that take a modern look at the classic. More recent menu additions include steak frites, a selection of vegetarian entrees, and a renewed focus on using locally harvested ingredients. The dessert tray here is always exceptional; the white chocolate mousse served in a champagne flute with fresh raspberries is this writer's favorite indulgence in the city.

### ✳GREY PLUME                              $$$
### 220 S. 31st Ave.
### (402) 763-4447
### www.thegreyplume.com

The newly opened Grey Plume approaches food from a seasonal, local perspective. The contemporary American menu has a true farm-to-table approach and the fresh, tasty food is simply delicious. The menu changes weekly depending on what's available and in season. Chef Clayton Chapman has worked at some of Omaha's finest restaurants (M's Pub and V. Mertz included) and he creates truly innovative food.

A recent menu included a charcuterie board with a delicious selection of handmade meats and local artisan cheese. A salad included local greens and pickled, seasonal vegetables. Locally sourced pork, chicken, and beef are prepared simply and presented beautifully.

The restaurant is decorated in cool hues of white, grey and green; the atmosphere is simple, quiet and contemporary. Service is impeccable, and the creativity in both the space and the food makes this spot a singular one. The dessert menu rotates regularly

and often includes a delectable selection of homemade ice cream.

Grey Plume is green from top to bottom. The takeout containers are sustainable. It recycles glass, aluminum, plastic and cardboard. Its menu is printed with soy ink on recycled paper. It composts food waste. In-house items for sale include roasted coffee, handmade pasta, charcuterie, flavored vinegars, gourmet ice cream, butter and artisan breads.

### INGREDIENT                              $$
### 3201 Farnam St.
### (402) 715-4444
### www.ingredientrestaurant.com

Ingredient is one of Omaha's newest casual eateries. Located in the Midtown Crossing development, Ingredient has a focus on simple, light food: sandwiches, salads, pasta, and more. Ingredient is a Kansas-based chain and has a number of locations there; this is its first in Nebraska. Fun light fixtures, lots of natural light from big windows, and a muted color scheme greet diners in the medium to large space, which seats more than 100. Ingredient has a great create-your-own salad bar and a number of signature house salads, as well as sandwiches, soup, and pizza. Asian flavors, as well as Italian leanings, find their way into the otherwise American menu, and dishes like the Vietnamese Dim Sum Chicken Wrap and wild mushroom pizza find harmony on the diverse list of cuisine.

### ✳LA BUVETTE                              $$–$$$
### 511 S. 11th St.
### (402) 344-8627
### http://labuvetteomaha.com

La Buvette offers one of the most charming spaces in the city to do some serious wine drinking and some serious people watching.

La Buvette is a retail wine shop, wine bar, and casual restaurant, but it's more than that: It's a place that locals absolutely cherish, and it's a place that always surprises newcomers and out-of-town guests. A simple menu of appetizers—cheese and meat plates; house-made charcuterie, including pâtés, rillettes, and foie gras; hummus; salads that are large enough to eat as a meal all served with delicious house-made bread and butter—are always available. A rotating special menu of entrees changes weekly and is focused on local ingredients and interpretations of fine French dishes. Though the food alone is delightful, the food when combined with the atmosphere becomes something entirely special. Exposed brick walls and uneven floors, weathered wood tables, and walls lined with wine bottles and candles make the space especially intimate; huge glass doors that open up to the popular patio in the summer make it irresistible.

**LE VOLTAIRE** $$–$$$
**569 N. 155th Plaza**
**(402) 934-9374**
**www.levoltaireomaha.com**
An accessible French bistro in West Omaha, Le Voltaire has a reputation for being one of the most romantic spots in the city. In an unlikely location—a West Omaha strip mall—diners quickly forget where they are once they get inside. A large wine cellar and secluded tables make sure diners get their own personal experience; the bar has a singular floral design. The restaurant's private room, with a cellar view, is a popular destination for parties and wedding rehearsal dinners. The waitstaff is friendly and accessible, and, above all, they welcome diners to ask questions about the wine list and the menu: There's no judgment for not knowing what

*Terrine de Manioc* means. The restaurant has a special that lets diners choose an appetizer and an entree or an entree and a dessert for $27; choose all three for four more dollars. Menu items include lamb, filet mignon, duck, and fish, along with a wide selection of appetizers and desserts. The vast wine list, focused on France, won't disappoint.

**LOFT 610** $$$–$$$$
**220 S. 31st Ave., #3107**
**(402) 885-6800**
**www.loft610.com/omaha**
A funky restaurant with a focus on drinks and good food, Loft 610 draws in a mixed crowd: young people wanting to check out the new place, people grabbing a drink after work, professional gatherings for large groups, and those in the mood for a long, romantic meal for two. Loft 610 is a bustling place, divided into two floors—an upstairs area focused on large groups, a bar, and a curtained off dining room. A wall of windows lends great views, and the main dining room butts up to the open kitchen area. Loft 610 also draws a solid lunch crowd from the adjacent Mutual of Omaha complex. The menu is modern American food, with a twist. The chef focuses on local ingredients, so expect lots of varieties of steak as well as a plate of six-hour shortribs. Other parts of the menu focus on home cooking: There's a variation on chicken pot pie, a creamy mushroom risotto, a duck confit, and other warm, filling entrees.

**✳M'S PUB** $$
**422 S. 11th St.**
**(402) 342-2550**
**www.mspubomaha.com**
M's Pub is quintessentially cool. An Omaha standard, the restaurant is a citywide favorite for both excellent food and a singular,

memorable atmosphere. The restaurant is one of the original businesses to open in the thriving historic Old Market neighborhood, and though the menu may have changed over the years, the vibe hasn't. It's casual but nice, friendly but hip. Lots of original wood; a long, green bar; strategically placed mirrors and windows; and well-worn, plain tables don't sound like much in words, but there's something in the friendliness of the waitstaff and bartenders, the familiar taste of the food, and the warm location that has kept patrons coming back since M's opened its doors in 1979. The lunch menu rotates weekly, as does a special, fancier dinner menu. The rest of the menu has lots of beloved standards. Check out the signature lahvosh pizzas, with a thin cracker crust and a wide array of toppings.

Three varieties of baked dishes are served in a miniature casserole dish with bubbly melted Havarti cheese on top. Spread the shrimp scampi, mushrooms, or escargot on one of the restaurant's house-made, yeasty rolls for a delicious appetizer. There's really nothing bad on the menu, but keep an eye out for the warm duck salad, the Omaha Grill sandwich, the carrot dog (yes, it's what you think it is), and the pesto pasta with chicken.

### ✳MARK'S BISTRO                    $$$
**4916 Underwood Ave.**
**(402) 502-2203**
**www.marksindundee.com**
Located in a turn-of-the-century house converted into a charming, second-floor neighborhood bistro, Mark's has a devoted Dundee following but is popular with the rest of Omaha, too. More than 50 feet of windows make up one wall of the dining room, and patrons in these seats have a bird's-eye

view of the usually bustling street scene below. The rest of the dining room is cozy and comfortable, and a private back patio that seats close to 50 under mature, beautiful trees is popular during warmer weather. Mark's signature dish—likely also its most popular—is the truly delicious macaroni and cheese. Served in a big bowl, the creamy four-cheese concoction is topped with a crunchy coating of panko bread crumbs. A set of daily embellishments rotate, but are likely to include things like steak, seasonal vegetables, and other meat or seafood. Mark's offers pasta, fish, chicken, and other main dishes on its dinner menu; one notable sandwich is a delicious vegetarian Tempeh Reuben that even meat eaters will like. Fish tacos; a sweet potato, beet, and spinach salad; and an absolutely delectable house-made whiskey bread pudding dessert (don't think about the calories, just enjoy) are all worth sampling.

### ✳RYAN'S BISTRO                    $$$
**17607 Gold Plaza**
**(402) 614-2202**
**www.ryansbistro.com**
Owner and chef Ryan Gish has created in his bistro one of West Omaha's best restaurants. Located in a shopping center, the inside of the restaurant instantly makes the visitor forget he or she is in the suburbs with its warm wood and brick, large fireplace, live music, and bustling bar. Ryan often circulates through the space, welcoming customers and socializing, and that personal touch brings much to the experience. The bistro recently started a daily happy hour, where select appetizers are $4.95, cocktails and house wine are $4, domestic beer is $2 and imports are $3, and small pizzas are $5 and mediums are $10. The happy hour

runs daily from 3 to 7 p.m., making it both one of the most generous in the city as far as items offered and length of time offered (most end by 6 p.m.). Ryan's is happy to accommodate gluten-free diners as well as vegetarians; his gluten-free pizza is one of the more popular menu items. Signature items include the peanut butter and bacon toast appetizer; excellent braised short ribs; and a great cioppino that includes clams, mussels, shrimp, and scallops in a flavorful tomato miso broth.

## URBAN WINE COMPANY $$–$$$
**1037 Jones St.**
**(402) 934-0005**
**www.urbanwinecompany.com**
A popular downtown wine bar, Urban Wine Company draws a mixed crowd to sample its vast array of vino: It serves 40 boutique wines by the glass and stocks more than 200 varieties by the bottle. The wine list comes to the table in a small booklet, and diners can choose to order a glass, a bottle, or a flight of smaller tastes for a fixed price. The food menu is made up of many small bites that together make a meal; if you're part of a large group, it's worth ordering quite a bit. Couples can get away with less, especially if an order or two of sushi is included. The menu includes Asian favorites (the aforementioned sushi, miso soup, tempura, and edamame) and Italian specialties like spinach and artichoke dip, bruschetta, and a capresi salad. Larger lahvosh pizzas include a variety of meat, seafood, and vegetable toppings. A customizable meat and cheese plate rounds out the menu. Urban Wine Company is popular for private parties and corporate events; visit the restaurant's website for more information.

## V. MERTZ RESTAURANT $$$$
**1022 Howard St.**
**(402) 345-8980**
**www.vmertz.com**
One of the city's truly romantic spots, V. Mertz is located in the underground Old Market Passageway. Its dim lighting, exceptional service, and elegant decor transports couples into a true fine dining experience. The environment at V. Mertz is authentically vintage, with old wood, worn brick walls and floor, and more modern glass and mirrors surrounding diners. Tables are shrouded in white cloth, and the chairs are classically outfitted with covers bearing the restaurant's moniker. Service here is top notch yet non-intrusive; prices are what one expects when enjoying fine cuisine. The restaurant puts together special menus when any holiday rolls around, and it's a popular spot on both Valentine's Day and New Year's Eve. Monthly dinner menus also rotate; a recent menu included a foie gras appetizer, parsnip veloute, entrees like a root vegetable tart and Oregon natural lamb chop, and an array of decadent desserts. Also a popular destination for business lunches, the restaurant has a set lunch menu with a popular Boursin stuffed chicken, among other dishes. An intimate bar in the back of the restaurant is a secret escape in the otherwise bustling Old Market; reasonably priced cocktails and wine by the glass are a small price to pay to enjoy the unique ambiance of V. Mertz.

## ITALIAN

### BELLA VITA RESTAURANTE $$$
**2620 N. Main St., Elkhorn**
**(402) 289-1804**
**www.bellavitane.com**

Bella Vita is a tiny, romantic spot in Elkhorn, a suburb on the west side of Omaha. It has the feel of a charming bistro with exposed brick walls, vintage furniture, and big wine barrels scattered through the space that act as podiums for dramatic floral arrangements. Pasta entrees include a Bolognese sauce infused lasagna and a cheese stuffed, marinara topped manicotti. Other house specialties include the grilled salmon risotto, pork osso bucco, and a portabella mushroom cap stuffed with cheese and mushrooms topped with a balsamic reduction and sautéed shrimp. Bella Vita has a happy hour Sun through Fri from 3 to 5 p.m. that features $5 wine, cocktails, and appetizers. On Steak Sunday and Monday, a 10-ounce ribeye is only $11, and on Wine-O Wednesday, guests get a free appetizer when they buy a bottle of wine.

**LO SOLE MIO RISTORANTE      $$–$$$**
**3001 S. 32nd Ave.**
**(402) 345-5656**
**www.losolemio.com/ristorante/**
Italian done the way it should be is what diners will find at Lo Sole Mio, a true Omaha classic. The family-owned restaurant is located in an otherwise residential neighborhood, surrounded by small homes and quiet streets; at one point in its life, the building was a local grocery store. Northern and Southern Italian dishes are on the vast menu, which is exhaustive. For those who can't choose just one dish, the Combination Platters offer variety: the Tour of Italy is spinach lasagna, portabella parmigiana, and chicken cannelloni; the Big Nick's Combo includes a breaded steak, Italian sausage, and sweet roasted peppers with linguini and meat sauce. The classics like chicken parmesan, veal parmesan, and

pasta alla carbonera are next to more innovative dishes like Pasta *con Aragosta e Gamberi,* which is langostino lobster and jumbo shrimp cooked in a cream tomato sauce with Asiago and fresh basil. The restaurant is decorated in a warm, welcoming manner, with lots of tables and a bar that doubles as a waiting room near the entrance. Because of the restaurant's popularity, diners can often face a long wait. Know that the food is worth it. Cocktails and appetizers are served in the waiting room, and will tide you over until a seat becomes available. It's an old-school Italian restaurant that's still hugely popular; the food is outstanding and the atmosphere memorable.

**MALARA'S ITALIAN RESTAURANT      $$**
**2123 Pierce St.**
**(402) 346-8001**
An Omaha favorite, Malara's is hidden in a South Omaha neighborhood but has enough atmosphere to be successful even in its unlikely location. Known for some simple favorites—people rave about the cheese sticks—and homemade pasta served in bountiful portions, Malara's serves simple Italian favorites and does them right. A number of Italian main dishes come as part of the daily special, which for one price includes the main dish, a salad with house-made Italian dressing, and a dinner roll. The specials are available in full and half orders (the half order is plenty big) and the main dishes change daily. Offerings include manicotti, fettuccini Alfredo, Mama Malara's naked spaghetti, and tortellini. The restaurant is simply decorated—it's nothing fancy—but the exposed brick walls, friendly staff, and devoted local crowd make it a welcoming destination.

## MANGIA ITALIANA          $$
### 6516 Irvington Rd.
### (402) 614-0600
### www.mangiaitaliana.com

Mangia Italiana is owned and operated by an Italian family that settled in Omaha's Little Italy neighborhood more than 75 years ago. Today, the bustling Italian restaurant does business in Irvington, just outside Omaha. Mostly known for takeout and catering, Mangia Italiana does Italian in the true Sicilian style. The restaurant is in a small grey house with a small waiting area; outdoor tables are popular in warmer weather. Mangia Italiana's popular Sugo sauce is sweet and flavorful, and they simmer it for hours before it's served. Mangia sells pasta, meatballs, freshly baked rolls (topped with toasted parmesan and available with a meal or by the dozen), and pizza. Those with different tastes in pizza will be happy to know that Mangia's will put different toppings on two halves or four quarters of the same pie. It also offers a few of its own signature pizzas, including the rosso, with five cheeses, tomato sauce, and a medium weight crust. The house-made cannoli come in a variety of flavors: chocolate, ricotta, lemon, chocolate-chocolate chip, and Oreo. Both crunchy and creamy, the cannoli are the perfect ending to a proper Sicilian meal.

## NICOLA'S ITALIAN WINE
## & FAIRE          $$–$$$
### 521 S. 13th St.
### (402) 345-8466
### www.nicolasintheoldmarket.com

A charming corner bistro on the outskirts of the Old Market, Nicola's is a downtown hidden gem. The restaurant's small kitchen creates each dish by hand, and the tasty results are worth waiting for. The menu is full of new Italian interpretations: All the pasta dishes come with a small salad featuring a sweet dressing and two slices of bruschetta with fresh tomato and basil. Delicious handmade ravioli are filled with a variety of things, including spinach, cheese, lobster, and meat. The light Spaghetti Aglio & Olio is a great summer Italian dish; its light sauce and kalamata olives are memorable. Nicola's is a tiny restaurant, with charming decor and lots of vintage posters; in nice weather, its large patio is the place to sit. It's just private enough but diners can still enjoy the sights and sounds of downtown. The restaurant just started offering desserts to go and the menu includes Italian favorites like tiramisu, cannoli, and Italian lemon cream cake. Cupcakes—including gluten-free cupcakes—come in regular and giant size. Designer cakes are available to order for a party or special event; contact the restaurant for more details.

## PASTA AMORE E FANTASIA          $$$
### 11027 Prairie Brook Rd., Rockbrook Village
### (402) 391-2585
### http://pastaamore.net

A family restaurant at its heart, Pasta Amore E Fantasia is owned and operated by the Fascianellas: Leo is the chef; his wife, Pat, runs the front of the house; and their three children cook, clean, and work in the space. Lots of creative entrees dot the otherwise traditional Italian menu. The rice salad includes cold rice, eggs, capers, artichoke hearts, tuna, and tomatoes in an olive oil dressing; the house favorite Linguine Amore includes mussels, clams, halibut, salmon, shrimp, calamari, and scallops in spicy red seafood sauce. The rest of the menu includes the standards diners expect from Italian restaurants, and the space itself is the same: A mural of Sicily adorns one wall and the simple decor and separated bar area all add up to a casual, comfortable eatery.

### SGT. PEFFER'S CAFE ITALIAN $-$$
**1501 N. Saddle Creek Rd.**
**(402) 558-7717**
**www.sgtpeffers.com**

What makes Sgt. Peffer's great (aside from the pizza) is its proximity to the Homy Inn and the fact that the restaurant delivers to the bar. Hungry Homy patrons often place an order for pizza and meatball subs and enjoy them at the bar. The pizza from Sgt. Peffer's is great and the neighborhoods surrounding the midtown location (there's a second location in Millard) are regular patrons. Lasagna, cannelloni, manicotti, ravioli, and other Italian favorites are on the menu; the sub menu includes the usual sandwiches that can be served cold or hot. The thick crust and specialty topping choices on the pizza menu are nothing out of the ordinary, but the somewhat sweet sauce and generous amount of toppings make the pizza memorable. The other location is at 13760 Millard Ave., Millard (402-932-6211).

### SPAGHETTI WORKS $$
**1105 Howard St., Old Market**
**(402) 345-7776**
**www.spagworks.com**

A family favorite, Spaghetti Works is one of the most affordable spots in the Old Market. With three locations in Nebraska and one in Iowa, the restaurants all offer lots of specials, including all-you-can-eat pasta starting at $5.99 and free meals for kids younger than 11 every Monday. The restaurant has been

operating in both Omaha and Lincoln for more than 30 years. The Ralston and the Old Market locations both have outdoor dining; the Old Market's vast outdoor seating area is on a converted loading dock that stretches almost a whole block and is popular in the summer. In all the restaurants, the salad bars are created out of old cars: Model T trucks in Lincoln and the Old Market and a vintage Chevy truck in Ralston. Other offerings include pizza, lasagna, a full bar, root beer on tap, and a wide variety of Italian sodas. The other locations are at 228 N. 12th St., Lincoln (402-475-0900) and 8416 Park Dr., Ralston (402-592-1444).

### SPEZIA $$$
**3125 S. 72nd St.**
**(402) 391-2950**
**www.speziarestaurant.com/omaha**

Omaha's Spezia is part of a Midwest-based chain of restaurants: there's also a Spezia in Sioux Falls, SD. The Omaha location is cleanly decorated, with simple tables and chairs and a great glass atrium that's a popular seating option for many diners. Spezia specializes in wood-fired items made in its large grill, and offerings include wood-fired flatbread pizza; roasted chicken, fish, pork, and beef; a vast selection of pasta, and a dinner menu with a number of singular dishes. Asiago-crusted walleye is served with Spezia mashed potatoes and roasted veggies, and the salmon pasta Spezia includes fettuccine Alfredo with prosciutto, baby peas, and a hunk of wood-grilled salmon.

### VINCENZO'S $$-$$$
**1818 N. 144th St.**
**(402) 498-3889**
**www.vincenzos-ne.com**

With a slightly varied menu at each of its three locations, Vincenzo's is one of eastern Nebraska's most popular Italian restaurants. The decor at the three locations—two in Omaha and one in Lincoln—is traditional, old-school Italian, with warm wood, dark red linens, checked tablecloths, and vintage photographs of Italian families decorating the walls. The menu, too, veers toward the classic, with appetizers like toasted ravioli and cheese bread, main dishes like lasagna, and a wide variety of pasta selections. The spicy Pene Diavolo is a popular choice, as is the chicken or veal parmesan. Each location has a private room, and the restaurant caters for special events; visit its website for more details. Other locations are at 1207 Harney St., Old Market (402-342-4010) and 808 P St., Lincoln (402-435-3889).

**VIVACE**                              $$–$$$
1110 Howard St.
(402) 342-2050
www.vivaceomaha.com

Owned by the same people who run the Old Market standby, M's Pub, Vivace is the neighborhood's answer to neo-Italian cuisine. The restaurant's interior has intimate tables, exposed brick walls, Picasso drawings scattered about, and a large glass window at the front that makes for great people watching year round. Sidewalk seating is popular in warmer months. A solid Italian menu features Neopolitan-style thin crust pizza and a make-your-own-pasta option, where diners choose from the shape of pasta, the sauce, and any meat or seafood they'd like. Sandwiches include grilled panini; Tramezzini, a Milanese bistro sandwich; and Piadini, a grilled flat bread wrap. The Parma Rosa pasta with chicken is particularly good; and for those who don't eat meat, the Garden Vegetable salad is an unexpected treat. The restaurant offers a kids' menu and a gluten-free menu.

**ZURLO'S BISTRO ITALIANO**            $$$
13110 Birch St.
(402) 884-9500
www.zurlos.com

Named after head chef Enzo Zurlo, Zurlo's Bistro is a fun West Omaha destination that's decorated in an eye-catching scheme of green, white, and silver. The menu is inspired by Chef Zurlo's Italian American heritage, and not only is his food tasty, it's artsy. The menu changes seasonally and the restaurant works to offer locally grown, sustainable items. The wine list includes 75 bottles and 30 by-the-glass selections, and the menu features brick oven pizza, pasta, and homemade desserts. An outdoor patio is a popular seating option in the summer. The restaurant has a number of gluten-free items; inquire with the waitstaff for a full list.

## MEXICAN & TAPAS

**CALIFORNIA TACOS**                       $
3235 California St.
(402) 342-0212
www.californiatacosandmore.com

An Omaha favorite, Cali Taco, as it's locally known, is a must-do for those wanting some simple but delicious Americanized Mexican food. After being featured on the Food Network's Diners, Drive-Ins and Dives, the restaurant experienced a surge in popularity but didn't change a thing. The restaurant is seriously casual, with tile floors and simple booths and tables, and the restaurant's episode of Diners, Drive-Ins and Dives runs on a corner television in a loop. The house specialty is the restaurant's namesake. The California Taco comes in a crisp fried shell with the diner's choice of beans, beef, chicken, steak, or fish and comes in at around five bucks no matter what choice you make. Other offerings include chimichangas, taco salads, enchiladas, and burritos, though most people choose the California Taco more than any other menu item. Bottle and tap beer, along with mega margaritas, are among the beverage offerings. During happy hour from 4 to 5 p.m. everything is half price.

### ✳EL DORADO                    $$–$$$
**5134 S. 24th St.**
**(402) 734-4947**
**www.eldoradomex.com**

Authentic, delicious Mexican food is what El Dorado does best. Located in the predominately Mexican neighborhood on Omaha's South 24th Street, the restaurant has a neighborhood, Spanish-speaking clientele but draws in people from all over the city to try its rich, authentic cuisine. A bright and colorful interior with televisions usually playing telenovelas or soccer matches, El Dorado in the evenings is filled with lots of large families happily enjoying the food. Oysters and ceviche are must-tries, as are the sizzling fajitas, which come with a variety of meat and seafood combinations. El Dorado's signature dishes include huge platters of grilled seafood and meat, served hot on a table-size grill with peppers, hot sauce, rice, and beans. The platters serve more than one and come with a fixed price per platter per person. A newer platter focuses solely on shrimp; most stick with the wide combination of food: beef, chicken breast, pork, Mexican sausage, quail, green onions, potatoes, breaded shrimp, shrimp wrapped with bacon, crab legs, clams, oysters, filet of fish, plantains, green onions, octopus, fish broth, abalone, or any combination thereof. These platters are simply delicious, and most of the diners who come from the surrounding Mexican neighborhood choose to feast on a few spread over a long table. Much of the menu is in both Spanish and English, and the waitstaff is bilingual too (to a degree). Even with this, they're friendly, open to questions, and happy to help diners choose what to eat.

### ESPAÑA                        $$$
**6064 Maple St.**
**(402) 505-9917**
**www.espanaomaha.com**

Omaha's best and most authentic Spanish tapas restaurant, España is located in the heart of the Benson neighborhood and was one of the businesses that began the area's resurgence in popularity. The menu includes a variety of tapas; house-made, signature paella (which takes longer to create but is worth the wait); and some seriously delicious sangria. España is small and romantic, with dim lighting, white tablecloths, and knowledgeable servers happy to answer questions even for long-time tapas fans. A rotating menu of ever-changing tapas specials, weekly and daily drink specials, and a variety of live music and dancing events keep people coming back. Every Tuesday from 5 p.m. to close, diners who buy two tapas will get a third one free. Wednesday night, select bottles of wine are half price, and Thursday night is ladies night, which features drink and tapas specials.

## GUACA MAYA                    $$–$$$
5002 S. 33rd St.
(402) 733-3440
www.guaca-maya.com

A fun fiesta of a restaurant, Guaca Maya serves up live music, dancing, and great, authentic Mexican cuisine. The huge South Omaha restaurant specializes in Mexican seafood, and there's a lot of it on the menu. The atmosphere at Guaca Maya is bright and colorful, with servers dressed in traditional Mexican garb, a full bar, pool tables, live music and dancing, and a private party room available for rent. Daily specials include a discounted buffet for military personnel, Tuesday discounted margaritas and Miller Lites, a Wednesday free buffet for kids younger than 10 years old, and a Friday night happy hour from 7 to 10 p.m. The parrilladas platters are a seafood smorgasbord and include all blends of seafood, meat, sausage, chorizo, pork, beans, and vegetables. All the whole cooked fish dishes on the menu are tender and flavorful. Each month, the chef prepares some special items; these also have special pricing. Guaca Maya has a regular buffet on the weekends from 11 a.m. to 3 p.m. for $6.99. A regular rotating schedule of bands, dancers, and other performers use the space regularly; check the website for the most up-to-date special events.

## ROJA MEXICAN GRILL              $$
1212 Harney St. (Old Market)
(402) 346-9190
www.rojagrill.com

Two Texas transplants own Roja Mexican Grill, and their heritage shines through in the restaurants' Tex Mex menu. The two Omaha locations are popular and serve tasty portions of fajitas, tacos, enchiladas, tostadas, tacos, and chimichangas, among other items. More than 80 tequilas are on the drink menu, and a wide variety of flavorful margaritas are, too. The atmosphere at both Roja locations is fun and funky, with a healthy dose of fire: Fire pits decorate the outdoor spaces of both locations, and the fire coupled with the indoor and outdoor red lighting makes the restaurants visible from a block away. Inside, the music is fun and the vibe is young and hip. Weekly specials include Margarita Mondays, where the drinks are $1.99 and Fajita Frenzy Wednesdays, where diners at the west location can buy one fajita, get a chicken fajita free. Happy hours take place Mon through Sat from 4 to 6:30 p.m., and Fri and Sat from 10 p.m. to midnight. A second location is at 17010 Wright Plaza, #100, (402) 333-7652.

# PIZZA

## BIG FRED'S PIZZA GARDEN         $$
1101 S. 119th St.
(402) 333-4414

A groovy chick and a beefy man adorn the pizza boxes at Big Fred's, which has been an Omaha standard since 1965. The pizza at Big Fred's is great: thin crust, cut into squares, and topped with just the right amount of sauce and cheese. The onion rings, too, are delicious: thinly breaded and thickly sliced, they have a flavor and texture that's irresistible. Rose's special double crust pizza, aka goudarooni, is also great. A central bar and a number of rooms full of tables and chairs make Big Fred's a good place for big parties, and it is super family friendly (I used to go here all the time growing up). Outside of pizza, the kitchen also serves up a wide variety of both Italian and American sandwiches, burgers, pasta, salads, and appetizers, including the best-selling Combo Plate, which includes zucchini sticks, mozzarella cheese sticks, jalapeno bottle caps, fried green beans, and onion rings, served with your choice of ranch, hot sauce, or spaghetti sauce.

## DANTE PIZZERIA NAPOLETANA    $$
**16901 Wright Plaza (Shops of Legacy)**
**(402) 932-3078**
**www.dantepizzeria.com**

Dante Pizzeria doesn't just say it's serving Neapolitan pizza, it has the paperwork to prove it. Nick Strawhecker, the owner and chef, is certified by the Associazione Verace Pizza Napoletana; the organization works to preserve the old-fashioned way of creating the thin crust, wood-oven-fired pies. Dante has specially crafted, Italian designed Mugnaini brick ovens that cook the pies, and the chefs prepare the crust on a specially crafted marble counter. The open air kitchen is visible to the diners, and it's truly the center of the establishment. Bar tables, booths, and other seats surround the kitchen. Patio seating is available in nice weather, and though the restaurant's West Omaha location doesn't make for the best outdoor people watching, the patio is pleasant, as is the dining experience. Pizza includes a wide variety of singular flavor profiles, including the Funghi mushroom pizza; the Paola, which features locally produced greens, roasted tomato, mozzarella, garlic, and olive oil; and the Monterosso, with potato, rosemary, garlic, crispy proschuitto and taleggio cheese. Pasta selections are also singular. Selections include a gnocchi with oxtail and roasted mushroom sauce topped with pecorino, and an herb roasted chicken livers bucatini topped with a sauce made of tomato, white wine, garlic, and chili.

## GOODNIGHTS PIZZA BAR + PATIO    $$
**1302 Mike Fahey St.**
**(402) 502-2151**
**www.goodnightsomaha.com**

Sure to become a favorite of College World Series fans, Goodnights opened recently in the Slowdown complex, across the street from TD Ameritrade Park, home of the series starting in 2011. The restaurant feels like a big chain, but it's actually locally owned, which makes the slick interior, large bar, and fast service even more impressive. The restaurant's signature thin pizza comes with a choice of parmesan romano basil crust or honey wheat crust, and the menu (or the waitstaff) can help diners choose which one would be tastiest with what toppings. The menu has all the standard pizza toppings one expects, along with creative choices: Twice Baked is modeled after a baked potato; Philly Cheese, Reuben, and Cheeseburger emulate the sandwiches; and Apple Walnut is almost like a dessert. The menu also includes a variety of salads. Goodnights has a weekly lunch special Mon through Fri from 11 a.m. to 2 p.m. that includes a slice and a soda for $4.99; a slice, salad, and soda for $6.99; or two slices and a soda for $7.99. In the evening, the bar has a popular full menu of shots and bombs, and the bar also has periodic specials listed on the Goodnights Facebook page.

**i** A Lithuanian grocer invented the Reuben sandwich in Omaha. Reuben Kulakofsky created the sandwich at Omaha's Blackstone Hotel in the 1920s as a treat for the players in his weekly poker game. The sandwich became famous when Kulakofsky added it to the Blackstone's restaurant lunch menu.

## LA CASA PIZZERIA $$
4432 Leavenworth St.
(402) 556-6464
www.lacasapizzaria.net

Thin crust pizza served on a plastic tray and cut into squares is the signature—and most popular—dish at midtown Omaha's La Casa Pizzeria. The other notable feature of La Casa is the original sign out front of a man strumming a mandolin; his neon hand strums up and down over his neon body and he's fondly known as Peppi. La Casa opened in its current location in 1950 and has a strong local following—the restaurant is decorated simply, with local artists' work on the walls, red and white checkered tablecloths, and a separate bar that doubles as a waiting area and overflow dining room on busy nights. The simple pizza is baked in a singular way and takes a bit longer, so expect a bit of a wait but know that it's worth it. Pizzas come with pre-selected toppings—think margarita, four cheese, and a delicious pesto pizza—or with the toppings of the diner's choice. For a real treat, consider the double crust pizza (which is just what you imagine it is). The toasted ravioli is a great appetizer, as is the antipasto plate. Other Italian standards round out the menu: lasagna, calzone, Italian sandwiches, eggplant and chicken parmesan, and Italian pasta dishes galore.

## ORSI'S ITALIAN BAKERY & PIZZERIA $$
2527 S. 10th St.
(402) 965-8029

Located in the heart of Omaha's Little Italy neighborhood, Orsi's serves delicious, filling pizza along with bread, meat, and cheese by the pound and desserts like cannoli and ricotta cookies. Orsi's is to-go only (there's no seating) and calling ahead

for pizza is the best thing to do, as the large square slabs covered in delicious sauce, cheese, and a choice of toppings take about a half hour to create (and are worth the wait). The pizza is incredibly filling, and one pizza is enough to feed a large group. Other menu items include a popular garlic bread; *goudarooni*, which is double crust pizza; and deli items including bacon, breadsticks, cannelloni, cheese, pepperoni, and sausages.

## ✳PITCH PIZZERIA $$-$$$
5021 Underwood Ave.
(402) 590-2625
www.pitchpizzeria.com

Owned and operated by a local pizza legend, Pitch does pizza (and atmosphere) right. This funky stop in the heart of Dundee has quickly become a place to see and be seen, as well as to eat good food and drink reasonably priced wine, beer, and house-made sangria. Owner Willy Thiesen started Godfather's Pizza—now a national franchise—out of a bar in the 1970s. Pitch is quite a departure from Godfather's, with sophisticated decor and a huge coal fire oven, the pizza is thin crust and comes in a few signature varieties as well as a make your own option. On Monday and Tuesday from 7 to 10 p.m. diners can get a pizza and a bottle of wine for $25. The Shrooms pizza, topped with mushrooms and a healthy drizzle of truffle oil, is to die for. The Mia (listed on the menu as Willy's favorite) is a pepperoni lover's dream topped with the signature meat, fennel sausage, cheese, and red sauce. Appetizers like the brussels sprouts with pancetta, the white beans, and a well-edited cheese plate are also palette pleasers. Communal seating, a friendly waitstaff, and a small but diverse list of beer and wine make Pitch a casual, hip stop on a night out.

## PIZZA KING                    $$
**1101 N. Broadway, Council Bluffs**
**(712) 323-9228**

An old-school pizza joint just across the river from Omaha in Council Bluffs, Iowa, the Pizza King does serve up pie, but it's also known for great steaks and seafood. The inside of Pizza King hasn't changed since the late 1970s, and it has the distinct feel of a Midwestern "old-school steak house." Think dark colors, a big fireplace, bricks, and lots of decor in the era-specific hue of old gold. Singular signature pizzas include one topped with cream cheese and jalapenos, though many diners stick to the old standbys: cheese and hamburger or just plain cheese. The menu at Pizza King is vast, and those looking for a finer experience can find it with a cut of beef, an order of onion rings, and a glass of wine or a beer, all for a more than reasonable price point. Pizza King is truly a Bluffs original, and it's worth the trek across the river for a memorable meal.

## PUDGY'S PIZZERIA                $$
**16499 Audrey St., Millard**
**(402) 884-7567**
**www.pudgys.net**

One of the only Omaha restaurants specializing in Chicago-style pizza, Pudgy's thick crust pizza emulates the deep dish so many know and love. Pudgy's sits in a neighborhood of West Omaha and definitely has the neighborhood feel the owners strive to achieve: It's casual and great for families. Deep dish pizzas include a variety of toppings: the Heat Treat includes hot sauce, chicken, jalapenos, tomato, and black olives; while the Austrian

Delight is a German-style deep dish that features Alfredo sauce, beef, Italian sausage, and hickory smoked Canadian bacon. Other menu items include all beef hot dogs, wings, bread sticks, and cheese bread. Pudgy's also offers a gluten-free crust and a thin crust option.

## VALENTINO'S                    $
**Numerous locations in Lincoln and Omaha**
**www.valentinos.com**

Valentino's started out in the late 1950s operating as a fruit market near the UNL campus. Its owners knew their tiny market was soon going to be eclipsed by larger supermarkets so they took a gamble into the pizza business. Armed with three pizza tins and a family recipe, they slowly built what's today become a franchise with nearly 40 restaurants in six states. Valentino's lunch and dinner buffets are one of the most popular choices, and a series of low-priced express lunches (think a slice, a salad, and a soda to go) make Valentino's a popular lunch destination. Valentino's has a family-oriented atmosphere and it's a popular destination for parents and children, especially for dinner. Pizza comes in both thick and thin crust, and signature pies include the popular original bacon cheeseburger option: hamburger, onions, pickle chips, lettuce, cheddar, mozzarella, and bacon, along with Val's secret sauce. The Val's Original Special, another popular pizza, has hamburger, sausage, pepperoni, ham, and mushrooms. The restaurant also offers pasta dishes, lasagna, salad, wings, and *zzagos,* which are pizza roll-ups that come with dipping sauce. The buffet and regular menu are available to go at Valentino's Express locations.

## ZIO'S NEW YORK STYLE PIZZERIA  $-$$
1109 Howard St. (Old Market)
(402) 344-2222
www.ziospizzeria.com

Zio's thin crust, New York–style pie could have been transferred from a city street stand straight into the hands of hungry Omahans. The restaurant's three locations all have similar decor: comfortable booths and big photos of past and present New York (including an impressively large image of the floor of the NYSE at the downtown location) borrow style from the city the restaurant emulates. Zios offers pizza by the slice to stay and by the pie to stay, for takeout or delivery from the downtown location only. It also sells half baked pizzas to go, and caters parties. More than 40 toppings adorn the make-your-own-pizza side of the menu, and Zio's also has a vast selection of specialty pies. The Thai Pizza is worth a try: toppings include marinated Thai chicken, bean sprouts, red onions, scallion, cilantro, and a special Thai peanut sauce. The crust has a thin center and a delicious, thick edge, perfect for eating alone or dipping in sauce. Zios also serves hoagie sandwiches, calzones, salads, and pasta. The other locations are at 12997 W. Center Rd. (402-330-1444) and 7834 W. Dodge Rd. (402-391-1881).

## SWEETS

### *ECREAMERY                    $-$$
5001 Underwood Ave.
(402) 934-3888
www.ecreamery.com

Known mostly for its customize-your-own-ice-cream-flavor service via the Internet, the Omaha-based eCreamery has only one brick-and-mortar store, and it's in the heart of Dundee. The place does a brisk trade in the summer, and, though the crowd thins down with cooler weather, eCreamery keeps the flavors coming year-round. The ice cream, gelato, and sorbetto are all made by hand on-site. The stand-alone store has a fun and funky vibe, with bright green tile walls and a long counter with customized flavors that change daily. If it's warm outside, expect a line out the door. The store sells coffee drinks in cooler weather and Soup Revolution soup for lunch every Tuesday.

**i** eCreamery isn't just loved locally; it's earned some serious national press. The shop's online customizable ice cream service has been featured on the *Today Show,* in Rachael Ray's magazine and in the *New York Times.* The store's website lets customers create their own ice cream, gelato or sorbetto, add personalized flavors and mix-ins, create their own packaging for the sweet treat and even come up with a personalized ice cream name. Visit www.ecreamery.com to check it out.

### TED & WALLY'S ICE CREAM SHOP      $
1120 Jackson St.
(402) 341-5827
www.facebook.com/pages/Ted-and-Wallys-Premium-Homemade-Ice-Cream

Ted and Wally's is an Old Market institution. The shop makes ice cream with rock salt, ice, and manpower in a machine that's on display next to the long soda shop counter. When a national ice cream shop chain moved in just across the street, many worried about the little guy's fate, but if anything, the competition made Ted and Wally's devotees even more persistent about supporting the local shop. The line regularly stretches clear out the door and into the parking lot on a hot summer evening, and the homemade ice cream is worth the wait. Ted and Wally's concocts delicious, singular flavors, and even the most traditional flavors are often infused with creativity, whether it be through nuts, fruit, or clever new incarnations of the familiar. Flavors vary every day, but a recent list included chai, pineapple coconut, root beer, peach granola, maple walnut, and green tea, along with the more traditional vanilla and Dutch chocolate. Mix-ins are pounded through the ice cream by hand, and portions are decidedly large.

## VEGETARIAN & NATURAL

**BLUE PLANET NATURAL GRILL**   $-$$
**6307 Center St.**
**(402) 218-4555**
**www.blueplanetnaturalgrill.com**
A locally owned restaurant with a focus on natural eating, vegetarian and gluten-free cuisine, and healthy options for meat eaters, Blue Planet is healthy fast food that's reasonably priced. Blue Planet cooks its food simply and healthily without using any additional grease or oil, without deep frying, and using whole grains, minimal processed items, and few preservatives. Tasty french fries are baked. Pizza crusts are made of whole grain. Meat is locally produced. This care is clear in the taste of the many yummy items on the menu, including the above three things. Burgers come as vegetarian or regular options, and wraps include lots of fresh ingredients. Bowls are another menu item, and they're basically a base of rice with a variety of toppings, either Thai, Chinese, Tuscan, southwestern, or American (macaroni and cheese.) The atmosphere inside the small restaurant is bright and colorful, if a bit

fast food inspired: Diners order at the counter and their food is delivered to the table. A nice outdoor patio offers tables and umbrellas for dining al fresco in warmer weather. Blue Planet also whips up a wide variety of fruit smoothies and has a well-edited list of wine and locally crafted beers.

**GREENBELLY**   $-$$
**12355 West Center Rd.**
**(402) 334-1300**
**www.thegreenbelly.com**
A healthy alternative to the regular lunch spots, Greenbelly aims to offer healthy food produced in an environmentally friendly way. Diners order at the counter and can make their own salad or choose from the set menu of pizza, soup, sandwiches, and signature salads. Greenbelly started as a catering company called The Cooking Club and now operates as its own business outside of The Cooking Club, which is separate now. Greenbelly packages all its food in environmentally friendly containers. Diners can choose from a vast array of ingredients at the make-your-own-salad bar: Diners pick their greens, choose a dressing from the long list, then choose 4 fresh fruits, vegetables, spices, and other toppings and finish it all off with a protein or other special topper. Salads start at a reasonable $7.99, and many of the other entrees have equally pocket-friendly price tags.

**MCFOSTER'S NATURAL KIND**
  **CAFE**   $-$$
**302 S. 38th St.**
**(402) 345-7477**
**www.mcfosters.com**
Primarily a restaurant for vegetarians and generally adventurous eaters, McFoster's does serve meat but does it responsibly:

free range chicken and fresh seafood only. About half the food served at McFoster's is locally grown and organic, and the restaurant recycles all its waste glass, tin, paper, aluminum, and plastic. (Diners who bring their own to-go container get a 10 percent discount.) The restaurant has a casual, funky vibe and is located in an old Tudor style building in a mixed use neighborhood. The servers are happy to help diners who may be unfamiliar with the food on the menu; in most cases, McFoster's offers the option to try something new. Lots of vegetarian and vegan items make up the bulk of the menu, and some are familiar: hummus, falafel, veggie melts and burgers, and Italian and Mexican food made sans meat. More innovative main dishes include curried greens with blackened tempeh, a vegetarian BLT sandwich, and a kasha salad. If you're in the mood for dessert, the tofu mousse is surprisingly creamy and delicious. From July to October, McFosters operates an organic farmers market on Sunday at 4 p.m.

# OMAHA NIGHTLIFE

Nightlife in Omaha is defined by good food, tasty drinks, lots of live music, and venues loaded with personality. The scenes, divided by neighborhoods, each offer a distinct style and vibe. The Old Market area is constantly popular, and each weekend people who don't live downtown can count on driving around for at least a little while before finding a place to park. Bars downtown are often connected to restaurants, but many are worth a visit even if you're only after a cocktail.

Midtown Omaha is home to a lot of dive bars, live music venues, and Omaha classics, including bars that have been standards for years and years. The new Midtown Crossing and Aksarben Village developments have brought lots of new hotspots to the city, and these two areas—one around 30th Street, the other around 60th Street—have suddenly become really popular. Blingy bars and swank lounges are the word of the day in West Omaha, and these newer outfits attract a mixed crowd of singles, young professionals, and older people out for an after-dinner drink.

What's clear about the nightlife scene is that it offers a wide array of diverse options: No matter what you're after, you'll find it.

## OVERVIEW

This chapter presents a wide range of night-life options, including bars, clubs, dance halls, and cinemas listed by geographic area of the city. There are, of course, lots of other options to be discovered in Omaha, and some of those are listed in the Arts chapter. The legal drinking age in Nebraska is 21, as in the rest of the United States. There are also plenty of restaurants in Omaha that are popular nightlife destinations; those are listed in the vast restaurants' chapter. This chapter focuses on listings of places where food is not the main draw. In some cases, restaurants with attached bars are mentioned, and that is because I felt they were exceptional enough to be mentioned. In those cases, the venue is listed in both the

restaurants chapter and here in the nightlife chapter.

Most bars in Omaha don't charge a cover, but when live music or dancing is involved, patrons can expect to pay anywhere from $3 to $20 for admission to a club or for a ticket to see a show.

Both Omaha and Lincoln are fairly spread out, and public transportation is limited. If you plan to go out drinking, be sure to use a designated driver or plan ahead by calling a taxi to get you to and from your bar or club safely. If you are a vacationer and plan to experience a lot of local nightlife, it might be wise to arrange your lodging options in the area you plan to visit most.

**i** Reverse happy hours have become a trend in Omaha. Many restaurants have half-price food and drink specials that begin at 10 p.m. or later; these specials are usually advertised on the menu. Many Old Market restaurants have happy hour specials on weeknights; keep your eyes peeled for special deals.

## OMAHA

### Downtown

#### BLUE JAY
**2416 Davenport St.**
**(402) 345-1979**
For fans of Creighton University sports, the Blue Jay is the go-to spot for post-game drinks. The recently remodeled bar is much improved from its former self, and the owners brought back food service after not offering snacks for a number of years. On non-game nights, the bar is predictably a huge hangout for Creighton students and alumni.

#### DUBLINER PUB
**1205 Harney St.**
**(402) 342-5887**
**www.dublinerpubomaha.com**
A big, kelly green rock marks the entrance to the Dubliner Pub, announcing its Irish heritage to everyone who passes by on the street. The basement bar is popular year-round (though, obviously, especially on St. Patrick's Day). The house band, The Turfmen, plays at least once a month, and their spirited Irish tunes keep the crowd on its toes year-round.

#### FARRELL'S
**902 Dodge St.**
**(402) 884-8818**

The main draw at Farrell's is easy to see when you walk in the door: A group of comfortably worn-in leather chairs sit in front of a wall of television sets that display every big game taking place each night. Free wireless Internet means patrons can check their fantasy teams while they tune into the games, and a selection of tasty bar food along with a nightly happy hour makes Farrell's a popular downtown destination for sporting events. In the spring and fall months, an outdoor fire pit surrounded by tables is a popular destination when the evenings are cool.

#### THE FOUNDATION
**1407 Howard St.**
**(402) 905-2270**
**http://foundationomaha.com**
One of downtown Omaha's most recent additions, The Foundation is a popular after work hangout for the city's young professionals. Nightly specials—Monday night is "guys' night," Tuesday is "service industry night—draw in mixed crowds. The Boxcar grill serves a variety of snacks, sandwiches, and other bar standards, and the bar has more than 100 bottled beers and 25 rotating tap selections. Pool tables live on the second floor.

#### *FRENCH CAFE
**1017 Howard St.**
**(402) 341-3547**
Though mostly known as a restaurant, the French Cafe has a charming bar on the east side that's a quiet spot for those after a pre- or post-dinner cocktail. The bar side doesn't have a set menu, though it serves the by-the-glass wine list that also serves the restaurant, and patrons can get just about any cocktail they desire from the vast selection of spirits. The amazing vintage bar is backed

by a sheet of glass that lends a glimpse into the restaurant side, and patrons can get a glimpse of the beautiful wall of black and white photography shot in Parisian markets by Omaha transplant Vera Mercer (also owner of La Buvette).

## HAVANA GARAGE
**1008 Howard St.**
**(402) 614-3800**
**http://thehavanagarage.com**

A menu of Cuban-inspired signature drinks (and cigars to match) make Havana Garage one of the Old Market's more exotic haunts. Slowly turning ceiling fans, thick leather chairs, and a warm, golden light fill this spot, where live bands often play Cuban music. A signature drink menu includes one named after the bar: says the menu of the Havana Garage Cocktail "If James Joyce and Che Guevara fixed a drink for Ernest Hemingway, this would be it." Other more traditional offerings include a mojito (mint, sugar cane, rum, lime, and club soda muddled in a tall glass); a Caipirinha (a Brazilian drink with Cachaca, sugar, and lime); and an old-fashioned Dark and Stormy (Gosling's Dark Rum and ginger beer). The bar also offers a wide selection of single malt scotch, single barrel bourbon, port, rum, and more than 100 cigar selections.

## *LA BUVETTE
**511 S. 11th St.**
**(402) 344-8627**

La Buvette is a little slice of Paris transplanted to Omaha. In the spring and summer, and during the downtown Omaha Farmers' Market Saturdays, its outdoor patio is the place to be, early afternoon to night, for a glass of wine or coffee. In the cooler winter months, its cozy interior, with uneven stone floor, creaky antique wood tables and chairs, and hundreds of bottles of wine lit by candlelight are indescribably lovely. Most wines by the glass (there's at least 20 on the menu daily) run less than $7, and any of the bottles can be corked for $4 and consumed on-site. The atmosphere is artsy and diverse, and though the service isn't always fast, La Buvette is a lovely place to sit, people watch, and enjoy good wine at a leisurely pace.

## MR. TOAD
**1002 Howard St.**
**(402) 345-4488**

Mr. Toad is like a library, but with drinking. Books line the walls of this downtown spot that's decidedly cozy in the fall and winter; the bar's outdoor patio—one of the Old Market's best—sits on a prime corner and is packed in spring and summer. In the fall and winter, the special coffee is the drink to order.

## NOMAD LOUNGE
**1013 Jones St.**
**(402) 884-1231**
**www.nomadlounge.com**

Candles, velvet curtains, lots of wood and pulsating music make Nomad Lounge the one true club in the Old Market. Regular events for things like New Year's Eve, Halloween, and other holidays often feature waitresses clad in body paint and not much more, along with cocktails created specially for each event. Resident DJs spin a wide variety of music; it's always progressive and can include deep house, trip hop, afro beat, disco, indie rock, and more. A gallery space, in the back of the bar, plays host to a regularly rotating docket of local artists who mostly exhibit two-dimensional work. A portion of all sales from the gallery go to support local charities.

**O'CONNORS**
**1217 Howard St.**
**(402) 934-9790**
**http://oconnorsomaha.com**
A countdown clock to March 17 is the first thing a viewer sees on O'Connor's website, and the Irish spirit at this supposedly haunted downtown bar is no joke. During the annual downtown Omaha St. Pat's Day parade, O'Connors is one of the most popular stops and is right in the center of the holiday madness as the evening begins. The current bar owner, Katie O'Connor, will tell you that the second floor of the space—which used to be a hardware store—is haunted by the friendly spirit of its original owner.

**❋ROSE AND CROWN**
**515 S. 20th St.**
**(402) 346-8242**
A sort of hidden gem right outside downtown Omaha, the Rose and Crown has a stellar outdoor patio complete with a handful of tables and old shade trees. It's off the major streets downtown and the fenced patio isn't visible from the street, but once you find it, you'll go back. Regular specials on beer and drinks and a neighborhood crowd make Rose and Crown a casual downtown hideaway.

**SAKE BOMBERS LOUNGE**
**416 S. 12th St.**
**(402) 408-5566**
**www.bluesushisakegrill.com/**
**sake-bombers-lounge/**
On the second level of downtown's Blue Sushi is Sake Bombers Lounge—a fun and funky space with mod decor, red lights, great views of the Old Market from a window seat, and daily happy hours, including an all day happy hour on Sunday. Food is on special,

but drinks are too: half-price martinis (the bar offers more than 20 exclusive house blends), cold sake or Morimoto Soba Ale, and $3 sake bombs included. Happy hours run Mon through Sat from 4 to 6:30 p.m., Fri and Sat from 10:30 p.m. to midnight, and Sun from noon to 8 p.m.

**SLOWDOWN**
**729 N. 14th St.**
**(402) 345-7575**
**http://theslowdown.com**
A show almost every week of the night, weekly events like pub quiz and science cafe, and regular drink specials make the Slowdown one of north downtown's most popular live music venues. On the rare night that nothing is happening at Slowdown, the free jukebox filled with great music and a shelf of dog-eared board and card games keep patrons busy.

**URBAN WINE COMPANY**
**1037 Jones St.**
**(402) 934-0005**
**http://urbanwinecompany.com**
With hundreds of glasses available by bottle and a regular selection of boutique wines available by the glass along with a great happy hour menu special, Urban Wine Company has become a popular downtown Omaha destination. The atmosphere is rugged and slick at the same time, and the outdoor patio is a popular seat in warm weather—it's recently been expanded to allow for more seating. The meat and cheese flight goes great with one of the two-ounce or five-ounce wine flights, which allow patrons to choose between red, white, or a mix. Appetizers are sized (and priced) for sharing. Locals who love wine might consider the annual wine club membership,

which includes regular tastings and events and free and discounted bottles of wine.

## Midtown

### BROTHERS
**3812 Farnam St.**
**(402) 553-9744**
Brothers bar is a hipster's dream. The dingy interior is flecked with kitschy decor. A couple of pool tables and an excellent jukebox are the bar's signature activities, and its signature drink is Moscow mules served in freezing cold copper mugs. A sometimes venue for occasional live music, Brothers is a locally owned joint (not to be confused with the big-time chain of the same name). It's one of midtown's most popular stops.

### CRESCENT MOON/MAX AND JOE'S/ HUBER HOUSE
**3578 Farnam St.**
**(402) 345-1708**
Locally known as "Beer Corner USA," Crescent Moon, Max and Joe's, and Huber House are truly a beer lover's paradise. The three bars—all connected—each have a specific focus. Crescent Moon focuses on locally crafted beers and ales, Max and Joe's on Belgian style beer, and Huber House—in the basement of the Moon—entirely on German beer. The bars are popular hangouts for Creighton University students, though on most weekend nights the crowd is a healthy mix of students, 20- and 30-somethings, and people there simply to drink good beer and watch sports on one of the large televisions scattered through all three spaces. Though they're connected, each bar has its own personality. Crescent Moon feels like a downright American beer bar, while Huber House has long wood tables and oftentimes patrons chug beer out of a giant

glass shaped like a boot. The calmer Max and Joe's is on the east end of the Moon and has a more laid-back atmosphere. The Moon sells packaged beer on-site that can be taken to go.

### ✳DUNDEE CORK AND BOTTLE
**614 N. 50th St.**
**(402) 934-2118**
A tiny wine bar with an excellent outdoor patio, Dundee Cork and Bottle is a beloved neighborhood bar, but popular with those who don't live in Dundee, too. On any given Friday night, it's full of locals—many who know each other—and a few newcomers just there to people watch. Booths sit outside, and even in cooler weather, they're popular. For those looking to eat, the bar has agreements with the restaurants around the area and takeout can be eaten inside the Cork and Bottle along with a glass of wine; bottles line the wall and a number of types are available by the glass for a reasonable price. On Wino Wednesday select bottles are half price.

### THE HOMY INN
**1510 N. Saddle Creek Rd.**
**(402) 554-5815**
Three words define the Homy Inn for most people: champagne on tap. And though the bubbly coming out of the fountain behind the bar is certainly a draw (it's served in pitchers and consumed from short wine glasses), the friendly atmosphere, funky decor, and cheap beer are what the locals come for. The Homy is a small place, with a few booths and large tables, and the decoration is decidedly one of a kind: vintage campaign buttons sit next to a Big Buck Hunter game; the walls are covered in yellowed newspaper; tchotchkes wrapped in plastic bags sit on a ledge near

the ceiling; table tops are decoupaged with themed clippings. If you live or visit Omaha and don't check out the Homy, well, you're missing out.

## *JAKE'S CIGARS AND SPIRITS
**6206 Maple St.**
**(402) 934-9633**
Jake's is a neighborhood bar at its finest, but with a serious dose of cool. The bar's laid-back vibe and friendly staff mean everyone would feel welcome here, but its great selection of beer, wine, and spirits along with its location in Benson, an up-and-coming artsy neighborhood, earns it some style points. A wide selection of cigars and an on-site humidor mean the aficionado will likely find what he or she seeks here. The bar is busy on most nights—especially weekends—and on slower nights it's a popular date spot or conversation spot: The noise level is the perfect pitch for talking. Package alcohol is available to go.

## JIMI D'S
**6303 Center St.**
**(402) 391-2011**
**www.jimids.com**
A popular spot for an after-work drink, Jimi D's has a daily happy hour from 3 to 6 p.m. with beer, wine, and drinks all on special. A sports bar that's a bit classier than most, Jimi D's aims to cater to both the corporate and casual crowds at once. A nicely decorated interior—think refinished concrete floors and modern lighting—meets a traditional round bar and loads of television sets tuned to the big game.

## LIV LOUNGE
**2279 S. 67th St.**
**(402) 884-5410**
**http://livlounge.com**

A regular schedule of events, live music, karaoke, and solid cocktails are what Liv, located in the new Aksarben Village development, is known for. The bar has a lounge-y feel, with comfortable seating clustered around low tables, a backlit bar, and an outdoor fire pit. An extensive cocktail menu—we're talking book length—means that whatever your fancy, you'll find it here.

## LYNX LOUNGE
**1604 NW Radial Hwy.**
**(402) 0553-8787**
If you like a jukebox filled with soul music and a decidedly retro vibe—think windows with pink curtains, mirrored walls, and a fireplace—the Lynx should be on your list of places to check out. Strong drinks for low prices along with atmosphere to spare make the Lynx one of midtown's most singular bars. It's hardly ever that crowded but is great to gather a large group or for those looking for a character-filled spot.

## NIFTY BAR AND GRILL
**4721 NW Radial Hwy.**
**(402) 933-9300**
An unappreciated, un-ironic dive bar, the Nifty is one of those places where the same working class sometimes rough-and-tumble regulars hang out almost daily, the bartenders have been there forever, and the jukebox plays solid music. The prices are cheap and if a dark dive bar is what you're after, that's what the Nifty brings to the table.

## PAULI'S
**4016 Leavenworth St.**
**(402) 345-7959**

## BARRETT'S BARLEY CORN
**4322 Leavenworth St.**
**(402) 554-5805**

During Omaha's annual College World Series, two bars are the epicenter for fun when the games are over: Pauli's and Barrett's. Pauli's sets up an outdoor patio in its parking lots, and sports fans hang out both inside and outside the two venues, which are just a few doors down from one another. Pauli's became a CWS tradition in the early 1980s, when the bar's owner painted a Chicago Cubs logo on the sidewalk outside the bar and drew an ESPN crew inside. More and more media started hanging out there during the games, and fans eventually followed; on a good night during the series, more than 3,000 people can pack into the bar. Barrett's is a hot spot for Louisiana State University fans—a perpetual CWS team—and the bar does itself up in Mardi Gras style (you'll see people everywhere wearing plastic beads; they got 'em at Barrett's).

## SIDE DOOR LOUNGE
**3530 Leavenworth**
**(402) 504-3444**

One of the city's newest bars, Side Door Lounge is owned by the same family that runs the popular Flatiron Cafe in downtown Omaha. It's still finding its footing, but the funky space is outfitted with lots of vintage materials—the floors, for instance, came from the old Orpheum Theater downtown—and a large mural by local artist Bill Hoover identifies the bar easily when approaching it from the west side. A schedule of live music and a newly developed craft cocktail menu are the most recent developments in the space, which looks to be an eventual spot for regular performance (including poetry readings and art shows) down the road.

## THE WAITING ROOM LOUNGE
**6212 Maple St.**
**(402) 884-5353**

The Waiting Room Lounge was one of the bars that helped Benson make its comeback as a trendy arts area. The live music venue, recently remodeled, has great acoustics and almost nightly events and drink specials. When live music isn't taking place at the venue, it plays host to themed movie screenings and other special events, which are all listed on its extensive online calendar.

### West Omaha

## BRIX
**225 N. 170th St.**
**(402) 991-9463**

A huge West Omaha wine store melded with a small restaurant and tasting bar, Brix offers the best of both worlds. Most of the shop's wine is competitively priced, and a backroom area offers some fancier reserve selections. The beer cases take up almost the entire back wall of the shop and, as you might imagine, the variety is wide. A wine tasting bar sits in the middle of the shop, and next door is an area with seats and table service that serves small plates to accompany a bottle of wine or a beer. Samplers can do a tasting from the bar's wine vending machines; this activity is popular and also quite fun.

## DJ'S DUGOUT
**636 N. 114th St.**
**(402) 498-8855**

With two locations in West Omaha and Papillion and a new downtown location, DJ's Dugout is one of the city's most popular sports bars. The downtown location is located on the corner of 10th and Capitol Avenue in the heart of the Old Market. The

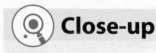

# Close-up

## ✳The Boiler Room

The bartenders at the Boiler Room (1110 Jones St., Omaha, 402-916-9274) have a serious love of the old-school cocktail. The beautiful, sunken bar in the sophisticated restaurant is worth a stop of its own. The lead bartender, Chris Engles, makes a delicious cocktail, but it's not the run of the mill gin and tonic. The Boiler Room focuses on creative, pre-prohibition drinks, and the menu rotates seasonally. (And you thought alcohol didn't have seasons.) Fresh squeezed juices, handmade syrups, creative interpretations of vintage drinks and some straightforward re-creations make this one of the best bars in the city, hands down.

The menu changes regularly, but some of the house-made cocktails are menu standards, and can be made even if they're not listed. A delicious interpretation of the champagne drink the French 75 is a standard and includes Ca' di Pietro Prosecco, Burnett's gin, simple syrup, lemon juice, lemon peel; it's refreshing in the summer and in the winter can be warmed up with the addition of brandy. A Jezebel Sling, one of Engles' creations, comes out a light shade of purple with an artful orange twist. It's delicious. A seasonal fall drink, the Harvest Sour, includes Laird's Applejack, Rittenhouse 100, Old Overholt, lemon, lime, simple syrup, and egg white.

The restaurant has a vast wine cellar, and the bartenders are knowledgeable about what's hiding in there; the wine list is the size of a thin magazine and they're happy to make recommendations according to taste.

When a rare slow moment rolls around, the bartenders are the kind who like to talk to the patrons, get to know their tastes and their lives. When it's busy, which it usually is, the bar itself is a spectacle. Bartenders are constantly in motion and the creation of the drinks is truly an art form: slicing and dicing of fruit, peeling of limes, vigorous shaking, and precise measurements make these drinks taste good. The level of care put into the craft makes them taste exceptional.

bar offers daily specials on bar food (Monday is buy-one, get-one-free burgers; a 9 oz. steak dinner is $7.99 on Thursday). A $7.50 bucket of domestic beer is on special from 3 to 7 p.m. every weeknight.

**HOLIDAY LOUNGE**
**7846 Dodge St.**
**(402) 391-4442**

**INTERLUDE LOUNGE**
**7643 Pacific St.**
**(402) 391-3060**

The Holiday Lounge and the Interlude Lounge could be long-lost cousins. Both have remained popular even while holding on to their mid-1970s vibe; these days, it's the very thing that keeps them both cool. Expect mirrored walls, 1970s vinyl chairs, half-moon shaped booths, and a mixed crowd that veers toward older patrons. People-watching is great at both spots. Don't let the respective bars' strip mall locations turn you off; each provides a fun—if not memorable—vintage Omaha experience.

## MAI TAI LOUNGE
**7215 Blondo St.**

Hidden in the basement of Mt. Fugi Inn—a Chinese restaurant—the Mai Tai Lounge harbors some of the strongest (and tastiest) drinks in the city. The space is somewhat predictably dark, though a neon glowing fish tank and tiki theme keep things interesting. The drinks are rated in terms of strength: GP (general public), R (Restricted), and (Adults Only); once you get to the  section, you're limited to two cocktails per visit. The coconutty Chi Chi is a delicious choice in the "R rated" section, while the  section has some of the Lounge's signatures, including its namesake Mai Tai, the Zombie (blended rums, pineapple juice, and grenadine), and the Navy Grog (blended rums, lemon, and grapefruit), which is delivered in flames (obviously not for the shy).

## Gay & Lesbian

### DC'S SALOON
**610 S. 14th St.**
**(402) 344-3103**

A slick finished wood dance floor takes up the bulk of DC's Saloon in downtown Omaha, and for good measure: Country dancing is the to-do activity in this gay bar. Weekly events—leather night, men-only nights—take place in the bar's basement, and, for those who don't know the country steps, lessons take place on a regular basis before the music starts for real. A well-stocked bar and reasonably priced drinks make DC's popular for cowboys and non-cowboys alike.

### FLIXX
**1019 S. 10th St.**
**(402) 408-1020**
**www.flixxomaha.com**

What started as a video bar has become one of the city's more popular gay bars. The lounge area includes a number of television screens playing dance music videos, and there's a Wii available for patrons to play, as well as a number of pool tables. The cabaret show bar plays host to Nebraska's best female impersonators as well as other weekly events including burlesque shows, Drag Queen Bingo, and other fun stuff. Check the Flixx website for an updated schedule.

### THE MAX
**1417 Jackson St.**
**(402) 346-4110**

Just inside the door of the Max is a sign that reads The Best Dance Club in the Midwest. Two dance floors, a handful of bars, and an outdoor patio complete with a rainbow color-change fountain make the Max a memorable club; the music and the anything goes atmosphere make it unforgettable. Go here on Halloween, New Year's Eve, heck, even Thanksgiving night to find a full-fledged dance party ready to welcome you into its open, loving arms.

## Country

### REDNECK SALOON
**3421 S. 84th St.**
**(402) 733-6365**

Boots and cowboy hats in every nook and cranny decorate the interior of this self-proclaimed "redneck cowboy bar." Dancing is the real attraction here, as the bar's center is occupied by a huge dance floor where patrons two step and line dance. Professional dancers on staff lead dance lessons and dance with shier patrons; most nights there's a $3 cover. Reasonably priced pitchers and a fun atmosphere make Rednecks a must-stop for country music lovers.

## WHISKEY TANGO
**311 S. 15th St.**
**(402) 813-6944**
**www.facebook.com/omahawhiskey
tango**

Downtown Omaha's most popular country bar, Whiskey Tango has tons of events that draw huge crowds. The way to be in the know is to become a fan of the bar's Facebook page, where a full schedule of events, concerts, viewing parties, and shows are updated on a regular basis.

## Casinos

Though Nebraska doesn't allow gambling, Omaha's neighboring city of Council Bluffs, Iowa, does, and its three casinos are popular destinations for those who live on the opposite side of the river. Though all three offer the same wide variety of video slot machines and table games and the same buffet-style and sit-down dining options, there are a few notable differences. Horseshoe has a poker room—the only one in the Bluffs—that's popular day and night. Blackjack tables are cheaper at Ameristar and Harrah's—some as low as $5 a hand. A regular slew of summertime concerts takes place in Harrah's outdoor Stir Concert Cove; the concerts are widely advertised and a list of upcoming shows is available on the casino's website.

## AMERISTAR CASINO
**2200 River Rd., Council Bluffs, Iowa**
**(712) 328-8888**

## HARRAH'S AND STIR CONCERT COVE
**1 Harrah's Blvd., Council Bluffs, Iowa**
**(712) 329-6000**

## HORSESHOE CASINO
**2701 23rd Ave., Council Bluffs, Iowa**
**(712) 329-6000**

## Cinema

✳**Film Streams** (1340 Mike Fahey St., 402-933-0259, http://filmstreams.org) is Omaha's only independent art house movie theater, and it shows a regular schedule of first-run and classic films as well as curated film series. Panel discussions and appearances by actors and directors are just a sampling of the theater's special events. The theater got its liquor license in 2010. It's located downtown and is part of the Slowdown complex. **Central Omaha's Dundee Theater** (4952 Dodge St., 402-551-3595) shows independent and first-run movies one at a time (the theater only has a single screen), and the historic nature of the building makes for a fun viewing experience. On Friday and Saturday, Dundee has midnight screenings of cult classics. **Midtown Crossing's Marcus Midtown Theater** (3201 Farnam St., 402-346-6900, www.marcustheatres.com) offers Cinedine, which lets viewers sit in a comfortable swiveling leather chair and eat a full meal (mostly bar food) or enjoy a cocktail during a first-run movie. Another big-box theater option includes the **AMC Star Council Bluffs 17** (3220 S. 23rd St., Council Bluffs, 712-325-8924), which is a great option for downtown Omaha residents or those who want to do dinner and a movie in the Old Market area. West Omaha giant theaters include the **AMC Oakview Plaza 24** (3555 S. 140th Plaza, 888-262-4386), the **Rave Motion Pictures Westroads,** located in the shopping mall (10000 California St., 402-393-9200), and the **Village Point Cinema** (304 N. 174th St., 402-289-4777).

# OMAHA SHOPPING

Omaha has lots of opportunities to shop. Locally owned boutiques—especially for women—decorate the scene in Omaha. Those, along with the national chain stores that Omaha has drawn in the past few years, have made the city a new destination on shoppers' lists of places to visit.

Specialty stores focus on more diverse goods: used books, locally owned music with a great selection of local bands, and carefully stocked clothing and accessory stores.

Specialty food stores, farmers' markets, and locally owned markets are all over Omaha. More often than not, consumers are after these locally owned places that carry locally produced goods. These shops do their part to give the consumers what they want.

A special Close-up section focuses on the singular pastime of thrift store and vintage shopping, for which Omaha (and Lincoln, too) are exceptional. People travel to Omaha from both coasts to find well-priced, well-taken-care-of beautiful examples of antique just about anything. Consignment, vintage, and thrift are all explored in this section.

Omaha has a wealth of aforementioned chain stores, big box stores, and national clothing and accessories retailers. Almost everything detailed here, though, is locally owned, operated, and appreciated.

## OVERVIEW

In these pages, you will find listings for a variety of shopping opportunities in Omaha. Of course, it would be impossible to list everything, so instead this list is curated. It provides examples of the best, most unusual stores in the city—places that stand out from the rest. Many national chain stores aren't listed here but Omaha has them: Target, WalMart, K-Mart, and dozens of others. These stores, along with hundreds of other mall stores and big box outfits, can be found with a quick Google search; Omaha, especially has been a magnet for chains like

J. Crew, Sephora, and other high-end stores in recent years.

## ANTIQUES

### *SECOND CHANCE
**1116 Jackson St.**
**(402) 346-4930**
Second Chance is the antique hunter's dream store. Packed—almost literally—from floor to ceiling, the store is organized by style of item: jewelry fills the central counter, glassware of all kinds fill a number of areas

in the store, and every corner is packed with books, quilts, antique linens, and thousands of tchotchkes in every nook and cranny. The store's staff is expert in their genre, and they also know the layout of the place like the back of their hand. Want a Bakelite bracelet, a vintage political button, or a piece of vintage Fiestaware? They'll point you in the right direction and answer your questions.

Don't miss the basement of Second Chance, which is stuffed with vintage clothes, costume jewelry, hats, gloves, fur coats, and shoes. Both men and women can find something special here—indie rock music plays from a boom box behind the counter and it's easy to get lost down here for hours on end.

## BOOKS

### *THE BOOKWORM
**8702 Pacific St.**
**(402) 392-2877**
One of Omaha's best locally owned bookstores, the Bookworm is also a popular place for readings of all kinds and keeps a full schedule of author appearances and in-person signings. Owners Phillip and Beth Black pride themselves on being independent and they stock a regularly changing selection of national best sellers, children's literature, books written by local authors, and gift items for people who love to read. They also employ people who love books, and inquiring customers are sure to find a good answer if they have any questions about the store or its stock. An attached coffee shop gives patrons the chance to sit and enjoy a hot beverage while reading their latest purchase. The store has a designated meeting room for book clubs, and well-behaved, leashed pets are welcome in the store.

### JACKSON STREET BOOKSELLERS
**1119 Jackson St.**
**(402) 341-2664**
NPR favorite and Omaha native Kurt Andersen fancies Jackson Street Booksellers so much, he wrote about it in the *New York Times*. That's true book-lover romance. Andersen isn't the only one who loves the place: It's a favorite of locals, too. The used bookstore—easily the best in the city—is packed full of books from floor to ceiling, books stacked on the floor and books filling chairs and corners. Like any good used bookstore, organization doesn't matter as much as what one comes across by chance, and there's lots of good stuff to be hunted out at Jackson Street. The characters you'll find working in the bookstore are almost as charismatic as the place itself. The bookstore is a cell phone free zone, and a sign posted on the store's front door says as much. Patrons would be well advised to turn their BlackBerry to vibrate and embrace a more old-school, printed word inside.

## BOUTIQUES

### Children's

### BELLY BUMP
**11045 Elm St.**
**(402) 502-5126**
**www.bellybumpmaternity.com**
The brainchild of a fashionable mom looking for clothing to suit her stylish sensibilities, Belly Bump is a popular maternity boutique that also has children's clothing. The West Omaha location has a sweet interior design painted in soothing hues of green and white. One of the store's most popular items is its line of premium denim made for expectant mothers: Seven for All Mankind, Citizens of Humanity, and Paige Premium Denim

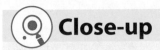

# Close-up

## Husker Outposts

On fall Saturdays in Nebraska, the city of Lincoln bursts at its seams with people, as at least 84,000 people descend on the town. Those people head to Memorial Stadium, where Nebraska Cornhusker football games have been consecutively sold out since 1962. The fans create a "sea of red" with their Nebraska gear of all shapes and sizes, but all of the same crimson hue.

A few shops in Omaha and Lincoln specialize in sales of Husker gear. Shoppers will find loads of sweatshirts, hoodies, T-shirts, hats, and other clothing. Almost everything you can imagine is branded with the Nebraska logo at these stores: water bottles, koozies, socks, winter coats, umbrellas, key chains—the list goes on and on. Two outposts on the University of Nebraska–Lincoln campus—just steps away from Memorial Stadium—offer a wide selection of Husker goods. The Nebraska Bookstore—just off campus—has two floors of Husker gear, and the University Bookstore, in the Nebraska Union on campus, has a wide selection, too. The University Bookstore also carries a limited selection of Victoria's Secret "Pink" gear branded with the Husker logo; most of the styles are exclusive to the store.

In Omaha, Cornhukser fans can choose between Husker Hounds and Husker Heaven, both of which have been going strong in the city for years. Husker Hounds offers a "one of a kind" section that boasts merchandise signed by former players and coaches and vintage game programs, among other items. Husker Heaven, in business for more than 25 years, has a whole section of Husker gear made especially for cars, so fans can make the 45-minute drive between Omaha and Lincoln showing their Husker pride to everyone on the road.

**Husker Heaven**
3926 N. 90th St., Omaha
(402) 572-8373

**Husker Hounds**
3003 S. 84th St., Omaha
171st and W. Center Road, Omaha
(800) 860-5844, (402) 758-0207

**Nebraska Bookstore**
1300 Q St., Lincoln
(402) 476-0111

**University Bookstore**
14th and R Streets, Lincoln
(402) 472-7300

---

are among the brands the shop carries. The clothing in the store is contemporary and fashionable; perfect for the expectant mother hoping to avoid looking unfashionable for nine months. The infant clothes in the shop are the kind of things you'd imagine a fashionable baby to wear: slogan T-shirts and onesies, cute hoodies, and puffy vests.

## Men's & Women's

### ✴DENIM SALOON
**4914 Underwood Ave.**
**(402) 885-8880**

This boutique in the heart of the historic Dundee neighborhood specializes in one thing—denim—and does it really, really well. Up-and-coming brands meet more well-established brands in this shop that has high-end offerings for both men and women. The decor fits the name, and the walls are plastered with vintage newspaper clippings and pictures of long-captured (or long-lost) outlaws. A selection of tops and jackets all work well with denim, and a neatly edited selection of scarves and bags make this shop key for creating casual but fashion-forward weekend looks. Jeans are arranged by style—skinny, bootcut, straight leg, legging, etc.—and the store owners—sisters Sarah Troia and Jenny Farha Galley—are knowledgeable and friendly.

## GARMENT DISTRICT
**16939 Wright Plaza**
**(402) 557-6100**
A chic, locally owned West Omaha boutique, the Garment District aims to give Omaha shoppers a taste of the East Coast. The store carries both well-known and emerging designers, and has a well-edited selection of casual and dressy clothes. The store itself is decorated in a fun yet welcoming scheme with touches of vintage—crystal chandeliers being the most obvious example. The store also offers wardrobe consultation and personal shopping for its customers, whether they need help for a special occasion or a complete closet makeover.

## NEBRASKA CLOTHING CO.
**1012 Howard St.**
**(402) 346-6114**
What used to be primarily an outpost for the Nebraska "Bugeaters"—the "bugeaters" being a previous name for the Nebraska Cornhuskers football team—has diversified into an eclectic boutique for both men and women. The shop still has a wide selection of Bugeaters gear, as well as casual men's clothing and accessories. But where things

have vastly changed is through Nebraska Clothing Company's selection of fashionable women's apparel at shockingly reasonable price points. Summer dresses, fashionable handbags, and cute jewelry make this a popular stop for Old Market visitors, especially on warm summer evenings. Be sure to scout the sale rack for even better deals on fun, casual clothing.

## NOUVELLE EVE
**1102 Howard St.**
**(402) 345-4811**
Nouvelle Eve is an Old Market icon. The small women's shop has been in business on the same corner of the historic Omaha neighborhood since 1973—since the infancy of the Old Market as it's known today. Owner Kat Moser had a dream of creating a one-of-a-kind shopping experience offering everything the modern woman might want when she opened the store, and she's stuck to the same formula for 35 years. Moser is also an artist and her photography serves as the branding for the store and is displayed throughout the eclectic space. A finely edited selection of women's formalwear, casual dresses, jeans, tops, and jewelry is melded with a small section of baby items and clothing inside the shop. Ancient wood floors and brick walls bring instant character to the shop, and a window looking into M's Pub, the store's neighbor, through a north wall window serves to remind shoppers where they are and make the space feel alive, especially on a weekend evening.

## ROOTS AND WINGS
**11046 Elm St.**
**(402) 504-4700**
**http://rootsandwingsomaha.com**

Roots and Wings aims to clothe the hip young woman in Omaha. The store is locally owned and operated, and carries singular, stylish clothes and accessories. A few of its flagship brands include Tom's Shoes, Havaianas flip flops, and Le Sport Sac bags. The clothing at the store takes a cue from what young women are wearing: casual wear from brands like B.B. Dakota, Blank Denim, Free People, and Gentle Fawn. The store is warm and welcoming, with big mirrors and stone walls; the employees are friendly and as cool as the store they work in.

### SHE-LA
**8733 Countryside Plaza**
**(402) 391-1880**
Sophisticated investment pieces melded with of-the-moment looks make She-la a stop for lots of Omaha's stylish women. High-end designers—think Elizabeth and James, Blumarine, Badgley Mischka, and Escada—meet an ever-changing docket of youthful, trendy brands. Accessories and handbags are also part of the merchandise lineup, and She-la stocks select lines of cosmetics. The store staffs a makeup consultant to help customers choose what's best for them, and the store's small, dedicated staff offers closet and wardrobe consultations by appointment.

### SOUQ
**1018 Howard St.**
**(402) 342-2972**
A few businesses in the Old Market have stood the test of time. Souq is one of them. An outpost for imported goods since 1972, Souq is still going strong with its lineup of incense, scented candles and oil, eclectic jewelry and ethnic clothing, shoes, and accessories. The store is at the front of the Old Market Passageway shops, and the area is truly ideal for its funky take on the world. The space is always richly scented and full of world music, and the vibe of the employees fits the space. Be sure to check out the cases of imported jewelry, as well as the scented soaps, candles, and home fragrances.

### TOGS
**16950 Wright Plaza**
**(402) 391-8335**
**www.shoptogs.com**
Togs has a West Coast feel about it: It has a clean, modern feel inside and carries casual sportswear brands like American Vintage, DaNang, Ella Moss, Juicy Couture, and Splendid, among many others. It also carries beauty brands—Bliss included—as well as select accessories and denim brands. The boutique is located in a sea of West Omaha chain stores and provides a welcome respite for contemporary casual wear.

### ✳TROCADERO
**1208½ Howard St.**
**(402) 934-8389**
Opened by New York transplant Alice Kim, the former accessories director for *InStyle* magazine, Trocadero brings a slice of New York City and puts it in the heart of Omaha. Kim has a knack for selecting items that are just exclusive enough to appeal to her Midwestern audience, and the shop is the only place in Omaha to get many things: Alex and Ani bracelets, Diyptique scented candles, and shoes from up-and-coming designers. Souvenirs from Kim's glamorous life in New York and Paris fill the shop—cards from Chanel designer Karl Lagerfeld, shoe master Brian Atwood, and from fashion weeks

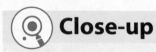

# Close-up

## Thrift, Vintage & Consignment

One of Omaha's best-kept secrets is its amazing scene for thrift store and vintage shopping. Coastal visitors to the city are often shocked by the vast array of items available and the rock bottom prices that go along with them. Like most cities, Omaha has a wide array of national chain stores, but the Goodwills and Salvation Armies are still worth checking out, especially for more experienced thrifters that know what they're after and aren't afraid to sift through thousands of other items to find it.

Both Omaha and Lincoln offer a handful of well-edited vintage and consignment outposts.

**Scout Dry Goods & Trade** (5019 Underwood Ave., Omaha, 402-964-2270) is one of the few shops in Omaha that's a blend of both consignment and vintage. The staff is similar to the stock at Scout: hip and on point, dressed in an eclectic blend of current styles, well-preserved vintage clothes, jewelry, and shoes and highlighted with a smattering of handmade goods from local artists. Scout is one of those vintage spots that regularly rotates out merchandise, and every Sunday the shop plays host to a $1 sale, where clothes are liquidated to make room for more stock; the store carries both men's and women's clothing. **The Black Market** (1033 O St., Lincoln, 402-475-1033) is the capital city's answer to Scout. Clothing is a mix of modern and vintage, and spans eras: Vintage dresses and suits meet modern denim brands here. A wide selection of sunglasses is mostly priced under $10, and the shoes and purses are often reasonably priced.

Goodwill's curated **ReServe** (501 S. 13th St., Omaha, 402-342-4102) and the **Flying Worm** (1125 Jackson St., Omaha, 402-932-3229) are the two Old Market outposts dedicated to pure vintage. ReServe is the Market's newest vintage shop. Operated by Goodwill Industries, it offers a specially selected group of the best of

around the world decorate the space in between the exclusive merchandise. But it's not all fancy: Trocadero stocks a wide array of books for both adults and children and fun Kid Robot toys that no one can resist, old or young.

## JEWELRY

### *BORSHEIM'S
120 Regency Pkwy.
(402) 391-0400

Borsheim's is an Omaha legend. Operating in the city since 1870 and owned by Warren Buffet's Berkshire Hathaway companies since 1986, the store is often called the Tiffany of the Midwest. It lives up to this name, with its gleaming, glossy interior, hushed music, professional employees, loads of diamonds, watches, and two separate departments dedicated to estate jewelry and fine gifts. The store's inventory maintains more than 100,000 items and on any given day, men search inside for the perfect engagement ring, people buy gifts of fine china, silverware, and other items, and the friendly staff behind the service counter change watch batteries and the best donations to stores around the city. Recognizable, high end brands are mixed with true vintage here, and the store serves a mix of home goods, accessories, shoes, clothes and an area for gently used and vintage wedding dresses. At the Flying Worm, clothing is divided by style, and every day the shop rolls one or more racks out onto the sidewalk full of discounted merchandise. Skirts, jackets, uniforms, and vintage T-shirts are on a regular outdoor rotation. Men and women can shop at both stores; the Flying Worm has an especially good selection of vintage men's jackets.

Lincoln's **Ruby Begonia's** (1321 P St., Lincoln, 402-438-4438) is a beautifully curated shop with a focus on vintage, most of which is in close to pristine condition. The old-style rotating jewelry case on the first floor is a must-do, as is the basement, which is about three times the size of the first floor and is stuffed with treasures, most more than competitively priced.

**The Giving Tree** (16902 Wright Plaza, Omaha, 402-884-1110) is a blend of lightly worn designer clothing and a well-edited collection of vintage. The store also has a buy-sell-trade program, which lets its customers trade clothes for cash, store credit, or credit to its sister store **BeYourself** (www.beyourselfonline.com/about).

Those looking for barely loved designer clothes and a collection of select vintage won't want to miss **Esther's** (805½ S. 75th St., Omaha, 402-391-1301). The shop has consigners from all over the United States who send gently loved designer—think Prada, Manolo Blahnik, and all the up-and-coming denim brands—to Omaha, where the store's knowledgeable staff prices them reasonably and puts them out into the store's neatly organized racks. Regulars wait the whole year for Esther's annual Superbowl Sunday sale. Everything in the shop goes on sale and it's the perfect escape to score a deal before the game begins.

clean rings. During the Berkshire Hathaway Annual Shareholders Meeting, which regularly brings 30,000 or more people to Omaha, Borshiem's plays host to the shareholder's reception, a rollicking party with food, wine, drinks, and, of course, lots and lots of shopping.

## GOLDSMITH SILVERSMITH
**1019 Howard St.**
**(402) 342-1737**

If custom jewelry is what you want, Goldsmith Silversmith is the place to get it in Omaha. Another one of the oldest businesses in the historic Old Market District—it opened its doors in 1974—Goldsmith Silversmith has earned its reputation for the ability to make almost anything its customers can dream of. Clients meet with a private jeweler and work to create a sketch of their piece, then the shop makes a wax mold using the sketch. Finally, one of the shop's artists creates the piece based on the client's design. A number of artisans create ready-to-wear jewelry for the store, and a selection is always available for immediate purchase.

**i** During the annual Berkshire Hathaway Shareholders Weekend, deals abound, as do stockholders with precious credentials. Discounts at Borshiem's Jewelry and Nebraska Furniture Mart draw throngs; the Oracle of Omaha knows stocks, but he also knows how to get people to shop. Non-shareholders can also find special Berkshire-related deals at boutiques and restaurants all over Omaha during the spring event.

## MUSIC

### DRASTIC PLASTIC
**1209 Howard St.**
**(402) 346-8843**
Drastic Plastic specializes in two things: vinyl and T-shirts, and they do both really well. In the past year, Drastic focused much of its energy on reissuing out-of-print vinyl, so it's an understatement to say that shoppers can find things here that simply don't exist elsewhere. In the front window, Drastic displays a selection of its Omaha-themed T-shirts printed with steaks, corncobs, and kitschy sayings. The store's owner also runs Impact Merchandising, a multi-million dollar company that prints T-shirts for thousands of rock and punk bands including the Clash, David Bowie, and Elvis Presley, among many others. The company also prints shirts featuring comic book characters and movie titles, and shoppers will see a selection of this merchandise in the store, too.

### HOMER'S
**1210 Howard St.**
**(402) 346-0264**
**www.homersmusic.com**
Homer's is one of those record stores that could have come straight out of a movie. Row upon row of neatly organized discs, including an impressive used section, fill the store's giant downtown space. With its creaky wood floors, ceiling to floor display of concert posters representing just about every type of music imaginable and staff of musically inclined hipsters, it fits the bill for the kind of locally owned music store people spend a lifetime searching for. During the summer, Homer's will put a big selection of used music on a table outside and sell it for dirt cheap. And for the superfan, the store has a list of people who request the band posters in the window; some are free, most go for a nominal fee. A second location is at 2457 132nd St. (402-334-8844).

## SPECIALTY FOODS

### NO NAME NUTRITION
**2032 N. 72nd St.**
**(402) 393-5812**
**http://nonamenutrition.com**
Though they feel like an old-fashioned market inside, No Name Nutrition's two locations are decidedly modern. No Name is Omaha's largest locally owned health food market, and it's been operating since 1976. It's a source for vitamins, supplements, and other natural remedies, but it's also an indispensible shop for people with food allergies—it has an amazing selection of gluten-free products—and those with other special dietary needs. The second location is at 14469 W. Center Rd. (402-333-1300).

## STOYSICH HOUSE OF SAUSAGE
**2532 S. 24th St.**
**(402) 341-7260**
**www.stoysich.com**

Anyone who loves beef jerky absolutely must visit Stoysich House of Sausage. The chewy rolls with a softly crispy outside and delectably chewy inside that bursts with flavor are one of my personal favorites; I lived for them as a child. Stoysich uses locally produced meat to make more than 65 varieties of sausage, cut meat, and processed meat. Many of the shop's recipes have been handed down through customers, and Omaha's ethnic neighborhoods—Czech, Polish, Mexican, Greek, Danish, Swedish, Irish, and Hungarian—color the shop's menu and make it a true reflection of the city's heritage. Another location is at 2502 S. 130th Ave. (402-333-7277).

## ✳WOHLNER'S GROCERY
**2289 S. 67th St.**
**(402) 551-6875**

Wholner's has been Omaha's beloved family-owned grocery store for more than 90 years. The store originally opened in the 1930s in a small building in the midtown Dundee neighborhood. In 2009, it opened a new store in the Aksarben Village development off 72nd and Center Streets, and has since opened a second outpost in the Midtown Crossing development, off 33rd and Dodge Streets. These two outposts—though much more modern than the original store, with its creaky wood floors and spice-scented air—have somehow managed to maintain the same aesthetic. Hand-cut meats, house-baked bread, friendly staff, and a focus on both producing and buying local make Wohlner's the anti–big box choice.

# FARMERS' MARKETS

## ✳OMAHA FARMERS' MARKET
**Sat 8 a.m. to 12:30 p.m.**
**In the Old Market District**

## HAYMARKET FARMERS' MARKET
**Sat 8 a.m. to 12:30 p.m.**
**In the historic Haymarket District, Lincoln**

Omaha and Lincoln each have one major farmers' market. For most of the markets' histories, Lincoln had the upper hand as far as range of products, size of market, and attending crowds. But in the past few years, Omaha has stepped up to the plate and expanded its Old Market Farmers' Market from the confines of a parking lot to three whole blocks in the Old Market. The two markets have many similarities when it comes to food vendors: Both stock locally produced vegetables of all sorts, which change as the seasons change; cheese; bread; eggs; meat; and specialty items like spiced nuts, local honey and jam, sweets, baked goods, and local popcorn. Lincoln's market has a larger focus on crafts, and many stalls focus solely on art and craft: Paintings, pottery, jewelry, baskets, soap, lotion, and wind chimes are among the many craft-focused booths.

## More Must-See Farmers' Markets

**BENSON FARMERS MARKET**
**Military Avenue, near 61st and Maple Streets**
**Sat 8 a.m. to noon**

**ELKHORN VALLEY FRESH FOOD MARKET**
**21330 Elkhorn Dr.**
**Wed 5:30 to 8 p.m.**

**PART 2: OMAHA**

**FLORENCE MILL FARMERS MARKET**
9102 N. 30th St.
Sun 11 a.m. to 3 p.m.

**MARKET AT AKSARBEN VILLAGE**
67th and Center, Omaha
Sun 10 a.m. to 2 p.m.

**MIDTOWN CROSSING**
31st and Farnam Streets
Sat 9 a.m. to noon

**VILLAGE POINTE FARMERS MARKET**
68th and Dodge Streets, Omaha
Sat 8 a.m. to 1 p.m.

# OMAHA ATTRACTIONS

maha is ripe with the kinds of attractions that draw tourists in droves. Military history, family attractions, historic architecture, horticulture, and the outdoors are all on display; it's fair to say there's something for just about everyone.

Historical attractions abound. Visitors can learn about military history, visit the birth site of the country's 38th president and one of its most famous civil rights leaders. They can learn the story of the Mormon's tumultuous winter spent on the banks of the Missouri River in the late 1800s, or go to the capital city and see Nebraska's state capitol, which is one of only three skyscraper capitols in the country.

Museums, too, offer lots of singular experiences. One of Omaha's oldest railroad stations has been turned into one of its most popular museums, where traveling exhibits from the Smithsonian show. Learn about Mexican history at a South Omaha museum, and visit the city's vast acreage of botanical gardens. Learn about strategic air command and Nebraska's famous astronaut, Clayton Andersen.

Nebraska's economy focuses on agriculture, and this means "agritourism"—tourist attractions with an agriculture bent—are big here. Get your hands dirty at a pick-your-own. Take a stroll out in the cropland. But have fun while you do it—these attractions are hardly just farms and instead offer lots of activities for kids and parents, too. Nebraska is a haven for the outdoorsman, and eastern Nebraska offers vast hunting opportunities. For a truly unique, "only in Nebraska" experience, consider tanking. What's that? Read on to find out.

Families will love learning about the history of Boys Town, Nebraska, which has its own zip code and post office. Outdoorsmen will love a visit to Cabela's, the world's foremost outfitter, and a hike through Bellevue's forest preserves. You can't go to Omaha without a visit to its top-ranked zoo; people of all ages will love it.

If a scenic drive is more your speed (which is probably slow), then you've come to the right place. The state has nine scenic byways, and many begin in eastern Nebraska.

Some of the more specific types of attractions are listed in separate chapters. For instance, art museums and galleries are in the Arts chapter, while other museums related to history and culture are here. Most outdoor spots are in the Parks & Recreation chapter, and places that kids will love can be found in the Kidstuff chapter.

## Price Code

The following price code has been included to give you a rough idea of what one regular adult ticket or entrance fee will cost at each of the following places. If the fees or costs associated with a particular activity or place are varied, no price has been given and you should use the contact information provided to find out the details. More specific pricing and discount information is included in the listings, where available.

$. . . . . . . . . . . . . . . . . . .Less than $5

$$ . . . . . . . . . . . . . . . . . . . .$5 to $10

$$$ . . . . . . . . . . . . . . . . . $10 to 2$0

$$$$ . . . . . . . . . . . More than $20

# MONUMENTS & HISTORIC PLACES

### GENERAL CROOK HOUSE AT
### FORT OMAHA                                      $
**30th and Fort Streets**
**(402) 455-9990**
**www.omahahistory.org**

General George Crook wasn't just a run-of-the-mill military man. Crook, a Civil War and National Indian Wars hero, is described as the "greatest Indian fighter in the history of the United States." Over his lifetime, Crook became a defender of Native American rights and was the defendant in the 1879 trial for Ponca Chief Standing Bear.

His home, built in 1879, sits in Omaha on what is now Metro Community College's Fort Omaha Campus. The Italianate style house, with its rust colored exterior and grand front porch, is full of Victorian furnishings from the 1880s. A living history museum inside the house includes costumes, art and craft, and period furnishings. Outside the house, a Victorian Heirloom garden features more than 100 varieties of flowers, trees, and shrubs native to Nebraska. Perennial plants create a mosaic design reminiscent of an Oriental rug, and walking paths invite visitors to stroll the grounds outside the home.

From early November through the end of December, the house is decorated for the holidays. Local designers and design students transform every room in the style of Christmas past. Groups of 12 or larger can take afternoon tea at the Crook House and enjoy homemade treats as part of a proper afternoon tea, a dessert tea, or a cream tea. Reservations for afternoon teas are required and must be made a minimum of two weeks in advance; call the Crook House for details.

The Crook House also has a bookstore and gift shop, and the selection includes one of the largest selections by and about Nebraskans anywhere in the city. Guided tours of the Crook House are available by appointment, and admission prices vary during the holiday season or during special exhibitions.

### GERALD R. FORD BIRTH SITE
### AND GARDENS                                  FREE
**3202 Woolworth Ave.**
**(402) 444-5955, (402) 595-1180 (to visit the Ford exhibit)**
**www.nebraskahistory.org/conserve/brthsite.htm**

The Omaha home where President Gerald R. Ford was born was one of the finest homes of its day. The 3-story, 14-room home was where Leslie King, Jr.—later known as Gerald Ford—was born on July 14, 1913. That home, demolished by fire in 1971, became a memorial site to the president after Ford became the leader of the United States in 1974. The birth site was dedicated in 1977 and the city planted a rose garden in 1978 to honor former First Lady Betty Ford.

Today, the gardens are located adjacent to the Gerald R. Ford Conservation Center, which specializes in the treatment and conservation of a variety of items: art, artifacts, archeological materials, books, photographs, paper, paintings, and textiles included. The gardens play host to an exhibit honoring the center's namesake, and a second exhibit, inside the conservation center, is open by appointment. The gardens are open early morning until dusk every day year-round, and are a popular site for private rental events, including weddings.

## MALCOM X BIRTH SITE                FREE
**3448 Pinkney St.**
**(800) 645-9287**
**www.malcomxfoundation.org**
A memorial to the late civil rights Leader Malcom X has long been the goal of the foundation formed in his name. Malcom X was born in 1925 in the heart of North Omaha; his birth home, located at 34th and Pinkney, has long since been razed. Omahan Rowena Moore's family owned five lots in North Omaha, including the one of Malcom X's birth home, and she single-handedly formed the Malcom X Foundation in 1971, saving her own money to stage events commemorating his birth and death. The foundation incorporated in 1983 and it placed a historical marker at the birth site in 1987. That same year, with the support of Malcom X's family, the foundation bought 10 acres of land around the birth site.

Today, the foundation is actively fundraising to construct a memorial at the site of the birth home, and to buy a building adjacent to the birth site that would be home to the International Headquarters and Visiting Center for the Foundation. It would be the first facility to house all of the foundation's operations in more than 30 years.

## MORMON TRAIL CENTER AT
## HISTORIC WINTER QUARTERS     FREE
**3215 State St.**
**(402) 453-9372**
**http://lds.org**
The Mormon Trail Center at Historic Winter Quarters marks one moment on the group's long exodus across the United States that eventually landed them in Utah. In 1846, the Mormons were driven from their homes in Illinois; they left in search of "a new Zion." They traveled by foot, many of them pulling handcarts, and after crossing through Iowa settled for the winter of 1846 on the Nebraska side of the Missouri River. They built hundreds of shelters along the river banks, and aimed to rest—the journey had been a harrowing one—at the site through the winter. Though the camp was cold and food was scarce, the real problems came with sickness: scurvy, tuberculosis, consumption, malaria, and other maladies plagued the group; by the end of the season, more than 600 people perished.

At the center, visitors can try pulling a handcart, learn about the hardships Mormons faced, and view the final resting place of the more than 300 people who died during the winter of 1846.

# MUSEUMS

## DURHAM MUSEUM                $$
**801 S. 10th St.**
**(402) 444-5071**
**www.durhammuseum.org**
The Durham Museum is located in Omaha's Old Union Station, which has been lovingly restored to the height of its art

deco–era glory. Entering the museum's vast vestibule instantly transports the visitor back in time, to when rail travel was both sensible and glamorous. Vintage train benches and train memorabilia decorate the lobby, and life-size (and lifelike) bronze sculptures are placed throughout the lobby. Some wait for trains, others stand at the ticket counter. A fully operational soda fountain is a museum favorite and phosphates, banana splits, and milkshakes are just a few of the items on the menu.

The museum has a relationship with the Smithsonian Institution, the Library of Congress, and the National Archives, so high-caliber traveling exhibitions make regular stops at Durham. The museum also has a regular docket of permanent collection exhibitions on display, including a series of restored train cars and 1940s era store fronts that museum visitors can stroll through. During the holidays, the museum transforms into a holiday wonderland, and Christmas at Union Station includes a giant decorated tree in the train station lobby.

**EL MUSEO LATINO**                              **$**
**4701 S. 25th St.**
**(402) 731-1137**
**www.elmuseulatino.org**
El Museo Latino has the distinction of being the first museum of its kind in the Midwest. Its collection and traveling exhibits focus on Latino culture in all its forms, including visual art, dance, music, and tradition. The museum offers almost all its programs in both Spanish and English, and it's located in the heart of the city's Latino District, just west of South 24th Street.

The museum makes creative use of an old school building, and has renovated the space into a series of galleries and performance spaces. It uses the classrooms for their original purpose and presents workshops, classes, and demonstrations. Performances from the CHOMARI Ballet Folklorico Mexicano are a highlight on El Museo Latino's schedule. During late October and early November, the museum celebrates Dia De Los Muertos, or the Mexican holiday Day of the Dead, with a wide array of events and an exhibition that always includes an authentic "Ofrenda," which is an altar designed to honor the departed.

**✳LAURITZEN GARDENS, OMAHA'S**
   **BOTANICAL CENTER, AND**
   **KENEFICK PARK**                        **$$**
**100 Bancroft St.**
**(402) 346-4002**
**www.lauritzengardens.org**
Located on what used to be a desolate area of Omaha's riverfront, Lauritzen Gardens now boasts more than 100 acres of flora and fauna coupled with a stunning view of the Missouri River valley. The botanical gardens are open year round and play host to a variety of special events including a yearly antiques show, a poinsettia show, and a regularly changing schedule of art exhibits from artists who focus their work on the natural world.

Outdoors, visitors will find a wide variety of meticulously groomed gardens. The rose garden is a popular destination for summer weddings. A railroad garden designed by landscape architect Paul Busse features replicas of buildings on the Omaha skyline created completely from natural materials as well as a to-scale model train that runs through the garden.

Kenefick Park continues the train theme and features a slice of Union Pacific and Omaha history. The park, located outside the museum gates, has free admission and houses two of the largest, most powerful locomotives ever to run on the UP line: Centennial No. 6900 and Big Boy. Interpretive signage tells the story of the trains, and natural grasses and plants decorate the landscape.

## STRATEGIC AIR AND SPACE MUSEUM $$
**Off I-80, exit 426, Ashland**
**(402) 944-3100**
**www.sasmuseum.com**

Located between Omaha and Lincoln, the Strategic Air and Space museum cuts a futuristic swath in the skyline of the eastern Nebraska plains. The vast building holds a variety of items chronicling the history of the Strategic Air Command, a joint military command that oversees the nation's nuclear weapons.

A giant SR-71 Blackbird—still considered the world's fastest aircraft—is suspended from the ceiling just steps from the museum's entrance and delights aviation fans, old and young. The plane has an intriguing history: its creation was shrouded in secrecy and the CIA developed it almost solely based on speed. Its titanium body and coal black paint make it intimidating, to say the least.

The museum cafe is situated to look into a glassed-off room where mechanics and other workers restore planes and jets of all kinds, maybe most notably a B-29 bomber. The museum's staff meticulously restored the bomber, from cockpit to instrument panels to paint job and engines and spent more than two years doing so.

Other interactive exhibits at the museum include a multi-axis trainer, which whirls the passenger through a series of spins, flips, and twirls as it simulates the flight pattern of a plane—warning, this is not for the faint of stomach! A permanent exhibit details the life of Astronaut Clayton Anderson, an Ashland, Nebraska, native. The show looks at his upbringing, his training to become an astronaut, and the two missions he completed in 2007 and 2010.

# WINERIES & BREWERIES

## LUCKY BUCKET BREWERY $$
**11941 Centennial Rd., La Vista**
**(402) 763-8868**
**www.luckybucketbrewing.com**

Nebraska is right on trend when it comes to the recent explosion of craft breweries and pre-prohibition drinks. Lucky Bucket Brewery is the state's newest offering in the genre, and its first three beers have become amazingly popular locally and are being distributed through Nebraska and Iowa.

A pre-prohibition-style Lager was its first beer, and the additive-free brew is both light and malty. Its India pale ale is created in a unique four-barrel stainless steel tank and has a hint of aromatic oils. Its third beer, Certified Evil, is complex and smooth and includes both molasses and honey in the brew. The brewery is working on its first batches of distilled spirits, and plans to eventually offer Nebraska-made vodka.

Tours are available on a regular schedule: Thurs from 4 to 7 p.m. and Sat from 10 a.m. to 1 p.m. Tours start at regular intervals and last about 45 minutes.

## NEBRASKA BREWING COMPANY $$
**7474 Towne Center Pkwy., Papillion**
**(402) 934-7100**
**www.nebraskabrewingco.com**

Nebraska Brewing Company is a West Omaha favorite, serving food and hand-crafted beer in a lodge-inspired restaurant. Its list of barley wines makes it stand out from the rest of the Nebraska brewing pack, and it's also taken home a fair amount of brewing awards in its own right.

The Fathead Barley wine's warming character and whiskey-inspired flavor make it a favorite. The Chardonnay French Oak Hop God is another singular offering: It hangs out in a French oak chardonnay barrel for six months before being served, and ends up with some citrus, grapefruit, and floral aromatics.

## RANCHES, FARMS & OUTFITTERS

### POOLEY'S PUMPKIN PATCH $$
**12020 N. 144th Plaza, Bennington**
**(402) 238-3663**
**www.pooleyspumpkinpatch.com**
One of eastern Nebraska's newer you-pick-it operations, Pooley's was a working farm for more than 80 years before morphing into an agritourism destination in 2004. A family-run attraction, Pooley's still raises cattle, pigs, ducks, horses, chickens, kittens, kids—and pumpkins. Pooley's aims to give its visitors the you-pick-it experience juxtaposed with an inside glimpse into life on a working Nebraska farm.

A hayrack ride takes visitors to the pumpkin fields and pumpkins run 35 cents a pound. Pooley's has a host of other activities, including face painting, a try at shooting the "corn cannon," pony rides, a pedal track, and a petting zoo that always includes pigs. The chicken coop is probably the most popular spot on the farm, and baby chicks, roosters, and mother hens let kids learn about the different types of chickens and their important role on a farm. On weekends, Pooley's plays host to both a magician and a storyteller.

With a reservation, Pooley's will build a campfire that groups can enjoy for a four-hour slot, from noon to 4 p.m. or 5 to 9 p.m. Most popular in autumn evenings, groups can not only enjoy the scenery but enjoy some gooey s'mores and hot cocoa. Seating allows for groups of up to 40, and Pooley's is happy to cater meals and provide drinks and the fixings for the aforementioned s'mores. The pumpkin patch has a no-alcohol policy.

### ROCA BERRY FARM $$
**16531 S. 38th St., Roca**
**(402) 421-2255**
**www.rocaberryfarm.com**
What started out as a you-pick-it berry operation has grown into one of the area's largest agritourism attractions. Each spring, visitors can pick their own strawberries at Roca, beginning around Memorial Day weekend and continuing for three weeks. During strawberry season, the farm offers a "harvest hotline" to keep visitors up-to-date on what can be picked each day and what the conditions are like. Berries cost 99 cents per pound, and you can either bring your own box or get one at the farm for 50 cents. School tours and summer camps are available but reservations are required.

The Roca pumpkin patch opens in late September and continues business until early November. Three haunted barns, two tricycle trails, a straw jumping pile, and a life-size Candyland game are just a few of what Roca offers in the fall. Roca's website offers a printable coupon for $1 off a pumpkin that weighs more than 10 pounds. At 6 p.m.

each night, the Roca Scary Farm takes over, and the main attraction is the Psycho Path and hayride, which includes four haunted houses. The night activities aren't recommended for children under 10 years old. Older kids and adults, though, get the bonus of a free s'more if they're one of the first 100 guests on a Friday evening.

## TANK DOWN THE ELKHORN
PO Box 45064, Omaha 68145
(402) 709-8963
www.tankdown.com

Tanking is one of those quintessential Nebraska activities that goes straight on the "must-do" list of newcomers. First, a bit of explanation: "Tanking," as it's known, started in the vast Nebraska Sandhills. Some inventive rancher decided to float a big, metal stock tank—otherwise used to give cattle water—down one of central Nebraska's shallow rivers. Throw in a picnic table and a six-pack of chilly beverages and you've got what's become one of the state's truly unique leisure activities.

The Elkhorn River is the only place in Eastern Nebraska where tanking is a regular occurrence, and the Elkhorn River Valley just happens to be pretty scenic. Tank Down the Elkhorn has 8-foot diameter stock tanks fitted with custom-made picnic tables that seat four adults. The current of the river moves the vessel downstream, so paddles aren't necessary.

Tanks are lightweight but sturdy, and they won't tip over in the water. Popular activities on-board include games, imbibing food and drink, and just generally hanging out and enjoying a warm Nebraska summer day. No glass bottles are allowed on tanks, so visitors should keep that in mind, and a standard size cooler is recommended, along with towels, a camera, snacks, sunscreen, and sunglasses.

Tank Down the Elkhorn is open from Memorial Day to Labor Day, seven days a week. Groups must rent a minimum of three tanks during the week and reservations are required. Tanks depart from 9 a.m. to noon and depending on river conditions, the average trip lasts about five hours. Life jackets, trash bags, and a paddle will be provided, though groups with children under 50 pounds have to supply their own life jacket.

Tanks cost $120 each, and a 50 percent deposit is required in advance. Monday through Thursday, Tank down the Elkhorn runs a $100 tank special. The business doesn't accept credit cards, so be sure to bring the checkbook or cash.

Cancellations are only accepted more than seven days in advance or when river conditions or weather become bad with the potential for danger. In those cases, the trip is either refunded or rescheduled. If you don't show up, you still pay for the reserved tanks.

## VALA'S PUMPKIN PATCH $$
12102 S. 180th St., Gretna
(402) 332-4200
http://valaspumpkinpatch.com

Vala's Pumpkin Patch started out as an eastern Nebraska pumpkin farm and has slowly become one of the most popular seasonal attractions in the area, hands down. The business is operated by the Vala family, and, in its early years, the Valas worked together to craft items to sell in the gift shop, construct buildings to house attractions, bake pies, dip caramel apples and grill hot dogs. A grandmother cut and painted signs that are still on display, and many of the food items are named after family members. Business meetings take place around the family's kitchen table. Today, the 152-acre operation plants nearly 55 acres of pumpkins a year, and thousands of people visit during the annual Fall Festival.

Pumpkin picking is one of the main attractions at Vala's, though it's certainly not the only one. Hayrack rides take people into the fields to pick pumpkins. A barnyard adventure ride lets kids see early farm life while riding in a John Deere wagon. Train rides travel around the grounds and pony rides are available, too. During the Fall Festival, families can look forward to pig races, a variety of live music and stage shows, and the ever-popular Pumpkin Chuckin' Cannon Show, which is just what you think it is.

Halloween activities are in no shortage when October rolls around. A pumpkin mine, storybook barn, and spook shed are tailored toward younger kids. The haunted Old Farmhouse—in the 100-year-old original farmhouse on the property—and 3-acre corn maze are created for more mature visitors.

## FAMILY ATTRACTIONS

### BOYS TOWN                                       FREE
**137th and W. Dodge Road, Boys Town**
**(800) 625-1400, (402) 498-1140**
**www.visitboystown.org**
Boys Town, Nebraska, isn't just a tourist attraction; it's a self-sustaining community that has its own zip code, along with a fire department, schools, police department, and churches. Founded in 1936 by Father Edward Flanagan, Boys Town is Nebraska's only National Historic Landmark District. It's also the headquarters for Boys Town Nebraska/Iowa, an organization dedicated to helping and caring for at-risk children and their families.

Most visitors start at the official welcome center, where self-guided audio tours and maps are available for free and a list of scheduled tours and events is also available. The Hall of History, housed in what used to be the Boys Town dining hall, tells the story of the organization and includes exhibits on its programs, mission, and artifacts from the movie *Boys Town,* which earned Spencer Tracy an Oscar for Best Actor. Guided tours of the Hall run year round.

The Father Flanagan house was where the Boys Town founder lived and its furnishings reflect late 1920s decor, replicating what it may have looked like when Flanagan lived there. A desk that residents of Boys Town made for Flanagan still sits in the study, and is made of more than 250,000 pieces of inlaid wood. The gothic Dowd Memorial Chapel sits at the center of Boys Town, and its Indiana Bedford interior and exterior play host to year-round mass that is especially popular during the holiday season.

Another religious structure, the Chambers Protestant Chapel, is made of terra cotta tiles designed by Boys Town residents, as well as stained-glass windows and cast bronze gargoyles. The two church structures are linked by a three-acre Garden of the Bible, which is maintained by Boys Town youth and includes more than 150 varieties of plants all mentioned in the Bible. The garden is a popular destination for picnic lunches.

### CABELA'S                                         FREE
**12730 Westport Pkwy., La Vista**
**(402) 861-4800**
**www.cabelas.com/lavista**
A Nebraska shopping icon if there is one, Cabela's outdoor store isn't just a hunting, fishing, and wooly sock purchasing mecca,

it's a statewide institution that many people count among the top tourist attractions. An Omaha-area outpost opened its doors in 2006 and spurred development along one of the southwestern-most parts of the city. The store encompasses close to 130,000 square feet of space, and much of it is devoted to museum-quality displays of animals. Trophy animals, like deer, bears, and big cats, sit next to big horn sheep, small mammals, and aquariums teeming with fish. The stuffed animals are displayed not in cases, but on realistic re-creations of their natural habitats. An indoor archery range rounds out the visitor experience.

The La Vista Cabela's is one of three in Nebraska, and the eastern Nebraska location also has a restaurant that offers wild game entrees and more traditional fare for lunch or dinner. Elk, wild boar, bison, ostrich, and venison all have a spot on the menu. All Cabela's locations have semi and RV parking outside, and the La Vista location also has a horse corral. Live bait is sold in the store, and a dog kennel is located on-site.

## FONTENELLE FOREST NATURE CENTER $$
1111 Bellevue Blvd., Bellevue
(402) 731-3140
www.fontenelleforest.org

## NEALE WOODS
14323 Edith Marie Ave.
(402) 731-3140, (402) 453-5615
Miles of dirt trails resting in thousands of acres of Nebraska forest make Fontenelle Forest Nature Center and Neale Woods a major attraction for bird watchers, wildlife enthusiasts, outdoorsmen, and families looking for a big dose of fresh air and nature. Trail maps are available at the visitor's desk and hikers are encouraged to explore the grounds on self-guided tours or as part of a guided hike experience.

Fontenelle Forest and Neale Woods are neighboring nature centers and together have 29 miles of dirt trails and 2,000 acres of preserved forest, prairie, and marshlands. Fontenelle Forest also has a one-mile long boardwalk with a view of the Missouri River, an indoor play area for children, picnic areas, and wheelchairs available free. Both the center and the boardwalk are wheelchair accessible. At Neale Woods, visitors will find the Millard Observatory, which is open seasonally for astronomy nights.

The two areas have been protected since 1913, and are a haven for bird and wildlife viewing. Oak savanna, prairie, and wetlands ecosystems all feature a diverse array of plants and animals each season. Activities abound year-round, for both adults and kids, and youngsters will enjoy themed hikes that include a silent night hike, where kids hunt for nocturnal animals; an "insect-a-hike"; and storytelling and nature detective programs. Adults can partake in yoga for hikers, birdwatching classes, and photography groups.

The forest is a popular meeting and event space, and a wide array of buildings and outbuildings are available for business meetings, staff retreats, and events like weddings or holiday parties. A full list of rates is available on the Fontenelle Forest website.

## HOLY FAMILY SHRINE FREE
Off I-80, exit 432, Gretna
(402) 332-4565
www.holyfamilyshrineproject.com
One of the area's most recognizable landmarks, the Holy Family Shrine sits atop a hill just outside of Omaha. The building has a striking façade that features a 49-foot-tall peak constructed of glass, arching wood

slats, and natural stone. The arching wood-work—meant to resemble waves of grain—also symbolizes the shrine's Catholic roots. Two streams of water flow past the pews and cut through the chapel's limestone floor. Twelve wood arches are meant to represent the 12 apostles; the holy family is etched into a pane of glass at the front of the space.

Though the building itself cuts a striking figure, the view of the Platte River Valley here is a singular one and the surrounding land's natural grass butts up to the glass windows, giving the visitor a feel of being smack in the middle of Nebraska's vast, open prairie.

The most recent addition to the shrine is a 45-foot crucifix statue visible from the interstate. The cross itself is 40 feet tall and the Christ figure is just over 8 feet tall; the entire piece weighs in at more than 500 pounds, certainly making it the largest sculpture in the area. Celtic circles surround the Christ figure, and symbolize infinite spirituality.

The shrine doesn't operate like a typical church. It won't play host to weddings, Sunday mass, or vow renewals. It will play host to retreats and anniversary celebrations, as long as groups provide their own clergy. The shrine does operate an on-site gift shop and each year it produces a 24-karat gold-on-brass holiday ornament designed by artist Gene Roncka.

## ✳OMAHA'S HENRY DOORLY ZOO $$$
3701 S. 10th St. at I-80 exit 454
(402) 733-8401
www.omahazoo.com

Interacting with gorillas, walking through a cloud of butterflies, and walking over an alligator-filled swamp are just a few of the many popular activities at Omaha's Henry Doorly Zoo, and they're also the kind of activities that make the zoo rank as one of the top in the nation. The zoo is home to the world's only indoor desert and rainforest (and all the creatures that live there) and it's renowned for its Hubbard Gorilla Valley, which lets visitors sit inches from a gorilla, separated only by a window. It's Scott Aquarium has a captivating walk-through tunnel that leads through a shark tank, and a pillar full of glowing jellyfish offers a favorite spot to take a photo.

New attractions include the Insect and Butterfly pavilion, which lets visitors walk through a room filled with, at any given time, 20,000 butterflies. The other half of the pavilion—the actual structure is shaped like a butterfly with a central body and two wings—houses all sorts of creepy crawlies. In the center, be sure to look for the hatching window, where if you linger long enough, you can see a newborn butterfly hatch from a gilded cocoon.

The zoo's newest exhibit was unveiled in 2010. Expedition Madagascar features some of the country's most unusual animals as well as a large habitat built especially for lemurs. The 15 indoor exhibits house a wide array of species including fish, reptiles, small mammals, and lemurs. The outdoor exhibits include a fossa exhibit, an island with ring-tailed lemurs living among man-made Baobab trees, a net covered exhibit where Coquerel's sifka leap among branches at eye level, and an exhibit of ruffled lemurs. The exhibition is closed during winter months and opens again each spring. Each exhibit is linked to an ongoing project in Madagascar, and the exhibit includes educational information about the conservation efforts the Omaha Zoo's Madagascar Biodiversity Partnership has been working on since 1998.

## SCENIC DRIVES

Nebraska has nine scenic byways, and each one provides a distinct experience that encapsulates a specific area of the state. A number of these drives in eastern Nebraska originate near either Lincoln or Omaha and make for a fun day trip or weekend adventure.

The Lewis and Clark Scenic Byway takes travelers north of Omaha in the footsteps of Meriwether Lewis and William Clark. The two took a journey, in 1804, along what is now the eastern border of Nebraska. The byway takes travelers through bountiful cropland and wooded bluffs around the Missouri River. The 82-mile route includes nature preserves, sights of migrating snow geese, bald eagles, and ducks. Winnebago and Omaha Indian Tribes once settled along this route, and their heritage is still here today. Annual powwows, historic attractions, and a tribal herd of bison are all things to stop and see or do along the way.

In the fall, Nebraska City is one of the most popular day trips and happens to be one of the best scenic drives this colorful time of year. Its Annual Applejack Festival is one of the state's most popular festivals, and usually takes place during the third weekend in September. The events include a parade, a classic car show, craft shows, and tours at the city's orchards (it's also home to Arbor Day). The Arbor Lodge, Arbor Day Farm, and the commercial orchards teach families about harvest and let them enjoy the spoils, like apple pie, caramel apples, cider, and lots of other food and goodies.

Brownville, which sits at the eastern end of the Heritage Highway, is a short jaunt south of Nebraska City and is another popular day trip, often coupled with a trip to Nebraska City. One of Nebraska's artsiest small towns, Brownville is a perfect day trip or weekend getaway. Visitors can run, walk, or ride down a trail near the Missouri River, see a play at the Brownville Village Theater, visit one of its four bookstores, or go to a concert in its concert hall. Antiques stores and galleries grace the main strip, and a visit to the Whiskey Run Creek Winery is the perfect afternoon activity. Brownville has a popular twice annual flea market—in May and September—that brings tons of people to town in search for the perfect antique.

Just outside of Fremont, Nebraska, sits the last original part of the Lincoln Highway, with the original bricks still intact. Highway 30 rolls all the way across Nebraska, from the eastern edge to the western, and would be an epic road trip if traveled in its entirety. For a getaway closer to home, here's how to find those original bricks, which are worth a drive over. Stick around Fremont for dinner or lunch; the small town has some great restaurants.

Take I-480 to the Dodge Street exit and follow it west. It later becomes Dodge Road.

About 2.5 miles west of Boy's Town, turn right at the LINCOLN HIGHWAY sign and drive on the original bricks laid down in 1920.

At Elkhorn, take NE 64 west to US 275 northwest to Fremont.

# OMAHA ARTS

O maha has a vibrant art scene. The city offers a diverse lineup of local theater, visual arts, and live music.

Omaha's historic Orpheum Theater and the new Holland Performing Arts Center work together under the fold of Omaha Performing Arts to bring a variety of events to Omaha, including traveling Broadway productions, music of all genres, dance, and outdoor programming in the summer. Small, passionate local theaters bring excellent productions to the city; many of their productions are based on scripts created by local writers featuring directors, actors, and behind-the-scenes people who are passionate about the city's local theater scene. Omaha's also home to the country's largest community playhouse, which has an avid following of its own.

Omaha also has a thriving independent music scene. Based primarily around the Saddle Creek Label, the city has many venues where shows take place almost every night, and within the past few years has become home to large-scale outdoor concert series in the summer months.

In the summer, Omaha's Jazz on the Green takes place at Midtown Crossing's Turner Park and draws thousands of revelers to enjoy music and a warm summer night. The visual arts, too, are thriving: The Bemis Center for Contemporary Arts has one of the nation's most renowned artist residency programs, the Joslyn Art Museum has a renowned collection of Karl Bodhmer prints, and Omaha is working to create a citywide art walk on the first Friday of each month.

## OVERVIEW

This chapter is designed to give you a broad overview of the many arts-related activities and venues in the Omaha area. Though not an entirely comprehensive list, these places and events catalogued here present the best of Omaha's arts community. The listings are presented in alphabetical order by heading and subheading.

It should be noted that the museums listed in this chapter are specifically art museums only. To find out more about the history, archeology, military, and other local museums around the area, refer to the Attractions chapter. Likewise, listings for bookstores have been kept to the shopping chapter. Also, since operating hours and entrance fees are always subject to change, they have been left out of these listings. Every effort has been made to procure correct information from these venues and organizations, including websites, so current hours and prices should be readily available.

Omaha has plenty of arts-related events that are geared toward children. These aren't included here, but can be found in the Kidstuff chapter along with plenty of other activities to keep young people busy.

## PERFORMING ARTS

### BLUE BARN THEATER
614 S. 11th St.
(402) 345-1576
http://bluebarn.org

Boundary-breaking theater is at the heart of the Blue Barn, and it's been tackling independent musicals and plays in Omaha since the late 1980s. A group of theater graduates from the State University of New York at Purchase got together and decided to create an urban theater outside of the constrains of New York City's commercial market. They joined forces with the Bemis Center for Contemporary Arts and produced *America in Three Pieces*, the first show that featured one-acts from David Mamet, Spalding Grey, and Sam Shepard. The production had a $75 budget and a set consisting of two white sheets and received an overwhelmingly positive response from the Omaha audience.

The theater group started producing independent scripts in the early 1990s and, after it was forced from its permanent home by a fire, roamed around for a few years and eventually settled in its current location, a 90-seat theater in the Old Market. The theater also opened an adjoining art gallery and established a bar in the lobby. The Blue Barn has produced more than 80 shows in its more than 20 seasons and remains a thriving outpost for local theater.

### ✳FILMSTREAMS AT THE RUTH SOLOKOF THEATER
1340 Mike Fahey St., Omaha
(402) 933-0259

http://filmstreams.org

When Omaha native Rachel Jacobsen moved back to her hometown, she did it in a big way. Jacobsen's Filmstreams—the city's only true art house theater—opened in July 2007 and spurred both local interest in art film and new growth in the city's North Downtown neighborhood (neither a small feat).

The nonprofit theater now plays host to a number of programs: the screening of first-run American independent films; documentaries and foreign films that don't play elsewhere in town; repertory film selections that focus on classic films, themed film series, or the history of cinema; arts in education programming that teaches high school students how to interpret classic films; and community outreach that includes lecture series, forums, and question and answer sessions with directors, filmmakers, and actors.

What once seemed like a wild idea in Omaha now has fans hooked: The theater's innovative programming and fearless screenings of artistic films isn't being done anywhere else, and Omahans realize it. Since Filmstreams opened, film series have been curated by director Alexander Payne, NPR host Kurt Andersen, and actor Laura Dern. Two theaters seat in total just more than 300 patrons, and films run seven days a week. The lobby's snack bar offers traditional movie fare alongside locally produced coffee and desserts, and, most recently, wine and mixed drinks. Current cinema options and showtimes are available on the Filmstreams website.

### JOHN BEASLEY THEATER & WORKSHOP
2505 N. 24th St., #201
(402) 502-5767

http://johnbeasleytheater.org

Omaha native and actor John Beasley—a regular on the WB series *Everwood*—opened his nonprofit theater and workshop space in his hometown with the hopes of bringing theater to underserved audiences and helping students develop artistic talent.

Beasley performed in his first theater production in Omaha, and pursued acting in community theater throughout college. After he raised his family, Beasley again began acting professionally, first in theater productions and then on television. Now, he regularly takes to the stage in his own theater, performing in such plays as *One Flew Over the Cuckoo's Nest, Come and Gone* by Joe Turner, and August Wilson's *Fences,* a show so popular it's been staged more than once in the space. Though plays are the mainstay at Beasley, other types of performance also happen here, such as musical performance, gospel singing, and musical theater.

Acting classes in stage and film for adults and children are offered on a regular basis. An updated schedule of shows and ticket information is available on the theater's website.

## OMAHA COMMUNITY PLAYHOUSE
### 6915 Cass St.
### (402) 553-0800
### http://omahaplayhouse.org

The Omaha Community Playhouse has the unique distinction of being the nation's largest community theater. A group of Omaha theater lovers started the organization in 1924, and its first production, a 1925 show called *The Enchanted Cottage,* starred Dodie Brando, Marlon Brando's mother; and Jayne Fonda, whose brother, Henry, was then living in Minneapolis. Henry Fonda starred in the Playhouse's second production, and many

others. Once Henry Fonda became a movie star, he gave back to the Playhouse, buying new seats for the theater.

Over the years, the theater continued to grow in popularity. The existing theater, at 69th and Cass Streets, opened in 1959 and the Fondas were instrumental in raising money for the building. Today, the Playhouse has two theaters: the 558-seat Howard and Rhonda Hawks main stage theater and the more intimate Howard Drew Theater, which seats just over 200. The Playhouse programs each space individually, and shows five productions a year on the Hawks main stage and the smaller theater plays host to more progressive shows that are called the Fonda McGuire series. Those shows run for one month each with four performances a week.

One of the Playhouse's biggest hits is its annual performance of *A Christmas Carol.* Each year, close to 20,000 people see the seasonal production, which sticks to the traditional story but has a few special touches that only the Playhouse uses.

The Playhouse has extensive education and outreach programs, and offers a wide variety of classes for people of all ages. The Playhouse is also home to the Nebraska Theater Caravan, which for more than 30 years has been traveling to more than 150 communities around Nebraska and to more than 600 communities in 49 states and Canada.

## OPERA OMAHA
### 1625 Farnam St.
### (402) 346-7372
### http://operaomaha.org

Opera Omaha is the state's only professional opera company. It started in 1958, and by 1970 was fully professional. While the opera regularly performs standby productions of the genre, it's also innovative in its own right: It produced Omaha artist Jun Kaneko's version of *Madama Butterfly*, and a production of *Aida* designed by Omaha sculptor Catherine Ferguson.

The most cost-effective ways to take in an Opera Omaha production are through its all-access previews, where artists, directors, conductors, and singers give the audience a taste of the upcoming mainstage production the night before the show opens. It's basically a dress rehearsal open to the public, and is great fun for opera lovers or those looking for a more casual performance. The preview begins at 6:30 p.m. and the sitzprobe rehearsal begins at 7 p.m.

The Opera also partners with Film-Streams to screen the Metropolian Opera at the theater live in HD. Filmstreams shows the Met's 12 yearly productions live and in high-definition, and Opera Omaha staff gives a talk that starts one hour before curtain. Ticket prices and season information are available on the FilmStreams website, http://filmstreams.org. A schedule of Opera Omaha productions and ticket information is available on the opera's website.

**ORPHEUM THEATER**
**409 S. 16th St.**
**(402) 345-0202**
**http://omahaperformingarts.com**

**HOLLAND PERFORMING ARTS CENTER**
**1200 Douglas St.**
Two of the city's largest performing arts venues—the Holland Center and the Orpheum Theater—both fall under the control of one organization: Omaha Performing Arts. Founded as a nonprofit organization in 2000, the group brings performing arts productions of all kinds to the city, including Broadway-caliber touring musicals, artists of all genre, dance, jazz, classical, and popular music performances, free outdoor entertainment in the summer, and programming aiming to specifically draw young, hip audiences.

Its broad sweep of programs means that there's almost always something going on at either the Holland or the Orpheum. The Orpheum has been an Omaha standby since 1927, when it was a vaudeville house, and recent $10 million renovations restored it to its original, art deco splendor, enhanced its acoustics, and bettered the views from around the auditorium. Today it serves as the home for most of the touring Broadway musical series as well as a regular schedule of concerts. Recent performances have included indie rockers Spoon and the Pixies, country pop band Lady Antebellum, and solo singer Melissa Etheridge, among many others.

The Holland Performing Arts Center is downtown's other performing arts venue, and with its modern façade of solid glass and strong, lean lines, it's definitely one of the city's most recognizable pieces of recent architecture. The building offers great views of downtown Omaha, the Gene Leahy Mall, and the Old Market. In 2010, the Holland opened Zinc, a full-service restaurant open two and a half hours before Omaha Symphony and Omaha Performing Arts events that take place at the Holland.

The 1200 Club at the Holland offers programming aimed at a younger audience, and recent acts included comedian Jeff Daniels, The Cherry Poppin' Daddies, and Miguel Zenon.

A full list of ticket prices and upcoming performances at both venues is available on the Omaha Performing Arts website.

## THE ROSE THEATER
2001 Farnam St.
(402) 345-4849
http://rosetheater.org

The Rose Theater lives in one of the most architecturally distinctive buildings in downtown Omaha. Its singular combination of Moorish and Classical architecture styles identifies it instantly; and in a past life, it was the city's grandest movie house. It originally opened in 1927 as the Riviera, and the original owner installed the Mediterranean tile wall murals. It also had a fountain, sculptures, friezes, and Oriental rugs and tapestries. The theater sold in 1929 after the market crash and stayed the Paramount Theater until the 1950s, when it closed. In the 1960s, it was the home for a professional bowling team, the Omaha Packers, and in 1962 it became the Astro Theater, which showed films until 1979.

Omaha businesswoman Rose Blumkin, of Nebraska Furniture Mart fame, bought the theater in 1981, and donated it to the Omaha Theater Company for Young People, gave $1 million toward its renovation and asked the gift be matched by the company. Today, the Rose is restored to its original 1920s-era glamour and is a popular destination for families and adults alike.

The Omaha Theater Company—the country's third largest professional children's theater organization—still operates in the space. Performances take place year-round at the Rose. More than 5,000 kids take a class there each year, and the space is also available for concerts and rentals. A complete schedule of shows and ticket information is available at the Rose website.

## *SNAP! PRODUCTIONS AND THE SHELTERBELT THEATER
3225 California St.
(402) 341-2757
http://shelterbelt.org

The Shelterbelt and SNAP! Productions together make some of the most risk-taking and challenging theater in Omaha. An intimate theater that places audience members a mere 15 feet from the actors, the Shelterbelt is located in the heart of central Omaha (conveniently next door to one of its more popular restaurants, California Tacos and More).

The Shelterbelt opened in 1993 when a local playwright asked the owner of a local coffee shop (on the site of what's now the theater) if he could produce a play in the space. The writer, Scott Working, produced the theater's first production, V of Geese, in the space and at the same time founded the theater. Named after a row of trees that protect a farmer's crops, the Shelterbelt has always aimed to create a sort of "safe space" for theater, and in 2001, it joined with SNAP! Productions to further that mission.

SNAP! has a simple mission: to support those suffering from the AIDS virus and educate about support, programs, and acceptance of AIDS. To wit, the group's first two performances were Bent, about a gay Jewish man sent to a concentration camp in Nazi Germany, and Jeffrey, a play about a young New York gay man who gives up sex only to meet the love of his life and decide if it's worth risking AIDS. SNAP! continued from there, offering challenging, thought-provoking, and sometimes controversial theater for the masses. Recent renovations have improved lighting, sound, and rigging and added a cash bar. The theater remains one of the most intimate, open-minded art spaces in the city.

## MUSIC

**✳JAZZ ON THE GREEN**
**Turner Park at Midtown Crossing**
**31st and Dodge Streets**
http://jazzonthegreenomaha.com
In 2010, Jazz on the Green—Omaha's largest summer outdoor music series—found a new home in midtown Omaha's Turner Park. For the first 25 years, Joslyn Art Museum played host to the jazz, but after it remodeled its sculpture garden, the series had to find a new home.

Turner Park turned out to be a perfect match for big crowds and live music, and the concerts are now positioned to be more popular than ever. Regular crowds at Joslyn were around 6,000 per concert; the first season at Turner Park drew more than 50,000 people during the season.

The events take place during the month of July and the first weekend in August, and the concerts are free. The park opens at 5 p.m. and concerts begin at 7 p.m. A makeshift dance floor almost always forms in front of the stage, and families, couples, and single people gather on blankets and in chairs to enjoy picnic fare, wine, and food, either brought from home or purchased from one of the many on-site vendors. Businesses around the park—especially bars and restaurants—become thriving hot spots during the month, and with more storefronts continuing to open in Midtown Crossing, the redeveloped business district adjacent to Turner Park, Jazz on the Green is posed to grow even more in the coming years.

**OMAHA SYMPHONY**
**1605 Howard St.**
**(402) 342-3836**
http://omahasymphony.org
Classical music is a standby for many Omahans, and the Omaha Symphony—which has been around for close to 90 years—is a local favorite. The Symphony presents a wide variety of concert types, but its Masterworks and Pops series are at the heart of its productions. Most of the shows take place at the acoustically advanced Holland Performing Arts Center; one exception is the more intimate Chamber series, which takes place at the Strauss Performing Arts Center on the University of Nebraska at Omaha campus.

The Symphony's Family series introduces kids to the orchestral experience, and activities in the lobby welcome kids to what may otherwise be an intimidating experience. The "Symphony Rocks" series takes on rock and roll music, and is aimed at both young professional and baby boomer audiences. The one-night-only shows have in the past tackled Michael Jackson, the Eagles, Paul McCartney, and Simon and Garfunkel, among others.

Ticket information and a full schedule of concerts are available on the Symphony's website.

**QWEST CENTER OMAHA**
**455 N. 10th St.**
**(402) 341-1500**
http://qwestcenteromaha.com
Omaha's Convention Center, the Qwest Center Omaha, has changed the city's live music scene: It brought the biggest acts that had ever played in Omaha to the city. U2, Bruce Springsteen, Cher, and many others have taken to the Qwest stage since its doors opened in 2003. The nearly

200,000-square-foot exhibition hall plays host to home shows, hunting and sports shows, and craft shows throughout the year. The concert arena seats just over 18,000.

Connected by skywalk to the downtown Hilton Omaha Hotel, the site also includes more than 4,500 parking spaces in an attached garage plus lots of surface parking, so finding a spot is never an issue. The Qwest also plays host to the UNO Mavericks hockey team, and the popular games make for an exciting evening.

Public tours of the Qwest are available and can be arranged in advance by calling the arena.

### *SLOWDOWN
**729 N. 14th St.**
**(402) 345-7569**
**http://theslowdown.com**
Omaha is known internationally for its independent music scene. Slowdown is one of two venues that are at the heart of the scene, and the guys behind Saddle Creek Records—Omaha's largest indie record label—opened the venue in North Downtown Omaha to give the label's bands a high-end venue to stage performances. North Downtown grew up around Slowdown and the complex it's located in, which is also home to the Saddle Creek Records offices, Filmstreams, shops, restaurants, and a coffee house.

Concerts happen at Slowdown just about every weekend, and both national and international touring acts make stops at the venue, which has a bar on one side and a stage on the other side. When live music isn't happening, the stage is closed off from the main bar and it becomes a popular hangout venue. The Tuesday night Pub Quiz is a popular, albeit competitive, pastime for lots of people, and the pool tables and board games keep patrons busy during the rest of the week. Regulars also love the Slowdown's diverse array of tunes loaded on the jukebox—best of all, the juke is free.

### THE WAITING ROOM LOUNGE
**6212 Maple St.**
**(402) 884-5353**
**http://waitingroomlounge.com**
The Waiting Room Lounge is one of the coolest venues in Omaha, and its central location in Benson, one of the city's recently revitalized neighborhoods, only adds to its hip factor. Strong cocktails, excellent acoustics, and a regularly rotating roster of some of the best independent musicians in the country make The Waiting Room the city's other musical hotspot.

The venue is an intimate one—fans can get right up to the stage—and cover charges are always reasonable on show night. Parking can be tricky on the main drag of Benson, so it's a good idea to check for parking in the surrounding residential neighborhoods, or else get to the neighborhood early and enjoy a drink or bite at one of the many bars and restaurants in the area. Locals love the bar even on non-show nights, as pints run a mere $3 and often The Waiting Room screens movies when a band isn't playing. Check the venue's website for a full schedule of concerts and other events.

## ART MUSEUMS & GALLERIES
### *BEMIS CENTER FOR CONTEMPORARY ART AND BEMIS UNDERGROUND
**724 S. 12th St.**
**(402) 341-7130**
**www.bemiscenter.org**
One of the nation's most well-respected artist-in-residence programs operates out

of Omaha's Bemis Center for Contemporary Arts. Each year, a select group of talented artists come to Omaha and create work as part of the program; all they're required to do at the conclusion of their stay is leave one piece of work at Bemis. Though the Bemis is known worldwide for its program, it remains a well-kept secret in its home city, and in-the-know locals love to share this gem of a space with visitors and the uninitiated. More than 20 shows debut each year in the Center's three main floor galleries, and residents live in 14 furnished studios on the upper floors of the Bemis' Old Market building. Bemis is celebrating 30 years in 2011 by expanding: it's adding 5 studios to to the newly renovated third floor.

The annual Bemis Auction is easily the best-loved and best-attended art event in the city, and it serves as the Center's largest annual fundraiser and also a rollicking party. Hundreds of artists donate work to the silent auction, and a select number of big-ticket items sell in a live auction that ends the evening.

In 2004, the Bemis Underground opened with the goal of offering exhibition space to the local community. The space has its own dedicated curator and director and a slew of lively exhibitions—also well attended— open in the space each month. Most Bemis events are free and a regularly changing slate of art talks, curator talks, open studio tours, and concerts take place in the space.

## HOT SHOPS ART CENTER
1301 Nicholas St.
(402) 342-6452
http://hotshopsartcenter.com
The Hot Shops Art Center is the area's most diverse arts center. It is home to 50 art studios, 4 gallery spaces, a glass forge, a

metalwork studio, and a kiln for ceramicists. The space is always bustling with activity. Art openings here are an event: the four galleries play host to four distinct openings and studio artists throw open their doors, inviting patrons inside.

Crystal Forge glass studio artists produce fused and blown glass pieces using stained glass fabricators on-site. Visiting the Forge during the holidays is a spectacular experience, as thousands of hand-blown crystal ball ornaments cascade from the ceiling, inviting patrons to try and purchase only one. The Forge holds a special holiday event the first Saturday of December to debut the newest ornaments, though a selection can be found year-round.

The Loken Forge produces all types of metalwork, from large-scale pieces that are part of art installations around the city to things people use every day in their homes, like stair railings, chandeliers, door pulls, and fireplace tools.

The four galleries: The Hallway Gallery, the Nicholas St. Gallery, the 1301 Gallery, and the Alley Gallery all produce their own docket of shows, and a complete exhibition calendar is available on the Hot Shops website.

**i** In 1981, artists Jun Kaneko, Ree Schonlau, Tony Hepburn, and Lorne Falke formed an artist industry program that today is known as the Bemis Center for Contemporary Art. Today, the program still focuses on removing artists from their everyday lives and gives the freedom to concentrate on creativity. More than 1,000 artists from around the world apply each year for a coveted spot in the program.

PART 2: OMAHA

## JOSLYN ART MUSEUM
**2200 Dodge St.**
**(402) 342-3300**
**http://joslyn.org**
Omaha's Joslyn Art Museum boasts the largest collection of work in the state, spanning from ancient times to today, with an emphasis on 19th- and 20th-century European and American art. Joslyn has a large and renowned collection of American Western art, and it's particularly notable for its Karl Bodmer watercolors, which document the explorer-artist's mid-1800s journey to the Missouri River frontier.

The Joslyn's art deco building houses its collection and also has a 1,000-seat concert hall, a fountain court, gift shop, cafe, and library. Outside the museum is a newly renovated sculpture garden, which includes a number of specially commissioned works created for the space and a garden created with children in mind. Special exhibitions take place year-round, as do musical performances, lectures, and art classes for all ages. One of the most popular times to visit Joslyn is on Saturday morning, when admission is free from 10 a.m. to noon.

## KANEKO
**1111 Jones St.**
**(402) 341-3800**
**http://thekaneko.org**
The KANEKO is Omaha's newest creative space and it doesn't fit into any one category.

It's an art space, a performance space, and a library. Its programming includes talks from artists, authors, newspaper reporters, and filmmakers. At the heart of its mission is "exploring the creative process" and, with that, KANEKO's slogan is "Open Space for Your Mind."

Omaha sculptor Jun Kaneko, known the world over for his ceramic work, opened the nonprofit organization and works with a staff to develop the innovative programming. He commissioned architect Mark Mack to convert a series of existing warehouses into the new space, which will eventually include a gallery where Kaneko will show his large-scale sculptures. The main performance space is a former truck garage that Mack transformed into the "Bow Truss" space. Internal steel girders support the curved roof so no columns or other support obstructs the room.

KANEKO's ongoing series of "great minds" lectures are a big draw, and the website has an up-to-date list of all its upcoming events.

# OMAHA PARKS & RECREATION

Omaha has a wide array of outdoor fun: urban parks, a developing trail system, and golf that includes some of the nation's top-rated courses.

Recreational activities abound. If it's a soothing experience you're after, consider a class at the Old Market's Omaha School of Yoga or at one of One Tree Yoga's two Omaha locations. Both schools offer a wide array of styles of yoga practice; One Tree Yoga is the city's venue for hot yoga.

Golfers will find a wide variety of courses: Omaha's selection includes greens fees at all levels, from bargains to high-end price tags, and everything in between. Amenities vary, and there's a course out there for the golfer of every skill level, too.

Spectator sports in Omaha culminate every summer with the NCAA College World Series; other sports include baseball, soccer, football, and hockey, among others.

This chapter covers city (and some state) parks and listing for recreational activities like hiking, biking, and running. The lodging section includes information on campgrounds, though this chapter includes lodging at state parks, including Mahoney State Park, a popular option for camping and cabin rental that's conveniently located between Omaha and Lincoln.

The Kidstuff chapter has more details on children's activities like fun centers and water parks, as well as information on children's sports leagues.

## Price Code

The following price code has been included to give you a rough idea of what a regular ticket or entrance fee will cost to each of the following places. If the fees or costs associated with a particular activity are varied, no price has been given and you should use the contact information provided to find out details. More specific pricing and discount information is included in the listings, where available. Every effort has been made to include a variety of activities across a broad spectrum of prices to cater to every possible budget. For the golf listings, no price code has been included because it proved impossible to cover the range of greens fees and membership fees for every golf club. Instead, check the individual golf club listings for information about cost and membership options.

| | |
|---|---|
| $................... | **Less than $5** |
| $$ .................... | **$5 to $10** |
| $$$ ................. | **$10 to $20** |
| $$$$ ........... | **More than $20** |

## PARKS

**EUGENE T. MAHONEY STATE PARK**   $$
**28500 West Park Hwy., Ashland**
**(402) 944-2523**
**http://nebraskastateparks.reserve america.com**

Located between Omaha and Lincoln, Mahoney State Park is Nebraska's most popular state park. Open year-round, the park lets visitors choose between camping in one of its campgrounds; renting one of its modern, furnished cabins; or bunking in the lodge. The Little Creek and Lakeside campgrounds both feature mature trees and a picturesque water view. Both have modern shower and latrine buildings and drinking water, and Little Creek has a coin-operated laundry facility. Lakeside campground also has free wireless Internet.

Cabins are a more secluded option, and also are available year-round. The heated and air-conditioned cabins all have a fireplace, television, fridge and range, microwave, deck, and grill and offer a decidedly contemporary idea of "roughing it." The Peter Kiewit Lodge has 40 rooms—most of which have decks with scenic views—and offers all the amenities of a modern hotel.

Mahoney offers its visitors a treasure trove of stuff to do: hiking and biking, birding, paddle boating, arts and craft programs in the lodge and other buildings on-site, a driving range, a fishing pier, miniature golf, a swimming pool and aquatic center, and horseback riding are just a few of the things families and visitors can do year-round at the park.

**HEARTLAND OF AMERICA PARK   FREE**
**800 Douglas St.**
**(402) 444-5955**
**www.cityofomaha.org/parks**
Nestled between the Old Market and the Missouri River front, Heartland of America Park connects to both downtown Omaha and the riverfront development via a number of walking and biking paths. The central attraction in the park is its Heartland of America fountain, which shoots water more than 300 feet into the air. Gondola and boat rides take visitors around the lake and past the fountain for a closer (and sometimes wetter) look at the light show and jets. Visitors can walk across the pedestrian bridge connecting the park to Lewis and Clark Landing, along the river, and eventually walk across the Bob Kerrey Pedestrian Bridge, which spans the Missouri from the border of Nebraska, over the river, and into Iowa.

**HEFFLINGER DOG PARK       FREE**
**112th and W. Maple Road**
**(402) 444-5900**
**http://omahadogpark.org**
Dogs of all sizes can run without a leash at Omaha's first dog park. The park used to be softball fields and recently was converted to a new use. The park is divided into two sides, one for small dogs and one for large dogs. Dogs that fall into the medium size zone should err on the side of the park that seems to best fit their personality. The park has water fountains for both pets and people, and on a warm weekend day upwards of 50 dogs might be in the space. Bag stations are positioned all over the park, so owners can clean up after their pets, and trash cans are also on the grounds. Pets should be leashed before entering and after leaving the park, and kids under the age of 14 must be accompanied by an adult at the park.

**MEMORIAL PARK              FREE**
**6005 Underwood Ave.**
**www.cityofomaha.org/parks**
In the heart of midtown Omaha, Memorial Park is one of the city's busiest public parks and, unless it's the dead of winter, is almost always full of activity. One of the park's busiest days happens every July 4, when the First

National Bank of Omaha–sponsored Fourth of July concert takes place; tens of thousands of people descend on the park for the free show and the fireworks that follow. On any given day, intramural sports teams play games in the green space on the north side of Dodge Street, and people run and walk with and without pets on the surrounding trails. The park butts up to the University of Nebraska at Omaha campus on the south side of Dodge. Visitors will find more trails, a playground, a pool, a ballpark, a large-scale sculpture by Omaha artist Leslie Iwai called *Sounding Stones,* and a paved pavilion and clubhouse that are a popular destination for summer weddings.

### ROBERTS SKATE PARK     FREE
**730 N. 78th St.**
**(402) 444-5900**
**www.cityofomaha.org/parks**
Omaha's first skate park opened in 1999 and has been going strong since. Local skateboarders worked with the city on the park's design concept, and many of their ideas made it into the final park. The park is 14,000 square feet and has ramps, stairs, quarter pipes, a grinding block, and a fun box. A snake run empties into a four-foot and seven-foot bowl. The busy park is especially full on summer evenings and weekend mornings, and is a destination for skaters of all levels. The park is open when weather is appropriate for skating during daylight hours only. Skaters use the facility at their own risk.

## GOLF COURSES & EVENTS

### BENSON PARK GOLF CLUB
**5333 N. 72nd St.**
**(402) 444-4626**

Benson Park is a city-owned 18-hole course in the south-central area of Omaha. Built in 1962, the par-72 course measures 6,771 yards. It features generous fairways and sizeable greens that are suitable for a bogey golfer looking to be challenged but not overwhelmed. Benson Park's other asset is its price. Since it's city-owned, the course's green fees are some of the cheapest in Omaha. Beware: Benson gets a lot of play, and like many other public courses it tends to get beat up by late summer.

### COX CLASSIC
**Champions Run Golf Course**
**13800 Eagle Run Dr.**
**(402) 498-8900**
**www.coxclassic.com**
The Cox Classic, played every August at Omaha's Champions Run Golf Club course, is an excellent, affordable way to watch some of tomorrow's top golfers. The Cox Classic is an annual event on the Nationwide Tour, the tour for professional golfers who have fallen just short of qualifying for the PGA Tour. In past years, future PGA stars like Bo Van Pelt and Jason Gore have won the event, wins that helped springboard them toward the big time. The galleries at the Cox Classic are large and boisterous for a nationwide event. The 19th hole, a makeshift night club set up near the clubhouse, becomes a hot spot every night after the tournament's four rounds.

### EAGLE RUN GOLF COMPLEX
**3435 N. 132nd St.**
**(402) 498-9900**
Eagle Run is Omaha's go-to spot if you are a golfing novice or want to play a round with younger children. The Links is Eagle Run's par-32 "executive course," a nicely manicured

2,211-yard layout that can be completed in around 90 minutes. The Meadows, Eagle Run's other nine, is a par-3 course perfect for kids. Eagle Run separates itself from the area's other par-3 courses because the course is generally green and well-kept and because the layout, while easy, isn't boring.

## INDIAN CREEK
**3825 N. 202nd St., Elkhorn**
**(402) 289-0900**
Indian Creek is a 27-hole course that suits a visiting golfer with a serious game. Indian Creek was built in 1990 in Elkhorn, a northwest Omaha suburb. What the course lacks in age it makes up for in quality. Here, you will find long, treacherous tee shots over water; challenging approach shots; and large, undulating greens. The course is nice—and difficult—enough to host state match play championships and US Open sectional qualifiers. The average golfer will likely dunk a few balls in the water here, as there are lakes or streams that come into play on 15 of the course's 27 holes.

**i** Say the name, "Johnny Goodman" today and a golfer will likely think of the 18-hole public course in South Omaha. Several generations ago, though, Omahans knew Johnny Goodman as the best golfer in city history. In fact, Goodman, the orphaned son of Lithuanian immigrants, pulled off one of the most stunning achievements in golfing history—in 1933 he won the US Open. Why was that stunning? Because Goodman was an amateur golfer and an insurance salesman, not a professional golfer. No amateur has won the US Open since.

## MIRACLE HILL GOLF & TENNIS CENTER
**1401 N. 120th St.**
**(402) 498-0220**
Miracle Hill is a comfortable place to enjoy a leisurely round with three of your buddies who are equally interested in golfing and socializing. The 6,412-yard layout is short and fairly easy, minimizing the chance that someone in your foursome will ruin a nice summer day with a string of profanity. And, unlike most public golf courses, Miracle Hill also features tennis courts where a spouse or child can get a lesson while you are on the course. Miracle Hill may be best known for its practice area. Its gigantic driving range and two practice greens are a perfect place to hone your game after a long workday.

## OMAHA COUNTRY CLUB
**6900 Country Club Rd.**
**(402) 571-7777**
It's private, but that shouldn't stop the obsessed golfer from trying to beg, borrow, or steal a tee time at OCC, one of the state's oldest and finest courses. The club, founded in 1899, really took off when the original course was redesigned by famed golf course architect Perry Maxwell in 1951. An 18-hole round takes you over rolling hills, past forested areas, and through the area's most perfectly manicured fairways and greens. OCC got another redesign in 2005, this one meant to toughen the course as well as restore some of the layout's original elements. The world's best over-50 golfers will soon get a look at the revamped OCC. The club is hosting the 2013 Senior Open.

**✳QUARRY OAKS**
**16600 Quarry Oaks Dr., Ashland**
**(402) 944-6000 or 888-944-6001**

Quarry Oaks is the best public golf course, hands down, in the Lincoln and Omaha areas. The 18-hole course is actually located near Ashland, a small town that's a half-hour drive from both Lincoln and Omaha. It's worth the trip—this course, built in 1996, is consistently ranked the best public course in eastern Nebraska. You can also find it on *Golf Digest*'s annual list of the 100 best public courses in the United States. It isn't hard to figure out why. Built next to the Platte River, Quarry Oaks has the sort of majestic elevation changes, spectacular views, and stunning scenery that most golfers simply don't expect to find in Nebraska. The course is more expensive than most Lincoln and Omaha public courses, but not by much. It's downright affordable compared to other golf courses of its ilk around the country. If you are a passionate golfer with an afternoon free, play Quarry Oaks. You won't regret it.

**SHORELINE GOLF COURSE**
**210 Locust St., Carter Lake, IA**
**(712) 347-5173**

Shoreline might be the best value of any golf course in the Omaha metro area. The 18-hole public course is located in nearby Carter Lake, Iowa, which is just minutes from downtown Omaha. It's actually on the way to Omaha's airport, allowing you to sneak in a quick round right before or after a flight. Shoreline's layout is full of the character and charm often missing from affordable public courses. Giant, ancient trees line the fairways. A lake comes into play on several holes, including one treacherous tee shot over water on each nine. And, from the back tees, Shoreline provides a difficult but fair test of golf that you rarely find for this price.

## YOGA STUDIOS

**✳OMAHA SCHOOL OF YOGA**
**1066 Howard St.**
**(402) 346-7813**
**http://omahayogaschool.com**

Located in the Old Market Passageway, the Omaha School of Yoga offers both singular classes and a singular environment in which to practice. The classes here focus on the ancient spirit of yoga, and the teachers focus on the meditative qualities of yoga. Classical, flow, and Vinyasa style classes are all on the school's docket, as well as their trademarked Hyp-Yoga program, created by the mother-daughter team Becky Grabner and Carly Cummings, along with fellow owner Kim Isherwood, which combines yoga with hypnosis to promote health and encourage weight loss. The school also offers massage and hypnosis treatments outside of its regularly scheduled yoga classes; call the school for further details or to schedule an appointment.

**ONE TREE YOGA**
**5020 Dodge St.**
**(402) 551-5020**
**www.onetreeyoga.com**

Omaha's destination for Bikram—or hot—yoga, One Tree Yoga operates out of two locations, its original space in midtown Omaha and a newer, larger space in West Omaha. The school offers a full slate of classes, mostly Bikram yoga, which is a series of 26 poses done in a heated room. Classes are available for all skill levels—beginner to advanced—and other styles of yoga, such as Vinyasa, Hatha, and Ashtanga, and classes focused on meditation are also available.

Teachers here are friendly and welcoming, and the school encourages students to leave their worries at the door and embrace the zen that can come along wth a regular yoga practice. Individual classes are available on a walk-in basis, and passes for a set number of classes at a discounted per-class cost are available. The other location is at 2420 S. 156th Circle (402-333-2420).

## ROCK CLIMBING

### SILO EXTREME
**3417 Vinton St.**
**(402) 614-1006**
Nebraska isn't exactly known for its mountain climbing, but it is known for ingenuity, and that's where Silo Extreme comes in. Omahans Rick Brock and Ron Safarik transformed silos they co-own into 180-foot climbing walls. The silos sit near busy I-80, so the duo use the silos farthest away from the highway for climbing. (The duo recently worked with the city to turn the rest of its silos into a public art project.) Other indoor climbing facilities are available around Omaha, including on the University of Nebraska at Omaha campus and at several fitness clubs, but no other spots offer an outdoor experience. Eventually, Silo Extreme plans to offer climbing on six to eight of the silos, a boulder climbing area, and an indoor climbing space.

## WINTER SPORTS

Sledding and cross-country skiing are popular activities during Nebraska's often snowy winters. Memorial Park is probably Omaha's most popular sledding outpost.

### Ice Skating

**CONAGRA FOODS ICE RINK**
**Open during the month of December**
**www.conagrafoods.com**
One of the city's best chances to take to the ice happens every December as part of the annual Holiday Lights Festival. ConAgra Foods erects a temporary ice skating rink on the outskirts of the Old Market, and it's become really popular. It's open until midnight on Friday and Saturday, and people of all ages take to the rink for a nominal fee, which is then donated back to the "Shine the Light on Hunger" campaign that gives back to people in need and supports the Food Bank of the Heartland. Skaters are also encouraged to bring non-perishable food items to place in on-site food collection bins, which are then distributed to Omahans in need.

**i** A racehorse named "Omaha" won the Kentucky Derby, Preakness Stakes, and Belmont Stakes in 1935, becoming only the third racehorse in history to pull off the Triple Crown. After being retired to stud, Omaha actually moved to Omaha, living out his days and serving as the de-facto mascot at Ak-sar-ben, the city's then-popular racetrack. When he died in 1959, Omaha was buried on the racetrack's grounds. Ak-sar-ben eventually perished as well, and now the great racehorse rests for eternity beneath Stinson Park, where you can find a plaque celebrating his career.

**UNO MAVERICKS HOCKEY**
**Qwest Center Omaha**
**455 N. 10th St.**
**(402) 341-1500**
**www.omavs.com**

Hockey, of all things, has helped the University of Nebraska at Omaha remove itself from the long shadow of its sister school, the University of Nebraska–Lincoln. The Mavericks, in fact, regularly pack the giant Qwest Center Omaha arena when they face off with bigger and more tradition-fueled hockey schools from Minnesota, North Dakota, and Wisconsin. Now, hockey isn't exactly native to Nebraska—it's cold here, but not cold enough to skate on a pond all winter long. But it's caught on like wildfire during what can be long and dreary Nebraska winters. What better way to break up an Omaha January weekend than by catching a UNO hockey match? Tickets are easy to come by, the atmosphere is electric, and they sell beer at the Qwest Center Omaha, located on 10th Street, just north of Dodge Street. Just don't call the school on the ice "the University of Nebraska." They will put you in the penalty box.

## SPRING & SUMMER SPECTATOR SPORTS

### Baseball

※**NCAA COLLEGE WORLD SERIES**
**TD Ameritrade Park, Omaha**
**www.tdameritradeparkomaha.com**
**www.cwsomaha.com**
The recreational vehicles start showing up in early June. License plates from Louisiana. Texas. South Carolina. They come bearing gifts of jambalaya and brisket, park in the nearest available parking lot, and prepare themselves for two weeks of unadulterated baseball. The passengers have trekked many miles to partake in an annual rite of passage, the College World Series, held each year since 1950 in Omaha.

The College World Series is an eight-team tournament meant to decide the country's best college baseball team. It enjoys a cult following, especially in the sun-soaked South and West where baseball can be played year-round. For Omahans, the Series is a unique chance to take a day off work, mingle with strangers from across the country, and watch some of college baseball's best players years before they make it to the major leagues. After six decades at Omaha's Rosenblatt Stadium, the series moved to the brand-new TD Ameritrade Park in downtown Omaha in the summer of 2011. While some old-schoolers are bothered by the switch, it presents an opportunity for the savvy traveler who can stay downtown, check out Omaha's Old Market, and then walk a couple blocks north to watch 'em play ball.

### OMAHA STORM CHASERS BASEBALL
**Werner Field**
**126th Street and Highway 370, Papillion**
**www.minorleaguebaseball.com**
The Omaha suburbs scored a major coup when they lured the newly named Omaha Storm Chasers, the AAA minor-league baseball team of the Kansas City Royals, to a new stadium in Sarpy County starting the summer of 2011. The Royals—er, Storm Chasers—have long called Rosenblatt Stadium home, but that grand old baseball park has been torn down to make room for the expansion of the Henry Doorly Zoo and a new downtown baseball stadium. So the Royals—er, Storm Chasers—decided to move to a new stadium in Papillion, giving the city's suburbs its biggest-ever sporting event. Minor league baseball is a cheap, family-friendly way to whittle away three hours on a summer weekday evening or a Sunday afternoon. The Storm Chasers, like most minor-league clubs,

are practiced in the art of all-ages entertainment. Mascots roam the stands. Promotions and games are held between each half-inning. And the new stadium, located near 126th Street and NE 370, has a massive playground for kids who don't care about the difference between a curve ball and a slider. For adults who don't care about playgrounds, the Storm Chasers have one of the best promotions around. During Thursday night home games, select beers and hot dogs are $1.

## Basketball

**CREIGHTON BLUEJAYS BASKETBALL**
**Qwest Center Omaha**
**455 N. 10th St.**
**(402) 341-1500**
**www.gocreighton.com**
Creighton, a Jesuit university known for its academic prowess, has built itself possibly the best—and certainly the most popular—college basketball program in the state. The Jays are a perennial power in the Missouri Valley Conference, a program that has made six NCAA tournament appearances in the past decade. And the Bluejays' crowd is more impressive than its record. Creighton annually ranks in the Top 20 in attendance, no small feat for a small, private school.

## Football

**OMAHA NIGHTHAWKS MINOR LEAGUE FOOTBALL**
**TD Ameritrade Park, Omaha**
**www.tdameritradeparkomaha.com**
**www.ufl-football.com/omaha-nighthawks**
The Nighthawks are the newest thing on the Omaha sports scene, and their first year proved that a minor-league football team can survive and even thrive in Nebraska's largest city. Omaha made its debut in the United Football League in 2010, joining a league that's the latest attempting to successfully play second banana to the NFL. The team, stocked with former NFL stars like ex-Husker Ahman Green and quarterback Jeff Garcia, sold out its first home game. It was the first sellout in the UFL's history. And the Nighthawks continued to pack the stands all season. Fans like the up-close-and-personal nature of the experience—the first row of stands is mere feet from the sidelines and end zones. The Nighthawks often play games on Friday nights, giving Omahans another weekend entertainment option. And the quick attraction to the minor-league football team proves that the city of Omaha is football crazy, no matter if it's the beloved Cornhuskers or the upstart Nighthawks. The Nighthawks are moving to the new TD Ameritrade Park, home of the College World Series.

**i** The city of Omaha produced a stable of elite athletes during the 1950s and 1960s. That group includes Bob Gibson, who won 251 games and two Cy Young awards during a dominating career as a St. Louis Cardinals hurler; Gale Sayers, one of the most breathtaking open-field runners in football history; and Marlin Briscoe, the first African American to start at quarterback in the NFL.

## Swimming

**OLYMPIC SWIM TRIALS (2012)**
**Qwest Center Omaha**
**455 N. 10th St.**
**(402) 341-1500**
**www.usaswimming.com**

The Qwest Center Omaha hosted the US Olympic Swim Trials in 2008, and the event was so wildly successful that US Swimming decided to return to Omaha in 2012. Michael Phelps and the country's other top swimmers will head to Omaha in late June 2012, for a weeklong event that decides who makes the US Olympic team and who doesn't. Omahans caught Olympic fever in 2008, buying a record 163,000 tickets for the weeklong trials and filling the Qwest Center each night. They weren't disappointed. Nine world records were set during the trials, with Michael Phelps breaking five. Phelps qualified for the team in eight events total in route to winning eight gold medals at the 2008 Olympics.

The 2012 US Olympic Swim Trials will be held from June 25 to July 2, 2012. They will begin right after the College World Series ends, making the summer of 2012 an exciting one for Omaha sports fans.

# OMAHA KIDSTUFF

Omaha is a family-friendly city. In fact, many locals won't hesitate to tell newcomers that they moved to Omaha—or moved back to Omaha—because they wanted to raise a family here.

Many of the activities in this section are competitively priced; some are even free. Two giant slides in the heart of downtown Omaha offer some of the best fun that money can't buy: the experience of spending hours going down the giant, wavy, mirrored monoliths is one that many Omaha kids remember for years. They relive the fun by taking their own children there, too.

Omaha's recently remodeled Children's Museum has activities for toddlers and bigger kids, too, and the locally owned Amazing Pizza Machine is basically a kid's mecca: buffets full of food, tons of games, and rides mean kids will be begging to check this place out, and parents won't mind the wallet-friendly price tag.

Youth sporting leagues are incredibly popular in the summer months (and some year-round) and the end of this chapter details a few of the most popular that offer soccer, baseball, and other sports to athletically inclined children and their enthusiastic parents.

Be sure to check out both the Attractions chapter and the Parks & Recreation chapter, which contain more listings that will probably be of interest to families with kids of all ages. Plenty of outdoor activities, recreation spots, and sporting events are listed in those sections. The listings in this chapter are all child-centric activities that kids are sure to enjoy. Teenagers will likely be interested in at least a handful of the sites listed below, too. The price code below gives you an idea of what entrance fees (if any) and costs will be like to attend or visit any of these places.

### Price Code

The following price code has been included to give you a rough idea of what a regular ticket or entrance fee will cost at each of the following places. If the fees or costs associated with a particular activity or place are varied, no price has been given and you should use the contact information provided to find out the details. More specific pricing and discount information is included in the listings, where available.

Every effort has been made to include a variety of activities across a broad spectrum of prices to cater to every possible budget.

| | |
|---|---|
| $. . . . . . . . . . . . . . . . . . | **Less than $5** |
| $$ . . . . . . . . . . . . . . . . . . | **$5 to $10** |
| $$$ . . . . . . . . . . . . . . . . . | **$10 to $20** |
| $$$$ . . . . . . . . . . . | **More than $20** |

## MUSEUMS & ATTRACTIONS

### AMAZING PIZZA MACHINE $$
13955 S Plaza
(402) 829-1777
http://amazingpizzamachine.com
The Amazing Pizza Machine is so big and shiny, it seems like a chain, but it's not. The Nebraska-owned entertainment complex has, since it opened in 2006, earned many "Best of Omaha" awards and one national award for the Best New Family Entertainment Center in the Country by the International Association for the Leisure and Entertainment Industry, a leading trade group. The business deals in excess: tons of games, lots of rides, scads of television sets, and no fewer than 100 items on the plethora of buffets make it a popular spot for families, teens, and birthday parties, especially on the weekends. Busy Works is an area devoted to younger children, with rides scaled to a smaller size and age-appropriate games. Teens gravitate toward the bumper cars and roller coaster. Adults can play glow in the dark golf, bowl, or drive a race car on an indoor track. A pizza bar, salad bar, and dessert bar are just the tip of the food-laden iceberg.

### OMAHA CHILDREN'S MUSEUM $$
500 S. 20th St.
(402) 342-6164
http://ocm.org
The recently remodeled Omaha Children's Museum is a true mix of new and old. The museum manages to maintain many of its exhibits that have been favorites of children for years—a pint-size grocery store complete with produce section, dairy freezer, and checkout stands at the top of that list—while adding new exhibits that continue to entertain young Omahans and their parents. The Charlie Campbell Science and Technology Center is home to the "Super Gravitron," which lets kids propel balls in and out of tubes using hydraulics, pneumatics, and mechanical tools. A set of recently renovated giant zoo animals has a special place in a lot of Omahans' hearts: They used to be in the play area of a local department store and recently were donated to the museum. The creative arts center is a mecca for the artistic child, and includes a wide array of art activities and dress-up games. The museum's third floor regularly plays host to a traveling exhibit.

**i** Did you know: *Parenting* magazine rated Omaha as one of the top 10 cities to raise a family, and *Redbook* magazine called it one of the 10 best cities for working moms. *Money* magazine ranked Lincoln as the 60th best city to live in the United States.

## WATERPARKS/ AMUSEMENT PARKS

### FUN PLEX
7003 Q St.
(402) 331-8436
http://fun-plex.com
Fun Plex is the state's largest amusement and water park. Divided into two sides— one devoted to dry activities, the other to water activities—Fun Plex is a popular destination for families but also for parties and company picnics. The land-locked attractions include a go-kart track and a slick track, a full-size roller coaster, a wide selection of carnival rides, an 18-hole miniature golf course, and a selection of children's rides. The water park side has a kids' pool, a

motion ocean, a lazy river, and five-story tall waterslides. The park is open from Memorial Day to Labor Day.

## PAPIO BAY AQUATIC CENTER          $$
**815 E. Halleck St., Papillion**
**(402) 597-2055**
**www.papillion.org**
Papio Bay Aquatic Center is five acres devoted to swimming paradise. Two waterslides, two diving boards, and a zero-depth pool are among the aquatic attractions. A sand volleyball court and sand play area, concession stands, and bathhouse round out the offerings, and a separate wading pool with a butterfly slide is perfect for younger swimmers. The center is open from Memorial Day to Labor Day.

## SPLASH STATION          $-$$
**3809 E. Fremont Dr., Fremont**
**(402) 727-2619**
**http://fremontsplashstation.com**
Six water-based attractions make Fremont's Splash Station a good stop for summer fun. Two tall waterslides make the park visible from afar: the yellow body slide empties into the main pool and a blue "speed slide" empties into its own long, skinny trough. A huge water tower dumps more than 500 gallons of water every two minutes into the park's zero depth pool area. A splashground for young children is adjacent to a small waterslide shaped like a train locomotive that's a favorite with kids. A wave action lap pool was designed especially for the facility. The outdoor facility is open during the summer months; check its website for current hours.

## PLAYGROUNDS

### ✳SLIDES AT THE GENE LEAHY MALL          FREE
**1098 Farnam St.**
**(402) 444-5955**
Sometimes it's the simple things that are the best, and, in this case, simplicity is king. The two giant metal slides sitting in a sunken area of downtown Omaha's Gene Leahy Mall have been the source of fun for kids of all ages for 30 years or more. Two metal slides, side by side, offer kids of all ages hours of fun, especially in warmer months. Steps on each side lead to the top of the slides, and kids land in a giant sand pit at the base. Discarded paper bags and pieces of wax paper—to add speed to a downward, bumpy ride—lay around the base of the slide, and kids can either bring their own or recycle someone else's piece. Either way, hours of free fun will prevail.

## SKATING RINKS

### SKATEDAZE OMAHA          $$
**3616 S. 123nd St.**
**(402) 333-3555**
**http://skatedaze.com**
Roller skating is so un-cool it's cool again, and SkateDaze does this retro hobby right. A huge skating rink plays host to themed nights every week, including a Tuesday night roller disco night for adults called "Adult Retro Night" and themed nights for kids the rest of the week. Close to 100 arcade games meet other activities that include a rock climbing wall, bumper cars, laser tag, and a roller coaster. A special $20 all access pass lets visitors consume as many hot dogs, pizza slices, and sodas as they desire.

## YOUTH SPORTS

### GLADIATOR BASEBALL
7222 Irvington Rd.
http://gladiatorbaseball.com
Focused only on baseball, the Omaha Gladiators is a large Omaha-based youth select sports program. The Gladiator program has its own fields located in central Omaha and plays host to a yearly tournament. Children must try out to be on the Gladiator teams, and a limited number of spots are available each year on the youth leagues.

### OMAHA SPORTS ACADEMY
11726 Stonegate Circle
(402) 504-1222
The Omaha Sports Academy provides a wide variety of sports to Omaha kids who are looking to play outside of school. Its facility has more than 30,000 square feet of space where kids of all ages regularly play indoors. Adults can use the space, too: The OSA offers adult fitness and training classes. Each year, OSA offers leagues, tournaments, camps, and clinics for basketball, soccer, and volleyball on both a summer and fall basis.

# Part 3

# LINCOLN

# Lincoln

**N 148TH ST.** / **S 148TH ST.**

HOLDREGE ST.

S 120TH ST.

A ST.

OLD CHENEY RD.

PINE LAKE RD.

■ Lancaster
Event Center

N 84TH ST. / S 84TH ST.

HAVELOCK AVE.

ADAMS ST.

N 70TH ST. / S 70TH ST.

FREMONT ST.

Nebraska
Wesleyan University

LEIGHTON AVE.

University of Nebraska-
Lincoln East Campus

N 66TH ST.

*Holmes Lake*

PIONEERS BLVD.

SUPERIOR ST.

E SOUTH ST.

N 56TH ST.

S 56TH ST.

COTNER BLVD.

NORMAL BLVD.

S 48TH ST.

Havelock
District

VINE ST.

S 40TH ST.

E VAN DORN ST.

Union
College

S 33RD ST.

N 27TH ST.

University of Nebraska-Lincoln
City Campus

Memorial Stadium

Lincoln Children Museum

S 27TH ST. / S 27TH ST.

CAPITOL PKWY.

SHERIDAN AVE.

PINE LAKE RD.

Haymaker
Park

Sheldon Museum of Art
Lied Center for Performing Arts
Historic Haymarket District

Pershing Auditorium

State Capital

S 20TH ST.

E SOUTH ST.

E VAN DORN ST.

OLD CHENEY RD.

Southpointe
Pavillions Mall

W. CORNHUSKER HWY.

S 13TH ST.

S 14TH ST.

S 10TH ST.

ROSA PARK WY.

Lincoln
Municipal
Airport

PIONEERS BLVD.

W 12TH ST.

WARLICK BLVD.

W 1ST ST.

S CODDINGTON AVE.

W A ST.

W VAN DORN RD.

Visitor
Center

Pioneer
Park

SW 40TH ST.

W DENTON RD.

NW 38TH ST.

NW 48TH ST.

**N**

0   2   4 mi.

0   2   4 km.

# LINCOLN ACCOMMODATIONS

Downtown Lincoln is the place many business travelers will want to stay, as the campus of the University of Nebraska–Lincoln is within walking distance and lots of the city's biggest companies are downtown, as are most of the state offices and the Nebraska State Capitol building.

Lincoln's historic bed-and-breakfasts offer personal service and lodging in a historic home or building; the character that comes with this type of lodging is unparalleled. Plus, who can turn down a home-cooked breakfast?

Most of Lincoln's hotels offer transportation to and from the regional airport; some offer transportation from the busier Omaha airport. The Getting Here, Getting Around chapter in Part 1 goes into full detail about transportation options to and from hotels to airports, as well as to and from Omaha and Lincoln for professionals who have business in Omaha or Lincoln and need a way to get back and forth.

Hotels and motels in Lincoln are relatively inexpensive, and travelers will find many of the hotels listed in this section on major discount websites; it's worth doing a bit of price comparison before booking.

## Price Code

The following price code has been included to give you a rough idea of what one regular double occupancy room or overnight stay will cost at each of the following places. When choosing a hotel, it is important to bear in mind that costs can vary greatly from high season to low, so you may be pleasantly surprised to find a lower price when you actually go to make the reservation.

Additionally, many of the hotels and accommodations here offer special rates, packages, and sales, so be sure to check around before you book.

$ . . . . . . . . . . . . . . . . . **Less than $70**
$$ . . . . . . . . . . . . . . . . . **$70 to $100**
$$$ . . . . . . . . . . . . . . . **$100 to $200**
$$$$ . . . . . . . . . . . **More than $200**

# DOWNTOWN

## THE CORNHUSKER, A MARRIOTT
   HOTEL                                 $$$
333 S. 13th St.
(402) 474-7474
www.marriott.com

One of the state's most well-known hotels, Lincoln's Cornhusker is one of Marriott's best properties in the country. The common areas and rooms have been recently upgraded, and the changes include comfortable new bedding and down pillows. The lobby is elegant and old fashioned, but the rooms themselves are decorated in a palette of green, gold, and white; the feel is decidedly modern. The 287 rooms in the Cornhusker are popular during Husker game weekends, and the hotel is a center in the city for conferences and large meetings, with a total of 46,000 square feet of meeting space. The hotel has two concierge levels, and the Five Reasons Lounge serves food for lunch and dinner as well as a cocktail in a secluded, quiet atmosphere. The Terrace Grille, on the main floor of the hotel, is open for breakfast, lunch, and dinner and is a popular brunch destination for locals.

## *EMBASSY SUITES HOTEL
   LINCOLN                              $$$
1040 P St.
(402) 474-1111
www.embassysuites.com

A hugely popular destination during Nebraska Cornhuskers football games, the downtown Lincoln Embassy Suites is one of the city's nicest hotels. The hotel is near the University of Nebraska–Lincoln campus, the Lied Center for Performing Arts, and the Haymarket district; all three are within easy walking distance, as is Memorial Stadium. Business travelers will find the hotel close to many offices. Each of the 252 suites have a bedroom and separate sitting area with a wet bar and mini-refrigerator. Wireless Internet is available in the common areas for free and for a fee in the rooms. The popular pool is a big attraction for families, as are the free evening cocktail and snack receptions and morning breakfast buffet. The hotel has more than 20,000 square feet of meeting space, making it a popular spot for conventions, large meetings, dinners, and wedding receptions. The Embassy Bar and Grille provides in-room dining and in the bar area of the hotel lobby.

## HOLIDAY INN LINCOLN
### DOWNTOWN                    $$$
**141 N. 9th St.**
**(402) 475-4011**
**www.holidayinn.com/lincolnne**

Recently remodeled, the Holiday Inn Downtown is on the fringe of the Haymarket and a popular stop when looking for a more affordable downtown option. Renovations brought a new indoor heated pool; an on-site fitness center, and the Red Onion Grill, a full-service restaurant that also provides room service to hotel guests. A 24-hour business center is available for guests, as is a free airport shuttle. On Monday, Tuesday, and Wednesday evenings, the hotel has a manager's reception with free beer, house wine, and appetizers. The lobby has a lounge open 24 hours a day where people can socialize. The new rooms include new beds and bedding, a large desk and workspace, free Internet, and a minifridge and microwave.

## SUBURBAN EXTENDED STAY HOTEL
### DOWNTOWN                    $
**1744 M St.**
**(402) 475-3000**
**www.suburbanhotels.com**

Close to the Nebraska State Capitol and the UNL Campus, Suburban Extended Stay Hotel Downtown is meant for those doing business in Lincoln for a longer stay, though is open to families on longer trips as well. The 51 rooms are simply furnished but clean, and the hotel is open to pets. Each room has a full kitchen including two burners, a full size fridge, and a microwave, as well as utensils and cookware. Housekeeping services are weekly. Free Internet, a fitness center, and laundry services round out the offerings.

# SOUTH LINCOLN

## HAMPTON INN LINCOLN          $$$
**5922 Vandervoort Dr.**
**(402) 420-7800**
**www.hamptoninn.com**

The 74-room Hampton Inn Lincoln is convenient for families visiting relatives who live in the newer developments in South Lincoln, or for business travelers working in the area. The hotel has free high speed Internet; simply appointed, clean rooms; free beverages and breakfast; and valet services; among other amenities. Though the hotel doesn't have a restaurant on-site, the neighborhood is home to many outside dining options, as well as a large amount of mall shopping destinations.

## RESIDENCE INN BY MARRIOTT    $$
**5865 Boboli Lane**
**(402) 423-1555**
**www.residenceinn.com/lnkri**

The brand-new Residence Inn by Marriott has 90 suites located in the heart of the newer South Lincoln neighborhoods. The rooms have a decidedly modern decor, with a full kitchen including a full-size fridge, two-burner stove, microwave, and kitchen implements, as well as a sleeping area and large bathroom with walk-in shower. A 24-hour convenience market on-site, an evening manager's reception with snacks and drinks, and free breakfast round out the offerings. The hotel also offers grocery service to long-term guests.

# NORTH LINCOLN

## STAYBRIDGE SUITES EXTENDED
### STAY HOTEL                  $$$
**2701 Fletcher Ave.**
**(402) 438-7829**
**www.staybridge.com**

Catering to business travelers in town for longer visits, Staybridge Suites has 109 suites. Free Internet access, a 24-hour business center, and two on-site meeting rooms make the Staybridge a popular corporate choice; it's also close to I-80, which makes it close to just about anywhere in Lincoln and a quick drive to Omaha, if business required. The hotel has a free breakfast every day and a manager's sundown reception, as well as a fireplace, heated pool, and spa. Outdoor facilities include a recreation and sports court, barbeque grills, and an outdoor pool. The hotel allows pets but does charge a pet fee, which varies depending on the length of the stay. The hotel renovated its health center in 2010 and updated all the equipment. Staybridge will work directly with companies that need 10 to 25 rooms; call the hotel directly for details.

## EAST LINCOLN

### CHASE SUITE HOTEL $$
200 S. 68th St. Place
(402) 483-4900
www.chasehotellincoln.com

Chase Suite Hotel Lincoln is located next to one of the city's best recreational trails and a manicured park; the relatively intimate space feels more like a bed-and-breakfast than a big hotel. The recently renovated spot has clean, well maintained interiors and manicured grounds. Guests can choose from a studio or a two-bedroom suite that includes a living room and kitchen. Guests can eat a free hot breakfast buffet, enjoy a daily social hour from 5 to 6:30 p.m. Mon through Thurs, and ride a free shuttle anywhere within Lincoln's city limits during weekdays from 7 a.m. to 7 p.m. On-site meeting space seats up to 40, and is often used for company retreats and special meetings.

### NEW VICTORIAN SUITES $$
216 N. 48th St.
(402) 464-4000
www.newvictoriansuites.com

Lincoln's New Victorian Suites offer guests an affordable stay for a weekend or an extended visit. Amenities include an indoor swimming pool, free breakfast, a 24-hour fitness center, free wireless Internet, and suites with the standard fixings. The hotel has a "suite deal guarantee" that ensures guests the hotel's rates will always be the same no matter the number of nights booked, the time of the week booked, or if it's on a holiday weekend. The hotel also has a small meeting and event room that comfortably fits 35; it's often used for wedding showers, baby showers, anniversaries, or family reunions.

## BED-&-BREAKFASTS

### ATWOOD HOUSE BED AND BREAKFAST $$$
740 S. 17th St.
(402) 438-4567
www.atwoodhouse.com

Decorated in charming Victorian-era style, the Atwood House Bed and Breakfast is in a downtown Lincoln house of the same name. The Atwood House is an 1894 Neoclassical Georgian Revival mansion in downtown Lincoln, just two blocks from the Nebraska state capitol building. The sizable mansion has three bedrooms, including the three-room Atwood Suite that's a popular destination for newlyweds. The mansion itself plays host to weddings, and the intimate setting has room for 40 guests. The other guest rooms all have private sitting areas as well as bedrooms. Breakfast is served in the formal dining room on bone china with sterling flatware and Waterford crystal glassware; the setting and presentation is entirely elegant. The L-shaped Frank W. Little suite is named after the house's original builder; Little owned the three-piece walnut bedroom set in the room, which dates from 1840.

### PRAIRIE CREEK INN          $$$
**2400 S. 148th St., Walton**
**(402) 488-8822**
**www.pcibnb.com**
Located just a short jaunt outside of Lincoln, the Prairie Creek Inn is owned by two lifelong Nebraskans, Bruce and Maureen Stahr. The couple moved the Bruce W. Leavitt home from the outskirts of Lincoln to Walton on a two-day, 11-mile jaunt that transported the 406,000 pound home to its current location. The 1911 home had been seriously vandalized before the move, and the Stahrs spent four years renovating the house and restoring period woodwork, marble, oak, and walnut. They refinished original floors, expanded the front porch, and added an elevator and a full basement. Today, the B&B has completely renovated guest rooms and also gives guests access to a 12-acre stocked fishing lake, three miles of hiking trails, and a full 75 acres of peaceful farmland. Two other buildings on-site are currently under renovation and eventually guests will be able to stay in a cottage house and a lakeside cabin.

### *WUNDER ROOST          $$
**14817 S. 25th St., Roca**
**(402) 794-6969**
**www.wunderroost.com**
Just a few minutes from shopping and eating in South Lincoln, Roca's Wunder Roost is a country farm that's close enough to the city to offer the best of both worlds. The century-old farmstead and country square is 8 miles from Lincoln. The Wunder Rosa

Winery is a short walk from the B&B and only two miles from the Jamaica Homestead Bike Trail. Wunder Roost has lots of amenities, including wireless Internet, a hot tub, a wood-burning stove, outdoor gardens, a private second floor entrance, and deck. The decor is decidedly country chic, with rustic yet comfortable chairs and seating, lots of blonde wood, and cozy handmade quilts.

**i** B&Bs, of which there are a handful in Lincoln, offer a charming stay perfect for a special occasion: newlyweds, couples on a romantic escape, girlfriends on a getaway, or the especially weary business traveler will enjoy the personal service, home-cooked food and memorable atmosphere. Packages are often available and specially priced; inquire with the innkeeper for details.

## RV PARK

### CAMP A WAY          $-$$$
**200 Campers Circle**
**(402) 476-2282**
**www.campaway.com**
A popular Lincoln campground, Camp A Way offers reasonable daily, weekly, and monthly rates for campsites and cabins, and a nightly rate for tent camping. The site has a number of large pull-through sites for large campers and fully furnished cabins for rent. Amenities include free wireless Internet; a heated swimming pool and indoor spa; an on-site park; flower gardens; cable television hookup; pancake breakfasts and burger cookouts for campers; and annual events that include a chili cook off, a harvest festival, and watermelon days.

# LINCOLN RESTAURANTS

incoln has a wide variety of restaurants—bar food, fine dining, ethnic cuisine, and one-of-a-kind foodie stops included. The city also has its own particular variety of late night college hangouts, where a plate of fries, a delicious gyro, and, in at least one case, endless cups of coffee, round-the-clock breakfast, and booths full of studiers are the everyday norm.

Lincoln's coffee houses shouldn't be missed: They brew locally made joe and each have their own independent personality and devoted clientele—not to mention cheap, hot coffee and tea that's hard to beat.

Small holes in the walls—hidden gems—are everywhere in the city. So are restaurants that masquerade as bars and serve delicious food.

The city also has a high per capita (or at least it seems that way) of delicious vegetarian food: Freakbeat Vegetarian serves some of the best soup this writer has ever tasted; and Bread and Cup is one of those locally owned restaurants that specializes in delicious, locally produced food that's both healthy and tasty—a rare combination.

## OVERVIEW

The restaurants in this chapter are presented by type of cuisine and in alphabetical order. The styles of cuisine are loosely categorized; some are rather difficult to categorize. A price code has been incorporated so you can find what you're looking for.

Lincoln has a strict smoking ban and smoking is not allowed in any workplaces, restaurants, or bars. No restaurants have smoking sections, but some have opened their patios or gardens to smokers.

There are thousands of restaurants in Lincoln, and this is just a small sampling of the types of cuisine and places diners can get it. Everyone has their own favorites when it comes to restaurants and food; many of the listings here are my favorites. You are encouraged to use this guide as

a jumping-off point and explore the city's foodie offerings for yourself.

### Price Code

The following price code has been included to give you a rough idea of what an average dinner of entrees for two will cost excluding cocktails, wine, appetizers, dessert, tax, and tip. Lincoln has a wide array of restaurants, including the very reasonable and ultra fine dining, and every price point in between. Unless otherwise noted, all restaurants accept major credit cards.

$................. **Less than $10**
$$ .................. **$10 to $30**
$$$ .................. **$30 to $50**
$$$$ ............ **More than $50**

## AMERICAN

**BARRY'S BAR AND GRILL** $
235 N. 9th St.
(402) 476-6511
www.barrysbarandgrill.com

Barry's is, historically speaking, the place to go before Nebraska Cornhusker football games. It's been around for more than 50 years, and sports fans crowd the place for pre-game fun every Saturday during the season. In fact, the bar's business is so good on game days, it could close for the rest of the year and still make a profit. Barry's is a popular lunch spot for downtown professionals, and to that end has a ton of daily specials. A punch card allows diners to buy four lunches, get the fifth one free. Friday night is steak night, and diners can buy an 8-ounce New York strip for $10.95. Barry's menu has all the bar food standards one expects: burgers and fries, sandwiches, soups, pizza, and appetizers.

**DOOZY'S** $
101 N. 14th St.
(402) 438-1616
www.downtowndoozys.com

Doozy's whips up some of the best sandwiches in downtown Lincoln. The restaurant is popular with University of Nebraska–Lincoln students as well as with professionals who work in downtown Lincoln. The crowd is really diverse: You'll see professionals in suits with key cards, grubby students, police officers, and university professors. The toasted bread at Doozy's with cheese baked inside is simply delicious, all the subs are hot and saucy, and one can't go wrong with just about anything on the menu. Most of the sandwiches offer meat; cheese; veggies; and melty, creamy mayo; there's a vegetarian sandwich, too. Doozy's also serves pizzas, though the hot sandwiches are the most popular item by far.

## *GREEN GATEAU $$
### 330 S. 10th St.
### (402) 477-0330
### www.greengateau.com

Green Gateau serves the most popular brunch in Lincoln. The restaurant is open for breakfast on weekends and lunch and dinner every day but Sunday, when it closes at 3 p.m. The name (French for "cake") is inspired by a green cake mentioned in Claude Monet's cooking journals. The restaurant's decor is inspired by the English countryside: mismatched chairs, stained glass windows, and a giant copper espresso machine take their cues from European country inns. The brunch menu is a mix of breakfast and lunch items, and the breakfast specialties seem to be some of the restaurant's most popular. Eggs Oscar, a take on Eggs Benedict, is a halved English muffin topped with crab cakes, asparagus, two poached eggs, and hollandaise sauce. The Gateau's potato pancakes are delicious: creamy and salty at once. The French toast, another popular item, is custard battered and served with syrup and powdered sugar. It also comes stuffed with strawberries, topped with whipped cream, and covered in strawberry sauce. The Gateau has a wide variety of sandwiches, salads, and specialty entrees it serves in the evenings, and its tasty dinner is probably a bit underrated.

## LAZLO'S $$
### 210 N. 7th St.
### (402) 434-5636
### www.lazlosbreweryandgrill.com

Lazlo's hickory-fire–fueled grill scents the air in Lincoln's Haymarket (and around its South Lincoln location) on a regular basis: The scent of the wood makes one's mouth start doing some serious watering. Both restaurants have a similar atmosphere of a rustic lodge meets a brewpub: fireplaces, lots of wood and rock, and ceiling skylights are the rule. Several servers work each individual table at the restaurant, so expect one person to take your order, another to refill your beer, and a third to bring your bill. Much of the menu uses that aforementioned hickory grill to create a singular flavor that's carried through many dishes: the burgers and a tasty swordfish sandwich both have the distinct taste. The rainbow chicken might be the most popular entree on the menu: It's a hickory grilled breast covered in tomatoes and green onions, then slathered with cheese. Baby back ribs, fish and chips, and some great french fries (try them dipped in honey mustard) are all solid choices. The pub brews its own beer—Emperyan Ales—and it's great. It's sold in bars and restaurants around Nebraska, and true fans can tour the microbrewery on the first non-holiday Monday of every month except December. The tours are free but super popular; the first 150 people are allowed through the tour, which starts at 7 p.m. Get there early. Lazlo's also has a weeknight happy hour from 3 to 6 p.m. at both locations in the bar and patio areas; check the website for updated specials. The second location is at 5900 Old Cheney Rd. (402-323-8500).

## LEE'S CHICKEN    $$
## 1940 W. Van Dorn St.
(402) 477-4339

You can't miss Lee's Chicken. It has a giant rooster out front, which is a good thing, because it's in an out of the way location on the very edge of Lincoln. The obscure location and the out of date decor (we can call it vintage chic) isn't the main draw at Lee's: It's the chicken. That chicken has kept Lee's in business for close to 70 years. Juicy and classically prepared with a crispy outside and moist center, Lee's knows what fried chicken is all about. Sides veer toward the classics: coleslaw, potatoes, and homemade rolls are the name of the game.

## MANHATTAN DELI    $
## 728 Q St.
(402) 476-7287
www.manhatdeli.com

Manhattan Deli serves the meatiest sandwiches in the city. It aims to emulate the old-school delis of New York City and it does a decent job. The lunch special includes a bowl of soup (flavors vary daily) and a half sandwich for just a bit more than $5. Sandwich choices include egg, chicken, and tuna salad; roast beef; turkey; ham; and what many describe as the best Reuben in the city, served with turkey or pastrami. Other sides include an array of salads (Russian potato salad is tasty and different) and the deli also makes blintzes and potato pancakes. Vegetarian sandwiches are marked on the menu, and the deli also makes a great deli burger—a homemade patty on toasted bread topped with provolone. End lunch with a tasty slice of chocolate or regular style cheesecake.

## PAUL'S OLD STYLE BBQ    $$
## 4724 Pioneers Blvd.
(402) 488-7427
www.paulsbbq.net

Lincolnite Paul Nevels founded his barbeque joint based on his St. Louis family's recipes. He first started cooking at a takeout window at 40th and A Streets, and eventually opened a full-service restaurant. Nevels slow smokes all of his meat every day on-site at the restaurant. He uses a variety of different woods to create singular flavor; the sauce is also homemade every day. He serves ribs, brisket, chicken, and smoked turkey. The meat is also available in family-style meals that include choices of sides including cornbread, coleslaw, potato salad, french or sweet potato fries, and more. Paul's is nothing fancy—a simple restaurant that serves food on paper and Styrofoam plates—but the homemade sauce and singular smoking techniques keep the customers coming in for more.

## TINA'S CAFE AND CATERING    $$
## 616 South St.
(402) 435-9404

Tina's Cafe is one of those locals-only hangouts that anyone who doesn't live in Lincoln doesn't know about. Tina's is an old-school hole in the wall diner; there's not much decor, but what is there is all NASCAR themed. Tina's makes some seriously large cinnamon rolls (think the size of your head) as well as great blueberry pancakes and breakfast food in the mornings. Smoky bacon, eggs cooked to order, and a wide variety of breakfast specialties are the most popular items on the menu. Tina's also serves lunch, including a great chicken fried steak.

## TWO TWINS CAFE                    $$
**333 North Cotner Blvd.**
**(402) 464-8946**

One of Lincoln's newest restaurants, Two Twins Cafe focuses on home-style cooking from scratch. The cafe serves breakfast, lunch, and dinner. An on-site bakery produces lots of goodies every day, including cinnamon rolls, muffins, scones, dessert bars, cakes, pies, cheesecake, and other specialty items that can be enjoyed at the restaurant or ordered to go. Breakfast items include a wide variety of hot egg dishes, oatmeal, granola, and things like French toast, pancakes, and a breakfast burrito. Lunchtime brings an array of burgers and some tasty sounding sandwiches, including parmesan grilled turkey taco and a toasted BLT. The atmosphere at Two Twins is laid back and friendly, and the two owners, who happen to be twins, are often there to welcome guests.

## THE WATERING HOLE                 $
**1321 O St.**
**(402) 438-3054**

The Watering Hole cooks up some of the best bar food in downtown Lincoln. It's known with locals for its hot wings, which are grilled or regular style, and are on special every Monday night three for $1. The rest of the menu, too, is solid: burgers, fries, grilled cheese sandwiches, and yummy sweet potato fries are worth a stop. The bar is a bit dingy, but it's crowded over the lunch hour, and college students and adults seem to love it as a hangout spot in the evenings. The wings come with a wide variety of sauce choices: hot, mild, extra spicy, apricot, BBQ, Hawaiian BBQ, spicy BBQ, sweet heat, and teriyaki. The bar also delivers to anywhere in the Lincoln metro area. Another location is at 1550 S. Coddington Ave. (402-477-2900).

## Asian

## CHINA INN                         $-$$
**27th and Cornhusker Highway**
**(402) 466-8242**

The *Lincoln Journal Star* named China Inn the best Chinese restaurant in the city, and Lincoln residents seem to agree. The small, nondescript hole in the wall serves great food prepared using authentic Chinese recipes. The menu includes items for the less adventurous eater—crispy chicken cutlets served with mild chili sauce and fried peanut butter chicken—as well as the braver diner. Think spicy Ma Po Tofu, Peking Duck, Salty Shrimp served with the head on, and Spicy Intestines in Hot Pot. The menu features the familiarized American Chinese food, as well as a back page of Chinese authentic dishes; the food is served family style, so sharing is encouraged. The menu is vegetarian friendly, too, and tofu can be substituted in many dishes. A selection of Korean dishes dot the menu.

## Coffee Shops

## THE COFFEE HOUSE                   $
**1324 P St.**
**(402) 477-6611**

College students simply love the Coffee House. The "CoHo," as it's affectionately known, is basically a study hall for hipsters. It's a classic college coffee house: wobbly tables, cushy couches, posters hanging everywhere, and students galore downing bottomless cups of brew. The space doubles as an art gallery, and lots of up-and-coming local artists stage casual exhibits in the space. The young, lively crowd fills the space every day and night; it's going to be busy. Baristas, while friendly baristas run a casual house, and sometimes conversation is more important than service. The house brewed coffee is tasty, drinks are created precisely, and the selection of teas can't be beat (sample the Monk's Prayer for a real treat). Free wireless, a singular atmosphere, and an interesting crowd will greet anyone who walks in the door.

**\*THE MILL**                                           **$**
**800 P St.**
**(402) 475-5522**
**www.millcoffee.com**

The Mill is the quintessential college town coffee shop. The downtown location is a place where students spend hours studying not because it's finals week but because it's a cool place to study. College professors go there to write, to work, and to socialize. Tables of regulars sit in the shop every morning, simply to talk. The College View location carries on that same cool coffee shop vibe. One of the best features about the Haymarket location is the outdoor seating: In the spring, students pack this area, smoke cigarettes, chat, and drink loads of joe. Inside, the brick walls, rickety tables and chairs, and constant whir of the espresso machine create a comfortable, cozy, and welcoming atmosphere. And aside from the can't-beat atmosphere, the Mill serves some really great coffee. It sells on-site roasted coffee and tea, which it also brews daily, featuring one flavor, one regular roast, and one decaf at a serve-yourself counter. Regulars know it's totally OK to leave the money on the counter and walk out the door with the joe to go. The Mill also sells locally made sandwiches and wraps, great scones and desserts, candy, chocolate, and everything one would ever need to brew coffee and tea at home. Pick up one of their signature ceramic mugs and take it home. It's the best coffee mug one

can drink out of. The second location is at 4736 Prescott Ave. (402-327-9391).

## ETHNIC

**AFRICAN RESTAURANT**                        **$**
**313 N. 27th St.**
**(402) 261-6673**

The simply named African Restaurant is the only place in Lincoln that serves Ethiopian (read: east African) food. It's not been long open, but already It has a dedicated following of adventurous foodies. The tiny menu only has a few items, and the owner, who is also the chef, will likely also be your server. The atmosphere is simple at this small restaurant. African Restaurant serves Ethiopian staples including Injera Bread, which is similar to a crepe; Beef Tibs, a saucy, meaty dish; goat meat and pepper stew; beef Kay Wat, an Ethiopian stew; and a vegetarian dish featuring cabbage and carrots. The restaurant offers takeout, and does have some outdoor seating.

**ALI BABA**                                            **$-$$**
**112 N. 14th St.**
**(402) 435-2615**

**GOURMET GRILL**                              **$-$$**
**1400 O St.**
**(402) 476-7147**

Nobody (well, almost nobody) likes both the Gourmet Grill and Ali Baba. The two gyro joints are right next door to one another in downtown Lincoln, and UNL students and O Street bar-goers usually give them both a try once and then form a lifelong allegiance. Think Coke vs. Pepsi, and you get the idea. To the untrained tongue the two seem very similar: gyros and gyro platters, falafel, french fries, Greek salads—all the traditional offerings. But true connoisseurs will point out subtle differences: steak fries at Ali Baba. Seasoned crinkly fries at Gourmet Grill. Service that defines the two restaurants and familiar faces they like to see over and over again. Subtle differences in the cucumber sauce. Diced tomatoes rather than sliced. Great cheeseburgers at the Gourmet Grill that lure some in more than the traditional Greek fare. You'll simply have to try both for yourself and make up your own mind. That's the way it's done.

## *BLUE ORCHID THAI
### RESTAURANT                    $$–$$$
**129 N. 10th St.**
**(402) 742-7250**

The Blue Orchid has a sophisticated, neo-Asian atmosphere and a great menu to match. The feel of the restaurant is decidedly modern. Lots of white paper-topped tables and booths sit in the airy, open space that's bright thanks to ceiling skylights. A small bar is a great spot to order one of the house-made martinis or cocktails while waiting for a seat; without a reservation on a busy evening, there's usually a bit of one. The menu offers lots of delectable Thai specialties, but the spicy-sweet panang curry is a true standout. The smoky flavor is perfectly seasoned with jalapeno and kaffir lime leaf, and the sauce comes with a good amount of rice and your choice of protein. The salmon is an interesting choice, and the fish muddles nicely with the spice of the sauce; if you choose tofu, ask for larger pieces, otherwise the spice becomes a bit overwhelming. The daily lunch special lets diners choose an appetizer and entree for just $10. Other tasty menu items include the spring rolls, the tom kha soup, pad thai, and the Thai Basil entree.

## THE OVEN                        $$$
**201 N. 8th St.**
**(402) 475-6118**
**www.theoven-lincoln.com**

One of the classiest Indian experiences in Lincoln (and in Nebraska, even), the Oven serves great food in a singular atmosphere. The Oven prepares Northern Indian cuisine, and the Haymarket location is a popular lunch option for businesspeople who work downtown and on the nearby UNL campus. It's a great spot, too, for a romantic dinner or a big party. The restaurants are decorated in a similar manner: Both are dim, cozy, and welcoming; and both feature decoration that looks like it came straight from India. The menu includes all the Indian specialties that diners will expect, though it is well edited and focused at the same time. Servers are excellent and happy to make recommendations to those less familiar with the cuisine. Tandoori cuisine from the Oven is great, and the appetizer menu as well as the naan menu includes a lot of tasty options. The Oven offers a set lunch special where diners can get a house favorite with soup or salad for a reduced price. The second location is at 4101 Pioneer Woods Dr. (402-488-0650).

## *THE PARTHENON                  $$–$$$
**5500 S. 56th St.**
**(402) 423-2222**
**www.theparthenon.net**

Owned by a local Greek family, the Parthenon is the best place to indulge in Greek food in Lincoln. The restaurant has a huge menu full of all kinds of Greek goodness. The Parthenon is a huge restaurant decorated with a Greek theme: think columns, lots of plants and tons of big tables perfect for large families or parties. The Parthenon plays host to a lot of special events, including regular special dinners (some are themed) and performances from belly dancers. The menu has expected choices like gyros, pasticcio, mousaka, dolmathes, and Spanakopita. Less likely choices include Greek inspired pizzas; Mediterranean spiked pastas, soup, and salads; and a selection of vegan items. If you're in the mood for dessert, you're in the right place, and the baklava and its half chocolate dipped partner are melt-in-your-mouth delicious. Check out the dessert counter and swoon; then try to choose just one.

## FINE DINING

**BILLY'S** $$$
**1301 H St.**
**(402) 474-0084**
**www.billysrestaurant.com**
Located just a few blocks from the Nebraska State Capitol building, Billy's is the lunch place to see and be seen during the legislative session. Politicos of all bents find their way here—senators and lobbyists sit elbow to elbow—and it's a fun experience even if you're not politically inclined. Billy's is in an old Lincoln mansion built in 1887. The house still feels like the grand old mansion it is, and hasn't been renovated unrecognizable. Tables sit in separate rooms, and that sort of antiquey vibe makes the experience what it is. The lunch menu is a mix of things like crab cakes, pasta dishes, salmon salad, and a variety of burgers. The fancier dinner menu includes a popular rack of lamb, pomegranate duck, and a variety of steaks. Billy's makes three signature drinks over the lunch hour: raspberry ice tea, cranberry sparkle, and cherry lemonade; any of the three is worth trying. Billy's offers a singular atmosphere and clientele, and is truly a Lincoln standard when it comes to dining.

**✳DISH** $$$
**1100 O St.**
**(402) 475-9475**
**www.dishdowntown.com**
Dish has had its ups and downs over the years, with menu changes, name changes, and changes in the kitchen, but it's come out of the rough waters as popular as ever. The restaurant has the type of atmosphere that most Lincoln restaurants aspire to. Walls of windows give a glimpse into the downtown streets, a long bar and high-top table seating are on one side, close tables keep things intimate. The warmly colored decor is modern meets art deco, with a large etched glass in the bar and retro antiquey chairs. Outdoor seating with large, vintage globe lights makes the patio a nice dining option in nice weather. Couples find their way here on Valentine's Day, and college boys wanting to impress a girl bring them here on a first date. Business lunchers make the noon hour busy. The menu is simple but tastes great. Appetizers include things like hummus, steamed mussels, bruschetta, and a cheese plate. A vegetarian shepherd's pie is a singular entree, and the choices with an Asian twist—crispy duck and pan roasted tofu—are flavorful. Dish also offers a gluten-free menu.

**JTK** $$$
**201 N. 7th St.**
**(402) 435-0161**
**www.jtkrestaurant.com**
JTK scored one of the best locations in Lincoln's Haymarket for its restaurant: inside the old train station. Full of charisma, the location has everything going for it: classy yet vintage surroundings; music at the perfect volume level; a clean, modern design that's inviting and still cool. Knowledgeable servers and good service have made this restaurant one of the best fine dining options in Lincoln. The most popular option at the restaurant—and what keeps people coming back—is the

"date night" promotion. For $50, a couple can get an appetizer, two entrees with soup or salad, a dessert, and a bottle of wine. The best part is that the promotion is good every night of the week—even Friday and Saturday. The promotion has a set menu that includes lots of notable items, including a pomme frites appetizer that gets rave reviews, a lemon shrimp entree, a shoulder tenderloin with horseradish mushroom sauce, and desserts that include bananas foster and crème brûlée. It's a good sampling of the restaurant's regular menu, which offers the same type of items, just more of them.

## THE LODGE AT WILDERNESS
   RIDGE                            $$$-$$$$
1800 Wilderness Woods Place
(402) 434-5118
www.wildernessridgegolf.com

Aptly named the Lodge at Wilderness Ridge, the restaurant inside one of Lincoln's nicest country clubs feels like a huge log cabin. The giant space can accommodate hundreds of people; it's a popular special event space and sees a regular crowd of business people in and out for daily lunch meetings. The menu is pricey but tasty, and the restaurant serves breakfast, lunch, and dinner. It also caters special events. Hearty but elegant food is the main focus on the Lodge's menu. Items like Neopolitan pizza, crab cakes, filling sandwiches served with fries, and seafood-and steak-centric entrees dot the menu. A selection of ala carte steaks can be paired with a signature sauce and a side item; the sides can be prepared to serve one or two people. The restaurant has a wine bar with more than 100 bottles available as well as seasonal wine flights that let customers try four wines not otherwise offered by the glass.

## ✳MARZ INTERGALACTIC SHRIMP
   AND MARTINI BAR                     $$$
1140 O St.
(402) 476-4847
marzbarlincoln.com

The name is rather long but the short of it is that Marz is a really cool downtown Lincoln bar and eatery. The small kitchen is sometimes rather slow, but the atmosphere at Marz encourages lingering, so be patient and enjoy yourself rather than fretting. Marz is dark and hip, with a long bar, friendly waitstaff, and lots of signature cocktails that please any palette. Giant glowing globe lights sit on top of huge poles; the singular style isn't like anywhere else in Lincoln. The small plate meals are great for sharing, and it's wise for a group to order a wide selection and encourage sampling. Tapas include things like coconut shrimp, sweet and sour chicken wings, dolmas, calamari, and handmade fries. Marz also serves pizzas and small-sized entree portions of things like macaroni and cheese, meatloaf, fish and chips, smoked pork pasta, and grilled tuna salad.

## MISTY'S                              $$$
200 N. 11th St.
(402) 476-7766
www.mistyslincoln.com

Misty's is a Lincoln tradition in the same way that Gorat's is an Omaha tradition. The steak house has two locations: the newer Haymarket location, which has a modern feel, and the Havelock location, which takes diners straight back into the 1960s. It opened in 1963 and gives the "old-school steak house" vibe that so many visitors to Nebraska are after. Nebraska fans still go to the Havelock Misty's the night before a Husker game to toast to the team's chance of a win during the "Friday Night Big Red Pep Rally"; it's truly an institution. The downtown location is a popular lunch spot for professional types. Steak or prime rib are the items to order at Misty's: It's what they know and what they do best. Misty's offers a number of specials, including half-price prime rib on Mon and Tues from 3 to 5 p.m. The other location is at 6325 Havelock Ave. (402-466-8424).

## VENUE $$$
**70th and Pioneers Boulevard**
**(402) 488-8368**
**www.yourvenue.net**

When Venue opened in Lincoln, it catapulted the city's restaurant offerings into a new zone. It's got a big city feel—modern decor, exceptional service, and a sophisticated menu—and quickly became the go-to place for young professionals and people looking for a singular dining experience for a special occasion. The Venue serves brunch, but the lunch and dinner menus are much better. It's the only game in town doing what it does, so the prices are rather high, but considering its uniqueness in the Lincoln dining scene, that's OK. Roma style pizza and lavosh are a popular entree at noon and in the evening, and Venue bakes them in a stone oven. Toppings like smoked duck, barbecue chicken, and a variety of cheese mean there's a pizza for the adventurous or the traditionalist. Classic entrees adopt a variety of flavor profiles. Baja fish tacos, blackened ahi tuna, jambalaya fettuccine, and a kobe beef hamburger are a few of the offerings. Venue also offers a number of entrees that can be prepared gluten free.

## ITALIAN

**✳CAFFE ITALIA $$**
**2110 Winthrop Rd.**
**(402) 489-4949**

One of Lincoln's best-kept secrets, the crowd at Caffe Italia is devoted to the tiny restaurant that seats just 40 diners. It's in a quiet Lincoln neighborhood and is open daily for lunch and serves a popular dinner one night a week, every Friday. The little Italian bistro is decorated with glass tables and metal chairs and gets most of its personality from its devoted patronage. The Friday night dinner varies—sometimes it's vegetarian, other times not—and patrons can call on Wednesday to find out what the special will be in advance. The dish is always tasty, and it's always Italian, those things you can count on. The dinners run a reasonable $12.95, and past specials have included all varieties of pasta, lasagna, and meatballs; the meal always comes with bread and salad. The dinners have become really popular: Diners get there at least a half hour before nightly service begins and the meals are first come, first served, so those who get there after 6:30 p.m. will almost always have to wait for a table. Early birds also get the appetizers, which vary weekly. Desserts also rotate. Tiramisu is available every week and the restaurant offers a special dessert to compliment the weekly entree. Those with patience and a love of good food and wine will want to add Caffe Italia to their list of must-visits. Be sure to end your evening with a delightfully chilly, tiny glass of Limoncello. It's the right thing to do.

## MEXICAN & TAPAS

**D'LEONS $**
**Numerous locations in Lincoln**
**http://d-leonsmexicanfood.com/**

D'Leons is a bit of an institution when it comes to Mexican food in Lincoln. The restaurant's three locations are all open 24 hours a day and serve breakfast round the clock.

D'Leons classifies itself as "Mexcian Fast Food," and the two menus fit that designation. For breakfast, D'Leons serves burritos filled with sausage, chorizo, huevo, rancheros, and other goodies. Steak ranchero and Spanish omelets are also there. Lunch and dinner brings burritos, tacos, enchiladas, tostados, quesadillas, Mexican sandwiches, and super nachos. The restaurant combines the above items into 24 different platters; all come with beans and rice. The restaurant has a busy drive-through, and diners can expect a crowd even in the middle of the night.

### ✳LA MEXICANA MARKET     $
1637 P St.
(402) 477-0785

La Mexicana serves great, authentic Mexican food. It's a grocery store in the front and a Mexican restaurant in the back, and the dual business plan makes dining there a real experience. Walking through the aisles of authentic Mexican grocery items on the way to eat some delicious food sets the perfect note; it's also fun to check out the foreign items and sometimes make a purchase on the way out the door. It'd be impossible to re-create the cuisine one gets at La Mexicana at home, though, unless you've got an amazing Mexican grandmother who knows what's up in the kitchen. On the menu: a burrito stuffed with tripe. Chorizo tacos. Salsa spiked with plenty of spice and cilantro. Margaritas that are large and strong. Friendly, fast service, gobs of atmosphere, and rock bottom prices make La Mexicana one of the best spots in the city.

### OSO BURRITO     $–$$
1451 O St.
(402) 477-1717

Oso Burrito offers a local alternative to nation-wide burrito chains, and its product is fresher and tastier. Diners get a huge burrito stuffed with all types of customized ingredients. Proteins include beef, chicken, fish, pork, tofu, or rice and beans. Special sauces include buffalo, pesto, and Thai peanut. Rice plates come with the diner's choice of toppings, but it's never a bad idea to ask the person behind the counter for suggestions—some are surprisingly good, like a curry rice bowl with tofu that's not on the menu but tastes great. The burritos here aren't traditionally Mexican—flavors are across the board—and creativity seems to be the goal more than fitting any one flavor profile. It's clear—in a good way—that this shop is locally owned. Keep your eyes peeled for weekly special burritos that aren't always on the regular menu; these are a welcome treat.

## PIZZA

### ISLES PUB & PIZZA     $$
6232 Havelock Ave.
(402) 464-1858

A busy neighborhood spot, Isles Pub & Pizza serves saucy, cheesy pizza at its best. A retro cool atmosphere and a mixed crowd make the vibe at Isles a fun stop; the menu includes specialty pizzas with singular toppings including the Leaning Tower, which in short is a meat lover's dream, and the Midwestern taco pizza. It's a popular spot on Nebraska Cornhusker Game Day, and the filling pie is the perfect thing to feed a crowd.

### ✳YIAYIA'S PIZZA BEER & WINE     $–$$
1423 O St.
(402) 477-9166
www.facebook.com/yiayias

A college friend of mine once attempted to drink every beer on the menu at YiaYia's Pizza and Beer. The only thing that stood in his way was the manager, who kept changing the list to keep the poor fellow from achieving his goal. The vast beer list, which includes beers from every corner of the world, continues to change; in 2010 it started offering a dozen beers on tap. The pizza at YiaYias is great too: thin crust, New York–style with a wide variety of toppings. The pizza mostly focuses on toppings: the restaurant goes light on the sauce (sometimes eliminating it all together) and coming up with singular flavor profiles on the set menu. Diners can also choose any variety of toppings, sauce, and cheese they like. The vibe at YiaYias is decidedly funky: exposed brick walls; well worn tables; a long, curved bar; and huge vintage posters adorning the walls. It's crowded at both the lunch hour and on the weekends, and pool tables in the back are popular after dark.

## SWEETS

### IVANNA CONE                               $
**701 P. St.**
**(402) 477-7473**
**www.ivannacone.com**
Ivanna Cone is in an old soda shop in Lincoln's Haymarket district, and is a hugely popular stop for its signature flavors of homemade ice cream. Old-style ice cream shop decor fills the space. A long marble counter and a few small tables and chairs decorate the space, though the bulk of Ivanna Cone customers take their cones outside during the hot summer months and enjoy them on the street below. Ivanna's ice cream makers are always coming up with new flavors, and a recent sampling included white chocolate Oreo, chocolate orange cheesecake, kesari cashew, rum raisin, amaretto strawberry, mango lassi, macadamia

custard, and rose. The store regularly updates its Facebook page with new flavors; become a follower to know what's new.

### UNL DAIRY STORE                          $
**38th and Holdredge Streets**
**http://dairystore.unl.edu/**
The University of Nebraska–Lincoln is known for lots of things, and ice cream ought to be one of them. The UNL Dairy Store makes some delicious, creamy concoctions and a wide variety of tasty cheese, too.

The store has a big location on the UNL East Campus and a smaller, satellite location in the Nebraska Union on the city campus. At the east campus location, vanilla, Bavarian mint, butter brickle, cappuccino chocolate chip, chocolate, karmel kashew, and scarlet & cream are the flavors always available. The store also creates a regular docket of rotating flavors that are sometimes available. It also produces a variety of seasonal flavors created for holidays like Valentine's Day and Christmas. A few seats in the two locations of the Dairy Store offer the chance for people to sit and enjoy their creamy goodness, though most people take theirs out for a walk on campus. The Dairy Store also offers online ordering of ice cream, cheese, and gift baskets, and to-go items at the East Campus location. It's closed on weekends, but opens two to three hours before all the Saturday home Husker football games. The second location is at 14th and R Streets, in the Nebraska Union on the UNL campus.

## VEGETARIAN & NATURAL

### ✳BREAD AND CUP                           $$
**440 N. 8th St.**
**(402) 438-2255**
**www.breadandcup.com**

Bread and Cup is a cute little restaurant on the edge of Lincoln's Haymarket that serves fresh, creative, healthy food. Simple in design—clean, modern tables, and an open kitchen—diners order at the counter and their food comes to the table. It's a hugely popular lunch spot, and offers a regular farm-to-table dinner option every Saturday night that's especially delicious and bountiful in the summer, but still tasty and seasonally appropriate in the fall and winter. Two soups are on the daily menu—one is always vegetarian—and the on-site bakery produces great baguettes and bread to stay or go. The peanut butter and apple butter sandwich is pure genius, and simply delicious. So too is the cheese plate, the olive bowl, and the pork sandwich. If you're in the mood for dessert, the chocolate bread pudding is a can't-miss.

### *FREAKBEAT VEGETARIAN $
### 1625 S. 17th St.
### (402) 474-0101

Can there be a better soup place in the entire country? If there is, I don't know of it. Freakbeat has its quirks: It doesn't accept credit cards, is closed on Mon and Tues, and only has one employee behind the counter, but nobody cares about any of that stuff once they spoon a bite of soup into their mouth. There's a line out the door of this place every single day. It's that good. The homemade soup is all meat-free but it doesn't matter. It's simple, flavorful, and downright addictive. Diners choose from a daily docket of four or five soups—the most popular are probably the Moroccan Tomato, which has a healthy dose of peanut butter and a thick, creamy, and smooth finish, and the spicy Santa Fe Chowder, which is chunky and chock-full of

corn and mixed vegetables and has a sweet, spicy finish. Each bowl of soup comes with a piece of bread, an apple muffin, or a cheese scone. If you know what's good for you, get the cheese scone, because it will blow your mind. Freakbeat recently started offering casseroles; most days a large vat of creamy macaroni and cheese is available, and it's tasty, though the rest of your workday will be null and void after you finish a bowl of it. Freakbeat has a funky interior, full of thrift store art, weird toys, and old posters. The guy behind the counter (part of the family who owns the business) regularly flips records on a turntable to give the soup gobblers a soundtrack. Freakbeat is one of a kind, and its vastly mixed crowd of young hipsters, old ladies, and middle-aged office workers like it just the way it is.

### MAGGIE'S VEGETARIAN WRAPS $
### 311 N. 8th St.
### (402) 477-3959

Maggie's is the Haymarket's answer to simply made, healthy, creative vegetarian food. A popular lunch spot, especially for to-go orders, Maggie's has a cute interior with a few indoor seats and a few outdoor seats. The menu changes seasonally, so ingredients for some items, like lasagna, can change pretty drastically from summer to winter. Warm and cold sandwiches and wraps are all great, and creative ingredients, like oven baked tofu, give vegetarians unusual options. Vegan muffins, scones, and cookies are made in-house using organic ingredients; the most popular muffin is probably organic apple cinnamon, but a wide variety of flavors are in constant rotation. Muffins are baked every morning and are ready by 8 a.m.

# LINCOLN NIGHTLIFE

incoln's nightlife scene is centered on University of Nebraska–Lincoln students and the sort of cool, classic bars that always seem to draw young people.

Lincoln's bar scene is centered in downtown, and many of the bars mentioned in this chapter are either in the city's historic Haymarket district or else along O Street, where the 21-and-over UNL students mix and mingle with Lincoln 30-somethings out for a martini bar experience, older crowds there to hear live jazz or blues, and people just simply there to take in a game and drink a beer.

On a Nebraska Cornhusker game day, the bars in downtown Lincoln become the place to be for Husker fans both pre- and post-game (when they're not tailgating, that is). A wide variety of sports bars offer constant game viewing for those who don't have tickets, and are packed even early in the morning before games begin.

## OVERVIEW

This chapter presents a wide range of nightlife options, including bars, clubs, dance halls, and cinemas listed by geographic area of the city. There are, of course, lots of other options to be discovered in Lincoln, and some of those are listed in the Arts chapter. The legal drinking age in Nebraska is 21, as in the rest of the United States. There are also plenty of restaurants in Lincoln that are popular nightlife destinations; those are listed in the vast Restaurants chapter. This chapter focuses on listings of places where food is not the main draw. In some cases, restaurants with attached bars are mentioned, and that is because I felt they were exceptional enough to be mentioned. In those cases, the venue is listed in both the Restaurants chapter and here in the Nightlife chapter.

Most bars in Lincoln don't charge a cover, but when live music or dancing is involved, patrons can expect to pay anywhere from $3 to $20 for admission to a club or for a ticket to see a show.

Both Omaha and Lincoln are fairly spread out, and public transportation is limited. If you plan to go out drinking, be sure to use a designated driver or plan ahead by calling a taxi to get you to and from your bar or club safely. If you are a vacationer and plan to experience a lot of local nightlife, it might be wise to arrange your lodging options in the area you plan to visit most.

### THE BAR
### 1644 P St.
### (402) 474-6592

The closest bar to the University of Nebraska–Lincoln's Fraternity Row, the Bar is a popular Greek hangout. On nice evenings, the Bar's large patio is a popular hangout spot; regular drink specials and live music round out the Bar's offerings.

## *BARRYMORE'S
**124 N. 13th St.**
**(402) 476-6494**
Located in the backstage area of one of Lincoln's oldest movie theaters (now operating as the Rococo Theater), Barrymore's is old-school in the best possible way. Many of the original backstage elements survived: A wall of colored lights and levers is at the hidden alley entrance, and lots of ropes and pulleys that once operated curtains and sets still hang from the incredibly high ceiling. More recent updates to the bar brought in new furniture, vintage posters, and television sets. The crowd skews older but still very hip. The list of house cocktails features modern takes on vintage drinks, and a number of house martinis are all good. When there's a concert happening at the theater next door, listen closely and you'll be able to take in a free rehearsal performance before the show begins.

## BODEGA'S ALLEY
**1418 O St.**
**(402) 477-9550**
If you're looking for a place that'll definitely be playing the Grateful Dead or Phish on the jukebox, then Bodega's is your stop. The bar's laid-back atmosphere and friendly staff and a clientele that definitely counts as casual make this a popular stop for college-aged patrons and older.

## THE BRASS RAIL
**1436 O St.**
**(402) 474-5741**
A big hangout for Nebraska Cornhuskers football players, students in UNL's Greek system, and Husker fans on game day, The Brass Rail is one of Lincoln's most well-known downtown bars. *Playboy* magazine ranked

it as one of its top 100 college bars in 2006, and was the only Nebraska bar to make the list. Specials on food and beer are offered on Nebraska game day as well as all the other weekend nights surrounding a game. Live bands often take to the stage, and the best way to keep up to date on the bar's schedule is to follow it on Facebook, where weekly updates are the norm.

## CLIFF'S LOUNGE
**1323 O St.**
**(402) 476-7997**
Cliff's is known for its powerful cocktails and vintage vibe. In operation since 1969, though now in a new, more modern location, Cliff's kamikazes are strong stuff. The drinks come in a variety of expected flavors (banana, watermelon, raspberry) and some creative ones (bongwater, gold digger, painkiller, and roaring lion, just to name a few). The most popular one, though, has to be the Sharkwater: an icy blue concoction that doesn't even carry a hint of alcohol in the flavor. Those looking for a more traditional beverage can check out the bar's weeknight happy hours from 4 to 8 p.m., which include half-price bottled beer and $6 buckets. Other specials include $5 kamikazes from 8 p.m. to close on Tues and Thurs, and free appetizers at 5 p.m. on Fri.

## DUFFY'S
**1412 E. O St.**
**(402) 474-3543**
Lots of bars do drinks served in fishbowls, but Duffy's does them right: The bar even trademarked the name "The Home of the Fishbowl." The drinks are available in more than 20 flavors including traditional choices like rum and Coke and 7 and 7. Some of the more exotic house blends

include the Alabama Slammer, which is amaretto, sloe gin, Southern Comfort, and a special blend of pineapple and orange juices; the Angel Kiss, which includes a secret mix of booze and cranberry; Blue Bomb Pop, which tastes like its namesake; the Russian Red Snapper, which includes vodka, amaretto, peach schnapps, and cranberry; and a fishbowl version of Cliff's Lounge's Sharkwater. Duffy's has a regular docket of events: live karaoke on Thursday nights with a band on stage and singers from the audience, comedy night, and live rock shows.

## DUGGAN'S PUB
### 440 S. 11th St.
### (402) 477-3513

Duggan's Pub posts its savory lunch specials every day on its Facebook page. With daily grub like meatloaf, all-you-can-eat spaghetti, chicken corn chowder, and enchilada casserole, the place is clearly popular for more than just drinks. It's a popular place for after-work drinks; and in the evening, it's a regular venue for live music.

## EMPYREAN BREWING COMPANY
### 729 Q St.
### (402) 434-5959
### www.empyreanbrewingco.com

Empyrean is Lincoln's answer to a craft brewery. Operating since 1997, Empyrean serves its brew at two restaurants: Lazlo's and Fireworks. The brewery is named after an ancient paradise that existed at the highest point in the universe, and the beers are inspired by this idea of paradise. All the beers are unfiltered, unpasteurized, and free of preservatives and animal products. Better World Wheat, Chaco Canyon Honey Gold, and Third Stone Brown are some of the more popular standard beers, and Empyrean also produces a wide variety of seasonal beers. Every few weeks, the brewery produces something limited-run; these special beers are only served at the restaurants.

## IGUANA'S AND VODA LOUNGE
### 1426 O St.
### (402) 476-8850

Iguana's is one of Lincoln's most popular college bars and Voda—a vodka and martini lounge—operates in the same space but with an alley entrance. Voda specializes in martinis, mojitos, and other cocktails, while Iguana's is focused on wings, beer, and more classic mixed drinks. Both bars run regular specials: Voda's Friday special begins at 4 p.m. and includes free appetizers and $2 off house martinis. Iguana's most popular special has to be its 75 cent draws of Coors Light and Miller on Thursday nights.

## ✳MARZ
### 1140 O St.
### (402) 474-6279
### http://marzbarlincoln.com

Marz is probably Lincoln's swankiest bar. From the outside, it's hardly noticeable: The flat front and dark windows don't give even a hint of the lushly colored, singularly lit space. Giant colored globe lights are strategically placed throughout the two-level space, which specializes in delectable appetizers and posh cocktails. People gather around the long bar or in the half-moon shaped booths along the bar's east wall. It's a popular spot for after work as well as late night, and the food is substantial enough to work as an evening meal.

## *O'ROURKE'S
1329 O St.
(402) 435-8052

A dive bar of the finest sort, O'Rourkes is the kind of place you never get tired of. Decor is not the name of the game, though it's what you would expect: rough hewn wooden tables carved deep with initials and words, worn red vinyl booths and bar stools, cheap drinks, and friendly, if not sometimes gruff, service. A giant Chicago Cubs banner hangs from the ceiling, and Cubs fans can watch every one of the team's games at the bar while throwing back a cheap Grain Belt and eating free popcorn from the giant bag propped next to the bar. The jukebox is full of Springsteen, the pool tables are bustling, and the dart games are fierce. O'Rourkes is a certain type of classic.

## SANDY'S
1401 O St.
(402) 475-2418

If you look closely at the door of Sandy's, you'll note that the spot used to be a McDonalds. And though the door (and the floor) of the restaurant remain, nothing else is the same, particularly the beverages. Sandy's is known for its Elk Creek Water, a drink concocted from a secret recipe; the result tastes like an amped-up version of a screwdriver. Served in pitchers or in a single cup, the drink is powerful, so be aware. Sandy's is a quieter stop on weeknights; expect large crowds and the potential for a line in the evenings when UNL students are in town.

## SIDETRACK TAVERN
935 O St.
(402) 438-7776

The only time—or at least the best time— to go to Sidetrack is on a Husker Football Saturday. It'll be jam packed, and the Sidetracks Band—Paul, Joyce, and guests—will be playing Husker-inspired versions of popular songs. Yes, it's for real and, yes, it's really popular. The bar itself is basically a shrine to the team: Husker posters, prints, license plates, and a giant mural showing fans inside Memorial Stadium are the basics of the decor. The beer is cheap and the crowd is rowdy; it's the perfect pre-game primer.

## THE STARLITE LOUNGE
247 N. 8th St.
(402) 475-8826

With a retro atmosphere (down to the furniture and lighting), the Starlite Lounge carries the 1950s theme straight through to the drinks. Customers truly feel like members of the Rat Pack as they order era-specific drinks (think gin martinis with a modern, fruity twist), free appetizers on some nights and game nights, which include prizes for winning teams. The music blends modern songs with period-era tunes, and the basement location makes patrons feel like it's always cocktail hour, no matter the time of day.

## TAM O'SHANTER
105 S. 25th St.
(402) 474-2394

There aren't too many bars that have red shag carpet covered walls. The Tam O'Shanter is one that's held on to its vintage decor as well as its vintage prices. Tuesday night is karaoke night, and there's a daily drink and lunch special. A regular "crappy beer night" puts cheap beer to even cheaper prices, and the "Tammy Tuesday" offers a 6-ounce sirloin for $9.95 all day. Friendly bartenders, pleasant servers, and a fun environment make the "Tam," as it's lovingly known, a city favorite.

## THE WATERING HOLE
**1321 E. O St.**
**(402) 438-3054**
The Watering Hole might be more famous for its buffalo wings than it is for its beer; though both are cheap and quite good. The grilled wings—a house specialty—are the most popular choice, and the hole-in-the-wall atmosphere only seems to enhance the tasty bar food and beer that's always on special. The Watering Hole is also a popular lunch spot, and it's especially crowded during the noon hour on weekdays. On weeknight evenings, customers who buy a regular price pitcher of beer can get a second one for just a penny.

## ZEN'S LOUNGE
**122 N. 11th St.**
**(402) 475-2929**
A classy cocktail lounge with understated decor and comfortable seating, Zen's Lounge is one of Lincoln's classier outfits. Delicious drinks like Bloody Marys and Moscow Mules sit aside house creations like the Raspberry Truffle, guaranteeing something for everyone's taste. Exposed brick walls and multiple levels of seating, along with comfortable leather couches, make Zen's a great spot for an after-work drink, a date, or a larger group of girlfriends.

## ✳THE ZOO BAR
**136 N. 14th St.**
**(402) 435-8754**
**http://zoobar.com**
For more than 35 years, the Zoo Bar has been bringing jazz and blues of the best kind to Lincoln. Built in 1921, the Zoo is a long, narrow space that's played host to some of the best jazz and blues men of the time. Intimate tables and seating at the bar make the Zoo a nearly perfect venue for listening to live music; the crowd ranges widely in age but all have one thing in common: a love for good music.

> **i** Lincoln's Zoo Bar has become truly legendary, playing host to live music since 1973. A sampling of its roster includes Bo Diddley, Buddy Guy, The Hacienda Brothers, Magic Slim, and Koko Taylor, among many, many more.

### Gay & Lesbian
## THE Q
**226 S. 9th St.**
**(402) 475-2269**
Lincoln's answer to a gay and lesbian night club, the Q is the city's home for regular shows featuring female impersonators, amateur strip night, cabaret, and other events. Nightly drink specials add to the bar's popularity, and often weeknights don't have a cover. Friday night's beer bust brings $2 beers with 50 cent refills. The atmosphere is dark and filled with techno music and flashing lights, with clientele of all ages.

### Country & Western
## THE PLA MOR BALLROOM
**6600 W. O St.**
**(402) 475-4030**
A Lincoln standby—it's been in business for more than 80 years—the Pla Mor has always been and will likely continue to be the place to do some country dancing. Both country and big band dancing take place at the Pla Mor, and special events (singles night, Elvis night) tie in with the dancing and live music. During its heyday, the likes of Count Basie and Lawrence Welk played the Pla Mor, and though those names are long gone, the cool atmosphere and serious dancing live on.

## Cinema

**Lincoln's Mary Riepma Ross Media Arts Center** (313 N. 13th St., 402-472-9100, http://theross.org) is on the University of Nebraska–Lincoln campus and has a regular docket of first-run and art-house films. The theater has special pricing on Tues and Wed nights and plays host to a regular schedule of special events; visit the website for more information. **The Joyo Theater** (6102 Havelock Ave., 402-466-2441) is a family-owned, independent theater that specializes in cult movies (including regular screenings of the *Rocky Horror Picture Show*) and inexpensive showings of children's movies in the summer. The homemade popcorn is a popular feature. Marcus Theaters runs most of the first-run theaters in town, including the **Lincoln Grand Cinema** downtown (1101 P St., 402-441-0222), the **Marcus South Pointe Cinema** (2920 Pine Lake Rd., 402-441-0222), the **East Park Cinema** (220 N. 66th St., 402-441-0222), and the **Edgewood Cinema Lincoln** (5220 S. 56th St., 402-441-0222).

# LINCOLN SHOPPING

L incoln's selection of independently owned shops skews wide in many directions. Clothiers look to attract the young college student with a loan check to spend. Used bookstores look to those students but also to connoisseurs and collectors. Specialty food stores focus on locally produced goods and exceptional variety.

Lincoln also has a wealth of chain stores, big box stores, and national clothing and accessories retailers. Almost everything detailed here, though, is locally owned, operated, and appreciated.

## OVERVIEW

In these pages, you will find listings for a variety of shopping opportunities in Lincoln. Of course, it would be impossible to list everything, so instead this list is curated. It provides examples of the best, most unusual stores—places that stand out from the rest. Many national chain stores aren't listed here but Lincoln has them: Target, WalMart, K-Mart, and dozens of others. These stores, along with hundreds of other mall stores and big box outfits, can be found with a quick Google search.

## BOOKS

### ✳A NOVEL IDEA
**118 N. 14th St.**
**(402) 475-8663**
Padric and Eddy are usually the first to greet visitors at downtown Lincoln's A Novel Idea. They're not authors, or employees, they're the store cats. A Novel Idea is the kind of bookstore that has lots of comfy, poofy chairs; is full of secluded nooks and corners; and is simply one of the most welcoming

bookstores for devoted readers. The two floors are full of thousands of neatly organized, smartly categorized books, and the knowledgeable staff can help the inquiring mind find just about anything to read. The store offers a waiting list of sorts for regular customers: Give them the name of an author you seek and your name, and they'll enter you into their database and give a call whenever a book by your author comes in stock. A section on local authors and an area of rare and out-of-print books are worth checking out. A sale rack of discounted books almost always sits on the street in front of the store; sometimes, a full box of books marked "free" takes its place. Be sure not to let the cats out when you leave.

## BOUTIQUES

### Children's

**DIVAS & DARLINGS**
**2801 Pine Lake Rd.**
**(402) 328-0512**

Lincoln's alternative to the big box baby stores, Divas & Darlings has clothing for the stylish mom and baby, as well as loads of baby accessories, including diaper bags, bottles, nursery items, and swaddle blankets. The fully shoppable website and the store are executed in a cute but classy way, and devoted moms also become devoted shoppers once they enter the store. Divas & Darlings has a wide array of wardrobe options available for moms: dresses, jeans, shirts, pajamas, and robes included, all in contemporary designs from modern brands.

## Men's & Women's

### ✳PATTINO SHOE BOUTIQUE
**3943 S. 48th St.**
**(402) 484-4193**

Hidden in a small cluster of retail shops near Lincoln's Union College, Pattino is one of the best—if unexpected—small shops in Lincoln. Focused almost exclusively on shoes (a few small hair accessories and pieces of jewelry are the only deviation), Pattino does it right. A well-edited selection of reasonably priced shoes, sandals, and boots, depending on the season, fills the shop, and the sale rack is one that can be counted on to hold something good, as long as you can find your size. A recent perusal of the shop showed an on-trend selection of combat boots, dressy heels perfect for a night out, and casual workday pumps.

### THE POST AND NICKEL
**4728 Prescott Ave.**
**(402) 477-5300**

A standby for men's and women's clothing since 1966, The Post and Nickel is one of the most popular downtown Lincoln shopping spots. The Post and Nickel is known for a handful of things: its decor, which is mostly wood with lots of antiques; its wide selection of women's formalwear and men's suits; and its premium denim selections. The shop's main level is devoted to menswear; the second to women's wear. The shop has great sales—usually a number of sales racks fill part of one room—and all the big premium denim brands for men and women are here. Great staples like T-shirts, boots, and accessories round out the offerings.

### ✳STELLA
**101 N. 14th St.**
**(402) 476-0028**

Co-owned by three young, fashionable women, Stella is just steps from the University of Nebraska–Lincoln campus downtown and is a favorite of its female students. The store is a mix of fashion, home decor, jewelry, and vintage, but the bulk of the space is devoted to fashion. Reasonably priced dresses, tops, and leggings are at the heart of the shop, and Stella has a cute array of all of it. Fun printed items, seasonal dresses, and party dresses fly out the door, and the small shop only carries a select few items of each type in each size, so you won't see yourself walking down the street when you leave.

### SUNNY'S BOUTIQUE
**14th and P Streets**
**(402) 476-3432**

Contemporary fashion for men and women is at the heart of what Sunny's does. Located in the neighborhood around Union College, the shop carries premium denim, tops, and accessories like belts, bags, and jewelry. Women's brands include William Rast, Alternative Apparel, House of Harlow, Kensie, and Three Dots, among others. Premium denim is also available for the fashionable man, as are brands like A. Kurtz, G-Shock, and District 91. The store is hard to miss—a colorful black, pink, and yellow awning decorates the front window—and inside the store is bright and cheerful, with a well-curated selection that appeals to college students and older shoppers both.

## SPECIALTY FOODS

### ✳LICORICE INTERNATIONAL
### 803 Q St.
### (402) 488-2230

Lincoln's Licorice International has its roots in Manhattan but has a new home in the heartland. Once a New York City–based mail order business, this business was bought by a group of Lincolnites who'd been regular customers. In February 2003, Licorice International opened a brick-and-mortar shop in Nebraska's capital city. Two years after it opened, the store relocated to a larger space in Lincoln's historic Haymarket district. The shop sells more than 150 types of licorice from 12 countries. (Several varieties are gluten-free.) The shop also sells chocolates, gourmet foods, and other types of candy. Free samples of licorice abound in the shop, and it's especially popular on Husker game days.

### OPEN HARVEST
### 1618 South St.
### (402) 475-9069

Open Harvest is a locally owned, locally sourced cooperative grocery store in the heart of Lincoln's Near South neighborhood. A progressive store to say the least, Open Harvest's members own the shop, and it's dedicated to supporting local producers, fair employment practices, and supporting sustainable agriculture. You could say it's been on the "buy fresh, buy local" bandwagon for more than 30 years. Everything in the store is healthy, and most everything is produced or grown in Nebraska. None of the store's products have artificial colors, flavors, or preservatives. The staff is also trained on natural foods so questioning customers can find answers. The more than 3,300 owners make sure Open Harvest lives up to its mission, and it could easily be considered the best locally sourced food outpost in the state.

## FARMERS' MARKETS

These farmers' markets are open every Saturday May 1 to October 9. See the Omaha Shopping chapter for more information.

### OMAHA FARMERS' MARKET
### 8 a.m. to 12:30 p.m.
### In the Old Market district

### HAYMARKET FARMERS' MARKET
### 8 a.m. to 12:30 p.m.
### In the historic Haymarket district, Lincoln

# LINCOLN ATTRACTIONS

Nebraska's capital city has lots to see and do—the capitol building itself being at the top of many lists. The beautiful building is one of only a few skyscraper capitols in the United States, and the interior is decadently outfitted in some amazing art and design.

Lincoln has some notable museums that get high rankings: an impressive collection of more than 3,000 quilts, the world's largest collection of historical roller skates, and a children's museum that consistently ranks in the nation's top 10.

Outdoor attractions focus on some of the area's unique environments and aren't just dedicated to sharing what Nebraska's outdoors offer, but work to preserve it, too.

Wineries and breweries offer a singular and tasty experience, along with memorable special events.

Some of the more specific types of attractions are listed in separate chapters. For instance, art museums and galleries are in the Arts chapter, while other museums related to history and culture are here. Most outdoor spots are in the Parks & Recreation chapter. And places that kids will love can be found in the Kidstuff chapter.

## Price Code

The following price code has been included to give you a rough idea of what one regular adult ticket or entrance fee will cost at each of the following places. If the fees or costs associated with a particular activity or place are varied, no price has been given and you should use the contact information provided to find out the details.

$.................Less than $5
$$ ....................$5 to $10
$$$ .................. $10 to $20
$$$$ ........... More than $20

## MONUMENTS & HISTORIC PLACES

✳NEBRASKA STATE CAPITOL    FREE
1445 K St.
(402) 471-0448
www.capitol.org
Nebraska's state capitol is one of the most singular in the country. Designed by architect Bertram Goodhue in 1920, it was the first vernacular state capitol; today it's one of only three "skyscraper" capitols. (The other two: Florida and Louisiana.) The capitol was the result of a nationwide design contest run by the state of Nebraska. Goodhue's building is the third to live on the site and it was the nation's first to depart radically from the traditional design of state capitols and instead use a tower.

Workers built the capitol in four phases over a 10-year period—1922 to 1932—and the building cost just under $10 million dollars. Goodhue personally selected artists to decorate the interior of the capitol, and these renderings are truly stunning. Tile and mosaic designs by Hildreth Meiere show the natural and social history of Nebraska's Native American heritage and pioneer settlers. Hartley B. Alexander helped the artists with thematic design, inscription, and symbolism; and sculptor Lee Lawrie created work for the vast space. The art in the dome of the capitol, especially, is captivating; the capitol tour guides are always friendly and able to answer any question about the stunning mosaic.

The outside of the capitol is designed as a cross within a square, resulting in four outdoor courtyards. The tower itself is 400 feet tall and is topped with a bronze statue. The building is decorated with frieze carvings showing the 3,000-year history of democracy and government. Tours are available; call for details.

## MUSEUMS

### INTERNATIONAL QUILT STUDY CENTER $$
33rd and Holdredge Street on the UNL East Campus
(402) 472-6549
www.quiltstudy.org

Quilts—which many people have already put in the category of "boring"—are hardly that at Lincoln's International Quilt Study Center. Instead of being mere craft, these quilts, part of the largest publicly held quilt collection in the world, take on the role of art. More than 3,000 quilts make up the vast collection. Dating from the early 1700s

to the present, quilt artists from more than 25 countries have work in the museum's archives. While the historic quilts dive into history and culture, contemporary quilts show the viewer how this medium has truly expanded into the modern world with the use of new materials and technology.

In the last 10 years, the center moved to a new location, on the University of Nebraska–Lincoln's East Campus. The building, a $12 million project designed by New York–based Robert A. M. Stern Architects, cuts a stunning visage. Made of swirling panes of glass, the center's reception hall has a curtain of glass and is popular for private events, receptions, and weddings. A large-scale sculpture by artist Linda Fleming greets visitors outside the museum; it was specially commissioned for the space and is surrounded by gardens that visitors can stroll through before or after taking in the exhibitions.

### NATIONAL MUSEUM OF ROLLER SKATING FREE
4730 South St.
(402) 483-7551
www.rollerskatingmuseum.com

The National Museum of Roller Skating is one of Nebraska's truly unique attractions. It's basically a shrine to the sport of skating on wheels. The museum collects, preserves, and displays just about everything that has to do with the history of roller skating. The museum's permanent collection has the largest collection of historical roller skates anywhere in the world. The earliest pair dates to 1819. It also holds medals, trophies, photos, artwork, films, videos, costumes, roller skating memorabilia, and a library of more than 1,500 books about roller skating. The museum has a selection of special exhibitions that include items from its permanent collection; these focus on inline skating, artistic skating, roller hockey, speed skating, and roller derby.

## UNIVERSITY OF NEBRASKA STATE MUSEUM OF NATURAL HISTORY AND MUELLER PLANETARIUM $$

**South of 14th and Vine Streets, in Morrill Hall on the UNL City Campus**
**(402) 472-2642**
**www.museum.unl.edu**

The University of Nebraska State Museum is on the UNL campus and is a museum experience that no kid should miss, for the sheer fact that every kid will love it.

The first floor of the museum has lots of hands-on exhibits that let kids do things like touch a magpie, hear a rattlesnake, and visit the Discovery room, full of hands-on natural wonders. The Hall of Nebraska wildlife introduces visitors to all the plants and animals that live in Nebraska. There's also a special Charles Darwin exhibit. The main floor of the museum is devoted to paleontology in Nebraska, and includes the main attraction: a collection of ancient elephants. Elephant Hall includes mounts of modern and ancient elephants, including one of the world's largest mammoth skeletons (I still remember seeing this in person as a child and being totally in awe). Visitors can touch a two-billion-year-old fossil and play paleontologist with interactive exhibits. The Mueller Planetarium gives regular shows; check the museum's website for show times and costs. The museum's third floor explores the heritage of Native American and African cultures. Colorful costumes, artifacts, and pottery show African and Native American people's contributions to world culture and the United States. The Cooper Gallery plays host to a number of traveling special exhibitions.

## WINERIES & BREWERIES

### EMPYREAN BREWING COMPANY
**729 Q St.**
**(402) 434-5959**
**www.empyreanbrewingco.com**

A brewpub and bar with tasty food, Lazlo's Brewery is home to Lincoln's Empyrean Brewing Company; the restaurant was Nebraska's first brewpub. The restaurant's popularity has steadily grown—it's almost always packed—and Lazlo's has expanded beyond its original site into a large restaurant with a bar, two dining rooms, and several areas for private or large parties. It's a standard stop in Lincoln's Haymarket district. Empyrean Ales are still brewed on-site by hand in small batches and are unfiltered, unpasteurized, preservative-free, and free of any animal products.

Empyrean brews a wide variety of beers as well as some seasonal special brews, available at different times of year. The Better World Wheat uses chamomile flowers, the Chaco Canyon Honey Gold includes a bit of Nebraska-made honey, and the Third Stone Brown Ale won the 2006 World Beer Cup for Extra Special or Strong Bitter beer. All of the beers are available by the glass at Lazlo's, in a 6- or 12-pack, and in a 5- or 15.5-gallon keg. Seasonal beers include Fallen Angel Sweet Stout, available in the late winter; an Oktoberfest selection; and the Lazlos Limited selection, which is only available in the restaurant.

Free brewery tours happen on the first non-holiday Monday of each month and begin at 7 p.m. Empyrean's head brewer leads the tours and guests get five beer samples on the tour, which is limited each month to the first 150 people to arrive at the restaurant. Cask Night takes place in conjunction with the tours from 4 p.m. to close, and the restaurant serves a special beer during the event.

Other Empyrean events include the Empyrean Beer Quest; a monthly dinner featuring home brew tastings created by local brewers; and Brewed Awakening, a five-course meal with beer pairings. Advance ticket purchase is required for both events.

### ✳JAMES ARTHUR VINEYARDS $
**2001 W. Raymond Rd., Raymond**
**(402) 783-5255**
**www.jamesarthurvineyards.com**
James Arthur Vineyards isn't just one of the best vineyards in eastern Nebraska, it's one of the state's best. Nebraska isn't exactly the next Napa Valley, but its wineries continually bring home medals from wine contests, and James Arthur is no exception. Located just outside Lincoln, James Arthur is a popular destination for wine tastings. Guests can choose to try four or six wines during a typical tasting; samples are one ounce per taste and the tasting fee includes a complimentary wine glass. A four-wine tasting is $4, a six-glass tasting is $5.

Though wine tastings are the main activity on the schedule at James Arthur, the vineyard also serves a wide variety of Nebraska foods and invites tourists to eat on its porch; in its tasting room; or out on the vineyard grounds, where tables, chairs, and swings are scattered about, making for many romantic, secluded spots.

Food is available a la carte or in a basket, which is designed to feed at least two people. Bread, meat, fish, cheese, and chocolate—all made by local vendors—are available. Visitors can enjoy their food with a bottle of wine, which the vineyard will open as long as the bottle is consumed on-site. During cooler months, guests are invited to enjoy their vittles in front of the large stone fireplace.

The winery doesn't offer a regular tour, but an observation deck overlooks the production area and is always open. Visitors are also encouraged to walk the trails through the winery grounds and take in the grapes first-hand.

## HUNTING

### CAN-HUNT SHOOTING PRESERVE $$$$
**Bee, 19 miles West of Lincoln**
**(402) 588-2448**
**www.organichunting.com**
Hunting and fishing are ubiquitous activities in Nebraska, and Can-Hunt, just outside of Lincoln, has more than 1,000 acres of private hunting land. The main attraction here, though, is that the land is full of native Nebraska grass, trees, and stubble fields and operates completely chemical-free. It's the only organization of its kind in eastern Nebraska, and hunters can take their pick of guided hunts for pheasant, quail, Chukar or other upland birds, deer, or ducks and waterfowl.

All the birds on-site are raised locally and fed organically. The preserve grows all the crops on-site and is certified organic: It has a document trail for more than three years showing it rotates crops properly, stores the feed properly, and grows it without chemicals. The grain is also of a quality that's fit for human consumption. The chemical-free rules result in a healthier environment and better tasting meat.

Can-Hunt also trains hunting dogs—it's done so for more than 30 years—and will sell or lease a dog to a group of hunters. Hunters can choose from a variety of packages and the preserve operates from September 1 to March 31 every year. Farmed birds are available year-round, as are live birds to go, dried pheasant pelts, and dog services.

A number of types of hunts are available, as are custom hunts upon request. Prices vary widely depending on what the hunters are harvesting, the length of the hunt, and the number of hunters. Waterfowl permits and hunting stamps are not available on-site, and hunters must get a permit from the Nebraska Game and Parks Division before arrival.

## FAMILY ATTRACTIONS

### LINCOLN'S CHILDREN'S ZOO          $$
**27th and B Streets**
**(402) 475-6741**
**www.lincolnzoo.org**
Learning is at the heart of almost everything that goes on at the Lincoln Children's Zoo. The zoo sits on nine acres of land in central Lincoln and features all types of animals. Kids can feed a goat, ride a pony, touch a butterfly, or get up close and personal with seals, gibbons, and the zookeepers that care for the animals. Keeper talks take place twice daily during the summer season and keepers talk at different locations about different animals on a rotating basis; each day the schedule is posted at the zoo entrance.

Interactive exhibits are everywhere at the zoo. The Firsthand Farm lets kid touch and interact with farm animals, while Laura's Butterfly Pavilion, renovated in 2008, lets kids try and get an insect to land on their finger. Critter Encounter lets visitors interact with one specific animal each hour and past animals have included a guinea pig and a dove.

Older kids can interact with insects in the Bug Buddies exhibit or learn about archeology at the Stego's Big Dig excavation site.

An on-site cafe and picnic facilities are available, as is a zoo gift shop.

### LINCOLN SALINE WETLAND NATURE CENTER          FREE
**Junction of I-80 and US 77**
**(402) 476-2729**
**http://lincoln.ne.gov/city/parks/parksfacilities/wetlands/wetlandsnc.htm**
The Lincoln Saline Wetland Nature Center is best experienced via its walking trail, which takes hikers straight through the dense ecosystem, one of the most productive in the world. Of Nebraska's four types of wetlands, the Saline Wetlands are the most unique and also the most endangered. Floodplains off the Salt Creek, Little Salt Creek, and Rock Creek drainages have saline soil, which means they're tolerant to salt, and therefore grow specific plants not seen in other areas.

During the last century, more than 200 species of birds have been documented in the wetlands, and as a result, wildlife and bird viewing are popular here; the area's two wetland ponds get lots of waterfowl visitors. The wetlands, which were restored in the early 1990s, include the Old Wyoming Bridge, which visitors can walk across and experience. The bridge is one of the last of its kind. Dating from the mid-1800s, it has bowstring arches.

The wetlands are open to the public; casual clothing, including pants, socks, and comfortable shoes are recommended. Visitors are advised to stay on marked trails and within designated areas to generally be considerate of the endangered environment. Open fires and all types of grills are prohibited in the wetlands, as is collecting plants and wildlife from the site.

## SPRING CREEK PRAIRIE AUDUBON CENTER $

**11700 SW 100th St., 3 miles south of Denton on 98th Street**
**(402) 797-2301**
**www.springcreekprairie.org**

Spring Creek Prairie Audubon Center offers a slice of scenic Nebraska prairie and some of the best wildlife viewing opportunities in the area. Preserving Nebraska's native tallgrass prairie is at the heart of the organization's mission; and at the education center, visitors can learn why this preservation is important in the first place. Since less than 2 percent of the world's tallgrass prairie remains intact, the distinctive nature of Nebraska's native landscape can't be seen in many other locations. The building itself maximizes solar exposure and is energy efficient and green, using straw-bale construction and low-flow toilets.

Hundreds of species of animals and insects live on the land, including birds, deer, butterflies, and dragonflies. Plants, too, thrive here, and more than 350 species reside at Spring Creek. Wildflowers, distinctive trees and shrubs, moss, wetland plants, and milkweed all thrive on the site.

Many buildings on the Center's land are available for rental use. Deposits and advance reservations are required. A regular schedule of classes, as well as an updated roster of wildlife and birds currently in view, are available at the Center's website. Admission is free on Tuesday.

# LINCOLN ARTS

**A** thriving visual arts scene, growing live music scene, and popular live theater houses make Lincoln a center for the arts in Nebraska.

The Sheldon Art Museum—one of the best venues in the state for visual arts is home to one of the best collections of 20th-century American art in the country—also puts on Lincoln's Jazz in June, which attracts thousands of revelers each week to eat, drink, and dance under the evening summer sun.

Downtown Lincoln's independent galleries participate in a popular First Friday art walk event that draws hundreds of people into art spaces each month.

The Lied Center for Performing Arts, on the UNL campus, provides a regularly rotating schedule of live music and theater, with the added bonus of free tickets available to UNL students. The Mary Riepma Ross Media Arts Center, also on the UNL campus, is the city's best independent movie house.

## LIED CENTER FOR PERFORMING ARTS
**12th and R Streets on the UNL campus**
**(402) 472-4747**
**http://liedcenter.org**
Located on the University of Nebraska–Lincoln campus, the Lied Center for Performing Arts offers a wide array of both performing arts and university-sponsored events that are frequented by theater lovers, Lincolnites, and UNL students alike. Broadway musicals, classical music, modern and classical dance, jazz, country, and long-running lecture series are all part of the Lied's ongoing programming.

The Lied Center opened in 1990 and immediately started presenting national and international artists of all kinds to its diverse Lincoln audience. Arts Across Nebraska, one of its largest programs, works with communities around the state to tour shows to areas of the state where no local theater exists. The Lied Center gives free tickets to university students, and reasonably priced tickets for the general public. A complete list of upcoming shows is available on the Lied website.

## *MARY RIEPMA ROSS MEDIA ARTS CENTER
**313 N. 13th St.**
**(402) 472-5353**
**http://theross.org**
The art of film is at the heart of all the programming at the Mary Riepma Ross Media Arts Center, on the University of Nebraska–Lincoln campus. The theater shows a mix of American independent work, experimental film, classic foreign cinema, and documentaries. Invited scholars and visiting lecturers augment that content, and an on-site research library is open to students and film scholars. The two screens at the Ross have a regularly rotating slate of movies—check its

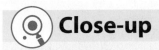

# Close-up

## ☀First Fridays

On the first Friday of every month, Lincoln becomes an art lover's paradise. The city's First Friday Artwalks have been going on for more than 20 years. Downtown Lincoln has more than 50 galleries, and most of them participate in the event. All of the galleries are within walking distance of one another, so art lovers can walk around downtown, from the 9th Street Haymarket area, to the UNL campus, up toward 14th Street and see new shows opening while enjoying wine and appetizers. The events begin each month at 5 p.m. and the last galleries usually close at 10 p.m.

Highlights include the **Sheldon Museum of Art,** which opens right at 5 p.m. and shows selections from its permanent collection along with challenging traveling exhibitions; recent shows have included a permanent collection exhibition featuring only the work of female artists, a traveling exhibition of women pop artists, and a contemporary Cuban art exhibition featuring work from the permanent collection along with pieces loaned to the museum by local Lincoln collectors. The space is beautiful to visit any time of year, and oftentimes the First Friday will include a gallery talk, an auditorium lecture, or a free film screening. Another must-stop are the **galleries at the Parish studios,** on the corner of 14th and O, where hundreds of people pack into a recently renovated second floor space to check out work from some of the area's most up-and-coming young artists. Two galleries—Tugboat and Project Room—anchor the space, which is also filled with a hair salon, artist's studios, and artsy businesses that sell things like T-shirts and posters. The vibe is hip and the crowd is vibrant; this is definitely a must-stop on First Friday. Lincoln's **Haymarket District** is another must-stop area. It's home to a handful of great, locally owned spots that show a diverse array of functional pottery, paintings, sculpture, jewelry, and art of just about any other medium one can imagine. Modern Arts Midwest is worth a stop; it's another space that's packed on First Friday.

The **Downtown Lincoln Association** has a convenient gallery walk map, which is handed out at galleries around downtown. Art lovers can also request one directly by calling (402) 434-6900. The Association also has a First Friday Artwalk passport program that lets participants enter into a drawing for a monthly grand prize. Players have to have their passport stamped at five galleries each month to be entered to win. Links to all this information, as well as a complete gallery listing, are available at http://downtownlincoln.org/firstfriday.

Omaha is working to get into the First Friday game itself. In 2010, the gallery owners at **The New BLK,** an Old Market space, created a Facebook page and website devoted solely to listing and promoting First Friday exhibitions. The Old Market is chockablock with galleries, many of which have First Friday openings. The movement in Omaha is still in its formative stages, but with the city's thriving arts scene and its many gallery lovers, it seems poised to take off in coming years. Learn more at www.omahafirstfriday.com/ and www.facebook.com/Omahafirstfriday.

website for the most up-to-date content—and the space is also home to the Van Brundt welcome center and the university's Film and New Media program. Classroom labs and editing suites are full of state-of-the-art technology used by UNL students.

**i** The Lincoln Arts Council maintains a website full of resources about the arts in the capital city. Performances of all kinds, visual art exhibitions, theater shows, and concerts are all listed on its comprehensive calendar. Visit http://artscene.org to get clued in.

## MUSIC

### THE BOURBON THEATRE
**1415 O St.**
**(402) 477-4776**
**http://bourbontheatre.com**
The recently renovated Bourbon Theater is poised to be Lincoln's brightest venue for live music. Not far from the University of Nebraska–Lincoln campus and nestled in between tons of popular bars and restaurants, the Bourbon has events almost every night of the week: one or two bands a night, movies, talks, and other special events.

Each fall, the Bourbon is the main venue for the Lincoln Calling music festival, which continues to grow and include more bands, more venues, and more people checking out the music. For information on the event, visit http://lincolncalling.com.

### JAZZ IN JUNE
**Sheldon Museum of Art**
**12th and R Streets on the UNL campus**
**http://jazzinjune.com**
A Lincoln tradition for 20 seasons, Jazz in June is Lincoln's summer music mainstay.

Thousands of people gather each Tuesday in June to listen to live jazz outside the Sheldon Museum of Art. The Phillip Johnson–designed building makes an artistic backdrop for local and national jazz and blues acts.

Concertgoers gather early for the free 7 p.m. concerts, and a festive atmosphere surrounds the shows, which often have a theme; the 2010 concerts had a "Havana Nights" theme, and Cuban sounds and Latin jazz were both on the menu. Usually, the series theme ties in with an exhibition in the adjacent Sheldon Museum.

The concert organizers make sure the event is green, and recycle bins are everywhere on the lawn. Drinks and food are available through a number of vendors, and the Jazz in June Marketplace starts before the concert begins, at 5 p.m. Local vendors sell their wares on the street next to the green space. Because UNL is a dry campus, alcohol is not sold or allowed on site. Dogs are not permitted unless they are service animals.

## ART MUSEUMS & GALLERIES

**✳SHELDON ART MUSEUM**
**12th and R Streets**
**(402) 472-2461**
**www.sheldonartmuseum.org**
The Sheldon Art Museum regularly presents some of the most challenging and thought-provoking exhibitions in the state. The museum's permanent collection comprises the Sheldon Art Association collection, founded in 1888, and the University of Nebraska collection, which began in 1929. More than 12,000 works make the permanent collection, and, at any time, a good portion of the art is on view. More than 30 sculptures by some of the most famous names in the game—Claes Oldenberg and Coosje van

Bruggen, David Smith, and Richard Serra included—live in the Sheldon Sculpture Garden, which is open year-round. The Sheldon opens approximately 20 exhibitions a year, and almost all of its events are free, as is museum admission.

The building itself is designed by famed architect Phillip Johnson and stands as one of the state's true architectural gems. A series of graceful arches and slender columns mark this distinctive structure, which is unmistakably recognizable. Inside, a travertine façade is dotted with large concave discs covered in gold leaf. The museum's great hall is one of the grandest spaces in Nebraska.

## LUX CENTER FOR THE ARTS
**2601 N. 48th St.**
**(402) 466-8692**
**http://luxcenter.org**
Arts education and exhibition space make the Lux Center one of Lincoln's most multi-use art venues. Art classes in practically any topic a burgeoning artist could imagine are offered at the Lux; the classes serve all ages and skill levels and are often really reasonably priced.

The Lux exhibition spaces are often full of work from local artists, though exhibitions from regional and national artists happen here, too. Lux also has an artist-in-residence program that aims to help burgeoning artists launch their careers.

The Gladys M. Lux collection is the center's permanent collection of work, and is named after its founder, who was a professor at Nebraska Wesleyan University. The collection includes more than 1,600 dolls, more than 450 prints, and a number of glass paperweights. Selections from the print collection are always on display in one of the Lux galleries.

# LINCOLN PARKS & RECREATION

Lincoln locals have a growing interest in the outdoors. The city continues to improve offerings in terms of local parks, hiking and biking trails, and other opportunities for residents and visitors to encounter and interact with nature. Lincoln has a high amount of parks per capita. Nature parks let families discover the outdoors and interact with the state's flora and fauna as well as some of the creatures that live here.

Nebraska is home to several golf courses routinely listed among the nation's top 100. Some of these courses are located outside the metro area, but many are in Lincoln. There may be a fee to use the public courses, but it's well worth it.

If you prefer to watch instead of play, Lincoln has options for lots of spectator sports, and this chapter includes information on spectator sports such as baseball and football.

## Price Code

The following price code has been included to give you a rough idea of what a regular ticket or entrance fee will cost to each of the following places. If the fees or costs associated with a particular activity are varied, no price has been given and you should use the contact information provided to find out details. More specific pricing and discount information is included in the listings, where available. Every effort has been made to include a variety of activities across a broad spectrum of prices to cater to every possible budget. For the golf listings, no price code has been included because it proved impossible to cover the range of greens fees and membership fees for every golf club. Instead, check the individual golf club listings for information about cost and membership options.

$..................Less than $5
$$ .....................$5 to $10
$$$ .................. $10 to $20
$$$$ ........... More than $20

## PARKS

**PIONEERS PARK NATURE CENTER FREE**
**3201 S. Coddington Ave.**
**(402) 441-7895**
Hiking trails, a wildlife sanctuary, and close to 700 acres of native Nebraska tallgrass prairie make Pioneers Park Nature Center one of the best outdoor spots in Lincoln. The park's eight miles of trail wind in and out of a variety of habitats and offer some great wildlife viewing opportunities. Two on-site interpretive buildings have hands-on small animal exhibits; a play area where kids can dig, build, and climb; prairie and herb gardens; and programming that includes nature camp, school activities, and classes for all ages. One of the park's newest attractions is the Hudson Cabin, which moved to the park in 2010. The cabin, built by Thomas Jefferson in 1863, was one of the grandest houses of its day in Lincoln. The house is open on special occasions and by request; the park itself is open year-round.

## RICHMAN'S RUN DOG PARK
**On the grounds of Holmes Lake**
**70th and Van Dorn Streets**

A stream for dogs to lap and play in runs through Richman's Run Dog Park, located in the city's Holmes Lake Park, and is one of the main features that draws dogs and their owners to the spot. Part of the 12 acres are fenced off for small dogs; the rest of the space is open to dogs of any size. Picnic tables and shade trees make the park a pleasant spot for pet owners, too.

## GOLF COURSES

### FIRETHORN GOLF CLUB
**9301 Firethorn Ln.**
**(402) 483-6099**

Two words that will get a golf fanatic's attention: Pete Dye. Dye, one of the world's foremost golf designers, shaped this patch of east Lincoln wilderness into the city's best 18 holes. And the news about Firethorn Golf Club gets even better for visitors willing to put in the effort—and put up the money—to get a tee time at this private course. In interviews, Dye has said that holes No. 11 to 14 at Firethorn might be the best four-hole stretch he's designed during his storied career. Its members call Firethorn a "prairie-style" course to emphasize how Dye used most of the land's natural contours and vegetation to create this golfing masterpiece. The fairways were created with minimal earthwork. The greens are guarded by all sorts of trouble and require an assortment of quality approach shots from anyone who wants to make par. And the rough—well, let's just say that you best stay far, far, away from the thick and tangled native grasses that have ruined many a good round. The course has challenged

some of the country's best young golfers when it hosted the US Women's Amateur, college national championships, and other top amateur events. Firethorn does have a less-illustrious 9-hole West Course (not designed by Dye) that is now run by Nebraska golf legend Jim White and open to the public. But the advice here is to pester the Firethorn assistant pros enough that they give you a tee time on the original 18. You won't regret it.

### HIGHLANDS GOLF COURSE
**5501 NW 12th St.**
**(402) 441-6081**

Highlands Golf Course may be the best bargain 18 holes in Lincoln. Highlands is one of the four courses owned by the city of Lincoln. There's much debate among the city's golfers about the best layout. Some prefer Pioneers Golf Course, an old course in west Lincoln. Others prefer Holmes Park in central Lincoln. (Few argue for the other city-owned course, Mahoney Park.) But Highlands, in northwest Lincoln, gets the nod here because of its interesting, links-style layout and its convenient location near I-80 as well as the city airport. Measuring 7,000 yards from the back tees, Highlands could be an extremely challenging test of golf if it were a private course whose members didn't mind tall and gnarled native rough. As it is, that native rough is mowed to a medium height that allows a bogey golfer to post a good score on a calm afternoon. Be advised, though: Like the links courses across the Atlantic Ocean, Highlands shows its teeth when the wind blows. And the wind blows quite often at this course, which sits atop a treeless Nebraska plain. No matter the wind, Highlands is surprisingly picturesque. And it's shockingly affordable. Like all of the

Lincoln-owned courses, you can play here for a song.

## ✳WILDERNESS RIDGE GOLF CLUB
**1800 Wilderness Woods Place**
**(402) 434-5106**
Wilderness Ridge is a public 18-hole golf course that immediately started to outclass Lincoln's older, city-owned courses when it opened in 2001. The University of Nebraska golf teams call Wilderness Ridge home. The 7,100-yard layout is nicely manicured and features 22 lakes, 4 waterfalls, and an ever-present stream that gobbles up golf balls as it winds its way through the course. While the course isn't shockingly distinctive, the award-winning clubhouse is—it's a 40,000-square-foot log lodge that includes a large restaurant, a bar, and a pro shop. The course has hosted numerous collegiate golf events as well as US Open qualifiers. It also features a 9-hole executive course good for children or beginning golfers. Wilderness Ridge is a tad more expensive than most of the city's other public courses. You'll need to decide whether you want to part with the extra dough for the well-manicured Wilderness Ridge.

## YOGA STUDIO

**HAYMARKET PILATES AND YOGA**
**  CENTER**
**311 N. 8th St., Ste. 210**
**(402) 477-5101**
**www.pilatesyogalincoln.com**
Haymarket Pilates and Yoga Center owner Cary Twomey is a New York City transplant who has been teaching yoga for more than 20 years. Her devoted students go to Haymarket Pilates and Yoga to practice as part of a group class or at a private pilates or

yoga session. Twomey spent her 10 years in New York as a professional dancer and has taught Kinesiology, Anatomy, Dance Injury Prevention, Modern Dance, Ballet, and Yoga at the Universities of Nebraska–Lincoln and The New School in New York. The studio specializes in rehabilitative yoga, ayurvedic nutrition and therapy, meditation, and a wide variety of workshops focusing on any of the above. Group classes all start at a reasonable $15, cards for a number of classes at a discounted rate are also available, and cost per private session or workshop varies depending on the event.

## SPECTATOR SPORTS

**LINCOLN SALTDOGS BASEBALL**
**Haymarket Park**
**403 Line Drive Circle**
**(402) 474-2255**
**www.saltdogs.com**
The Saltdogs are an independent minor league baseball team that shares Lincoln's Haymarket Park with the Cornhusker baseball team. The Saltdogs, like all independent teams, are not affiliated with a major-league club. That means that Saltdogs players have no clear path to the big leagues—these players are playing because they love baseball, not because of any future multimillion dollar contract. The skill on the field isn't bad, Haymarket Park is charming, and the best part about the Saltdogs game is the cost—you'll be hard-pressed to find a cheaper option in Lincoln.

**NEBRASKA CORNHUSKERS BASEBALL**
**Haymarket Park**
**403 Line Drive Circle**
**(402) 474-2255**
**www.huskers.com**

Outside of the College World Series, the state's best baseball experience might just be a Saturday afternoon inside Lincoln's Haymarket Park. The Nebraska baseball team, after decades of irrelevance, built a Midwestern baseball power in the past decade. They opened a pristine little ballpark across the street from Memorial Stadium. And they started to win baseball games, success that culminated in several trips to Omaha's College World Series. Joba Chamberlin, now a Yankees reliever, suited up for Nebraska. So did Brian Duensing, Alex Gordon, and several other Huskers who now play in the major leagues. The Husker baseball team, like all of the university's sports teams, is moving to the Big Ten conference in 2011, and it remains to be seen how the move will affect the program. But this much is certain: A slice of Valentino's pizza, some sunshine, and a seat along the third-base line during a Cornhusker baseball game makes for a great spring day.

## ✳NEBRASKA CORNHUSKERS FOOTBALL
**Memorial Stadium**
**10th Street and Stadium Drive**
**(402) 472-2263**
**www.huskers.com**
Husker football is pretty much religion from one end of the state to the other. On fall Saturdays, Lincoln's Memorial Stadium is packed with more than 80,000 red-clad fanatics, many of whom made the bumper-to-bumper drive down I-80 from Omaha. In fact, Memorial Stadium has been sold out every game since Nov. 2, 1962, a sellout streak that long ago set a national record for its longevity and seems unlikely to end anytime soon.

The Huskers dominated the 1990s under legendary coach Tom Osborne, winning three national titles and sending dozens of players to the NFL. Nebraska has struggled to return to college football's summit since then, but the fervor of the fan base hasn't diminished at all.

If you like sports at all, attending a Nebraska football game on a crisp fall Saturday needs to be on your bucket list.

The tailgating starts early in the morning in the bars and parking lots around the University of Nebraska–Lincoln campus. If you tell a cluster of Big Red fans that you are a newcomer you'll likely be holding a complimentary beer and just-grilled burger in seconds.

And there is absolutely not a sporting moment in this country like the moment when you emerge from a Memorial Stadium tunnel and get your first glimpse of 80,000 people, forming a proverbial Sea of Red, awaiting kickoff as one.

Things have changed—ticket prices are edging toward the triple digits, and the Huskers haven't won the national title in 13 years, and Nebraska just ended decades-long rivalries with Oklahoma, Missouri, and Kansas when it joined the Big Ten conference.

But that moment—your first glimpse of Nebraska's state religion—has remained, and it's why you should consider shelling out whatever it costs so you can see it for yourself.

# LINCOLN KIDSTUFF

Lincoln's Children's Museum is one of the top rated in the nation, and it's at the forefront of the city's family-friendly activities. A wide array of fun stuff that's also educational is what made the LCM one of *Parents* magazine's top 20 children's museums in the nation.

Lots of the attractions mentioned in other chapters of this book are also great for families.

Be sure to check out both the Attractions chapter and the Parks & Recreation chapter, which contain more listings that will probably be of interest to families with kids of all ages. Plenty of outdoor activities, recreation spots, and sporting events are listed in those sections. The handful of listings in this chapter are all child-centric activities that kids are sure to enjoy. The price code below gives you an idea of what entrance fees (if any) and costs will be like to attend or visit any of these places.

## Price Code

The following price code has been included to give you a rough idea of what a regular ticket or entrance fee will cost at each of the following places. If the fees or costs associated with a particular activity or place are varied, no price has been given and you should use the contact information provided to find out the details. More specific pricing and discount information is included in the listings, where available. Every effort has been made to include a variety of activities across a broad spectrum of prices to cater to every possible budget.

$....................Less than $5
$$ .....................$5 to $10
$$$ .................. $10 to $20
$$$$ ........... More than $20

## MUSEUMS & ATTRACTIONS

**AGER PLAY CENTER**        $$$
**1300 S. 27th St.**
**(402) 441-6792**
**http://lincoln.ne.gov/city/parks/
programs/info/ager.htm**
Little kids will find an exciting day of play at the Ager Play Center, a facility designed exclusively for small kids and toddlers. Ager restricts entry to kids smaller than 48 inches tall or under 3 years old. Two levels of play areas include a maze of tunnels, lots of slides, three pools full of balls, and a number of outdoor activities. A toddler area for kids younger than 2 is enclosed and gated for safety, and includes a smaller-scale ball pool, play equipment, and toys built the right size for toddler hands and bodies. Outside food is not allowed in the center, and kids are required to wear socks during play. Ager

offers classes on arts and crafts, music, and for special needs children; visit the center's website for cost information and a full schedule.

**CHAMPION'S FUN CENTER** $$
**1555 Yolande Ave.**
**(402) 434-7066**
**championsfuncenter.com**
Champion's Fun Center is Lincoln's answer to an amusement park. The family-owned business has all the rides and attractions one would expect, on a scale that can easily fill a whole day. Miniature golf, batting cages, go-karts, more than 75 arcade games, and regular and cosmic bowling are all there. The four-story free fall ride is singular to Champion's, as is the water wars game, where dueling teams use a giant boomerang to shoot a water balloon at the opposing team's target.

**✻LINCOLN CHILDREN'S MUSEUM** $$
**1420 P St.**
**(402) 477-4000**
**www.lincolnchildrensmuseum.org**
Ranked in the top 20 children's museums in the nation by *Parents* magazine, the Lincoln Children's Museum is all about hands-on exhibits and encouraging a child to imagine. Exhibits let kids pretend to be a firefighter, police officer, or other public servant; climb a three-story tall apple tree; perform on a real stage with costumes and lights; or fly a full-size Cessna airplane located inside the museum. A prairie dog town that lets kids crawl around and a section devoted to tiny Nebraska Cornhuskers fans remind visitors they're in Nebraska. The hands-on water exhibit has a number of boats, a turning water wheel, and a kid-size dock.

## Appendix

# LIVING HERE

In this section we feature specific information for residents or those planning to relocate here. Topics include real estate, education, health care, and much more.

# RELOCATION

Congratulations on your choice to move to Nebraska! Lincoln and Omaha are the state's fastest growing cities. Omaha is Nebraska's largest city and the 40th largest city in the United States. Its metro area population is close to 850,000. Land speculators founded Omaha in 1854 and it officially became a city in 1897. It's named after an Indian tribe and its name means "those going against the wind or current."

Many move to Omaha to work at one of its many Fortune 500 or 1,000 companies, including Berkshire Hathaway, Union Pacific Railroad, ConAgra Foods, Peter Kiewit Sons Construction, Mutual of Omaha insurance, TD Ameritrade, West Corporation, Werner Enterprises, or Valmont Industries. Omaha is a leader in the telecommunications and information services industries, with 1,000 companies employing more than 50,000 people. When you call to make a hotel reservation, there's a good chance you're calling Omaha: It's home to Hyatt, Marriott, Radisson, and Omni reservation centers.

Lincoln is Nebraska's state capital. The city has many big city amenities but offers a small town, affordable quality of life. It's home to the University of Nebraska–Lincoln, and the campus draws visiting scholars and students to the city, both of whom add to Lincoln's rich cultural fabric.

Both Lincoln and Omaha offer steady economies, low crime rates, costs of living that rank below the national averages, and low unemployment.

Lincoln and Omaha are both exciting, entertaining places to live with much to offer. Nebraskans are lucky enough to enjoy all four seasons: warm summers; temperate springs; cool falls; and cold, snowy (yet beautiful!) winters. West Omaha and South Lincoln are ever expanding neighborhoods and many people choose to live in these booming suburbs. Both cities have also enjoyed redevelopment in their downtown regions, like new living options such as condos and apartments and an ever growing list of entertainment and eating venues.

## OVERVIEW

This chapter is divided into several sections designed to orient you when you first arrive in Omaha or Lincoln, as well as help you begin your search for a home, whether it be a house, apartment, or condominium. Listings for the respective Chambers of Commerce and Convention and Visitor's Bureaus will give you a basic set of information about the city.

Contact information for the local association of realtors can start you on the way to buying a home. Also included are the phone numbers and websites for utilities hookups, including water, gas, and electric, so that once you do move, you will be able to get easily connected. Descriptions are also included for Omaha and Lincoln's neighborhoods.

Information about vehicle licensing, applying for a local driver's license, voter registration, and libraries is also here for your review.

## INFORMATION FOR NEWCOMERS

### Chambers of Commerce & Visitors Bureaus

Omaha and Lincoln both have active visitors bureaus and chambers of commerce. The chambers are focused on business development and drawing major conventions to the respective Nebraska metro areas. Visitor's centers are great stops for newly relocated residents and their worth in sheer information alone—brochures, city and statewide guides included—make them worth a stop. The Omaha and Lincoln chambers both have active groups for professionals, including dedicated groups for young professionals, so newly relocated business people can make connections with other career-driven types in their new home.

### *Omaha*
**OMAHA CHAMBER OF COMMERCE**
**1301 Harney St.**
**(402) 346-5000**
**http://omahachamber.org**

**OMAHA VISITOR INFORMATION CENTER**
**10th and Farnam Streets**
**(402) 444-4660**
**http://visitomaha.com**

### *Lincoln*
**LINCOLN CHAMBER OF COMMERCE**
**1135 M St., Ste. 200**
**(402) 436-2350**
**http://lcoc.com**

**LINCOLN VISITOR'S CENTER**
**7th and P Streets**
**(402) 434-5348**
**http://lincoln.org**

## METRO GOVERNMENT

The cities of Omaha and Lincoln both have extensive, mostly user-friendly websites divided into loads of sections, many of which have information that a new resident—or a new homeowner, for that matter—would probably want to know. The city of Omaha divides its site into sections for visitors, residents, and businesses. The city of Lincoln's website isn't quite as succinct, but the information is there in both cases: information on snow removal, taxes, employment, pet licensing, city council news and trash pickup, among many other topics.

**CITY OF OMAHA**
**Omaha-Douglas Civic Center**
**1819 Farnam St.**
**www.cityofomaha.org**

**CITY OF LINCOLN**
**555 S. 10th St.**
**(402) 441-7511**

## DEPARTMENT OF MOTOR VEHICLES

The Nebraska DMV has several locations throughout Omaha and Lincoln. License applicants must present two forms of identification for address verification. Licenses are then mailed within 7 working days, and applicants receive a temporary ID good for 30 days while the plastic card is being processed. New Nebraskans who want to drive in the state must get a license within 30 days of establishing residence. Licenses are valid for five years and are renewable up to 90 days before the expiration date if a driver is 21 years old or older.

**Omaha Locations:**

Omaha office locations are open from Mon to Fri from 8 a.m. to 4 p.m.

- 4208 S. 50th St., (402) 595-2039
- 7414 N. 30th St., (402) 595-2040
- 5730 S. 144th St., (402) 595-2424
- 2910 N. 108th St., (402) 595-3106

**Lincoln Locations:**

- 500 W. O St., (402) 471-2823 (open Mon to Fri, 7:30 a.m to 4 p.m.)
- 625 N. 46th St., (402) 471-3008 (open Mon to Fri, 7:30 a.m. to 4:30 p.m., no testing).

## Vehicle Registration

The Nebraska DMV requires proof of registration and motor vehicle insurance when registering a vehicle. For newly purchased vehicles, also bring the sales receipt and a signed title. Different counties have different registration requirements and fees; contact the offices directly for the most up-to-date information.

**DOUGLAS COUNTY TREASURER**
**1819 Farnam St., Civic Center, Omaha**
**(402) 444-7103**

**LANCASTER COUNTY TREASURER**
**625 N. 46th St., Lincoln,**
**(402) 441-7497**

## VOTER REGISTRATION

Nebraska residents can register to vote in the state the same day they become a resident. Registration is required to be eligible to vote; the only exception is for a person who has recently moved to the state and wants to vote using a Presidential-only ballot. To be eligible to vote in Nebraska, residents must be 18 years old, live in Nebraska, and not be a convicted felon, or if a convicted felon, be two years past the completion of the sentence, including parole. Registration is available at any county clerk or election commissioner's office during normal business hours. Residents may also register by mail, and applications are available at many places throughout the state; a complete list of locations is also available online. Those registering for the first time by mail must provide a copy of a current photo ID showing the same name and residence address provided on the application. Nebraska also allows people to register to vote when they apply for a driver's license at the Nebraska DMV.

Nebraska voters can choose from one of three party affiliations: Democratic, Republican, or Libertarian. Those who do not declare a party affiliation are not allowed to vote in primary elections, and at other elections only receive a non-partisan ballot.

Residents must re-register when they change their name, address, or party affiliation. Those who complete the forms will receive a voter registration card in the mail once the registration is complete.

For information on early voting and polling places or online forms, visit the **Nebraska Secretary of State** website, www.sos.ne.gov or call (888) 727-0007.

## LIBRARIES

Omaha and Lincoln both have an extensive web of public libraries located all over both cities, making a visit convenient no matter what part of town you decide to call home. Getting a library card is simple. In Omaha, any resident of Douglas County can apply online for a card and it will be mailed to the provided address. Applicants automatically get temporary online privileges for two weeks to review the library's catalog. Those who provide an email address will receive their card number and temporary pin within two to three days to gain online access.

In Lincoln, applicants need to provide a photo ID in person to get a card. In both cities, library cards are free and never expire.

Lincoln and Omaha libraries have a free reciprocal card program. The card must be applied for in person; a sticker is applied on the owner's library card to allow them to use the card in both cities. The reciprocal program is also available for Council Bluffs, Iowa, residents and libraries.

## Libraries in Omaha

**ABRAHAMS**
5111 N. 90th St., Omaha
(402) 444-6284

**BENSON**
6105 Binney St., Omaha
(402) 444-4846

**FLORENCE**
2920 Bondesson St., Omaha
(402) 444-5299

**JOHNSON (ELKHORN)**
13214 Westwood Ln., Elkhorn
(402) 444-4848

**SADDLEBROOK**
14850 Laurel Ave., Omaha
(402) 884-7473

**SORENSEN**
4808 Cass St., Omaha
(402) 444-5274

**SOUTH**
2808 Q St., Omaha
(402) 444-4850

**SWANSON**
9101 W. Dodge Rd., Omaha
(402) 444-4852

**WASHINGTON**
2868 Ames Ave., Omaha
(402) 444-4849

**W. DALE CLARK (MAIN LIBRARY)**
215 S. 15th St., Omaha
(402) 444-4800

**WILLA CATHER**
1905 S. 44th St., Omaha
(402) 444-4851

## Libraries in Lincoln

**BENNETT MARTIN PUBLIC LIBRARY**
136 S. 14th St., Lincoln
(402) 441-8500

**BESS DODSON WALT**
6701 S. 14th St., Lincoln
(402) 441-4460

**CHARLES H. GERE BRANCH**
2400 S. 56th St., Lincoln
(402) 441-8560

**DAN A. WILLIAMS**
5000 Mike Scholl St., Lincoln
(in the Arnold Elementary School; enter from West Cuming Street)
(402) 441-8580

**LOREN COREY EISELEY**
1530 Superior St., Lincoln
(402) 441-4250

**SOUTH**
2675 South St., Lincoln
(402) 441-8570

**VICTOR E. ANDERSON**
3635 Touzalin Ave., Lincoln
(402) 441-8540

## Utility Contact List

**Omaha Public Power District (OPPD)**
444 S. 16th St., Omaha
(402) 536-4131
http://oppd.com

**Metropolitan Utilities District (MUD)**
1723 Harney St., Omaha
(402) 504-7000
http://mudomaha.com

**Lincoln Electric Services (LES)**
1040 O St., Lincoln
(402) 475-4211
http://les.com

**Cox Communications, phone and cable in Omaha**
11505 W. Dodge Rd., Omaha
(402) 933-3000
www.cox.com

**Time Warner Cable, Lincoln**
5400 S. 16th St., Lincoln
(402) 421-0300
www.timewarnercable.com

## RENTING & APARTMENTS

Omaha and Lincoln are both listed on the major rental sites like Apartment Guide (www.apartmentguide.com), Apartment Finder (www.apartmentfinder.com) and apartments.com. These sites list long- and short-term rentals as well as more traditional rental opportunities for apartments in all parts of the city and of all sizes.

Craigslist for Omaha and Lincoln is a good place to seek out real estate, as is Lincoln's college newspaper, the *Daily Nebraskan*, which regularly lists apartments for rent and roommate openings. Both the *Omaha World-Herald* and the *Lincoln Journal Star* also have extensive listings of properties for rent.

## REALTORS

Buying a home is a daunting process, and finding the right realtor is a huge part of the experience. The Nebraska Association of Realtors (nebraskarealtors.com) is a good place to start. Founded in 1908, NAR now has more than 1 million members all across Nebraska who work as salespeople, property managers, appraisers, counselors, and other real estate professionals. Members of the group are held to a professional code of conduct and a standard of practice code. Most of the major real estate agencies in the state have agents who are members of this growing group.

## RETIREMENT

### Services & Organizations

**AARP OMAHA INFORMATION CENTER
1941 S. 42nd St.
(402) 398-9568**
The American Association of Retired People has been around for more than 50 years and has locations in all 50 states, Nebraska included. It's the country's biggest organization of its kind—directed at people 50 years and older—and gives its members discounts, information on health and wellness, and more. Contact the local office or visit the AARP website for membership information.

**EASTERN NEBRASKA OFFICE ON AGING
4223 Center St., Omaha
(402) 444-6444
www.enoa.org**
The Eastern Nebraska Office on Aging provides a wealth of services for seniors based in Omaha. The agency works to inform its

constituents about already existing services, and to make sure they're taking advantage of all the available programs in their area. Programs include nutrition, case management, employment counseling, volunteer opportunities, and community services, among others. ENOA also has a monthly senior-focused newspaper called *New Horizons*. The ENOA is also an Omaha-based provider of Meals on Wheels, which delivers more than 850 meals a day to seniors and others around the metro area. Weekend meals are available and delivered on Thursday or Friday.

### TABITHA HEALTH CARE SERVICES
**4720 Randolph St., Lincoln**
**(402) 486-8520**
**http://tabitha.org**
Care for older adults—including adult day services, home care, hospice, meals on wheels. and rehabilitation—are at the core of what Tabitha does for Lincoln residents. It's headquarters are in the city, and it has a number of regional locations around the state. Tabitha's website goes into vast detail about all its various programs, and includes information on how to take advantage of them.

## EDUCATION & CHILD CARE

### Colleges & Universities

### UNIVERSITY OF NEBRASKA–LINCOLN
**1400 R St.**
**(402) 472-7211**
**http://unl.edu**
In the heart of downtown Lincoln, the University of Nebraska–Lincoln is also at the heart of higher education in Nebraska. It's the NU system's flagship campus, and it's also home to the University of Nebraska

press, the Sheldon Museum of Art, and the majority of the state's college students. UNL established the world's first undergraduate psychology laboratory. It was the first institution west of the Mississippi to award doctoral degrees—the first in 1896 in physics. Ecology as a course of study began at UNL.

Today, UNL is one of the nation's leading teaching institutions, and is a leader in research, with grant-funded projects in the sciences and humanities. *Prairie Schooner* literary magazine comes out of the University of Nebraska Press, and Sheldon is home to one of the world's most significant collections of 20th century American art.

In 2010, UNL became part of the Big Ten Conference, which raises the school academically—the Big Ten Conference is recognized for world-class academic institutions—and athletically, as the Nebraska Cornhuskers will now play a slew of new competition.

UNL offers more than 150 undergraduate majors and close to 300 graduate programs; more than 400 student organizations make campus life broad and active for students no matter their interest.

### UNIVERSITY OF NEBRASKA AT OMAHA
**6001 Dodge St., Omaha**
**(402) 554-2393**
**http://unomaha.edu**
The University of Nebraska at Omaha was once a commuter campus offering mostly night school to people with full time jobs; it's evolved into a thriving campus with an active student body, on-campus housing, and a wide variety of majors, including the renowned Peter Kiewit Institute. UNO offers 125 bachelor's degree programs, 40 masters programs, and five doctoral degree

programs. The PKI includes two colleges: Information Science and Technology and the College of Engineering and Technology. Since its establishment in 1996, the PKI vaulted UNO into a groundbreaking institution for information technology and engineering education.

UNO has four new on-campus housing options for students. Maverick Village includes 95 four-bedroom apartments with full bathrooms and kitchens; University Village offers apartment-style living for close to 600 students on campus; Scott Village, near the PKI, is a ten-building complex of apartment-style living that opened in late 2010; and Scott Residence Hall, also opened in late 2010, provides easy access to the PKI as well as the new Aksarben Village neighborhood. The complex includes mostly four-bedroom suite-style living with shared bathrooms in each unit.

## UNIVERSITY OF NEBRASKA MEDICAL CENTER
**600 S. 42nd St., Omaha**
**(402) 559-6468**
**http://unmc.edu**
The University of Nebraska Medical Center offers education to prospective health care providers and also acts as a busy hospital in the city center. It's Nebraska's only public academic health sciences institution, and has six colleges and two institutes with more than 3,000 students. UNMC is nationally recognized for its rural health medicine program and its primary care program; other top programs include nursing, physician's assistant, physical therapy, and pharmacy.

## CREIGHTON UNIVERSITY
**2500 California Plaza, Omaha**
**(402) 280-2703**
**creighton.edu**
Known locally for its powerful basketball team, its bluejay mascot, and it's abundance of law graduates, Creighton University is Omaha's only Jesuit Catholic university. Creighton is one of the top ranked small private colleges in the nation. More than 7,000 students go to school at Creighton, which has a 130-acre campus adjacent to the North Downtown Omaha business district. More than 50 undergraduate programs and 20 graduate programs are among the school's academic offerings, with the bulk of Creighton students pursuing a degree in its arts and sciences college. Other schools include business, law, medicine, dentistry, nursing, pharmacy, and a graduate school.

Creighton has 14 Division I intercollegiate sports teams that compete in the Missouri Valley Conference; tickets are widely available.

## UNION COLLEGE
**3800 S. 48th St., Lincoln**
**(402) 486-2600**
**http://ucollege.edu**
Centrally located in Lincoln's scenic College View neighborhood, Union College is a Seventh-day Adventist campus with programs focused on the health care industry. The 50-acre campus is tree lined and beautiful, and a small business district across the street includes many popular student hangouts. Its programs are top rated: In 2008, 100 percent of its pre-med graduates got accepted to medical school. Volunteerism and service learning is a focus, and many of Union's students practice medicine abroad for those in need while also working as

student missionaries. Union offers a bachelors and associates degree, as well as a Master of Physician Assistant Studies; the school offers more than 50 majors and minors in close to 30 areas.

## Technical Schools

### CLARKSON COLLEGE
**101 S. 42nd St., Omaha**
**(402) 552-3100**
**http://clarksoncollege.edu**
Health care is the primary focus of study at Omaha's Clarkson College. It offers undergraduate and graduate degrees in nursing, allied health, health care business management, and professional development—health care is the focus no matter what.

### COLLEGE OF ST. MARY
**7000 Mercy Rd., Omaha**
**(402) 399-2405**
**www.csm.edu**
The College of St. Mary is the only Catholic all-women college in the five-state area. The school offers associate, bachelors, and masters degrees in nursing, education, engineering business, and a number of other topics. The environment is centered on faith, and the roughly 1,000 students at CSM can attend daily services and are required to take theology as part of the college's core requirements. Prayer, retreats, and faith are a regular and important part of campus life. Some singular programs include a nursing program aimed specifically at creating bilingual English-Spanish speaking graduates, a masters program focused on strengthening women's leadership qualities, and the region's only four-year paralegal studies program approved by the American Bar Association.

### GRACE UNIVERSITY
**1311 S. 9th St., Omaha**
**(402) 449-2800**
**www.graceuniversity.edu**
A prayer group belonging to ten Mennonite ministers eventually grew what today is known as Grace University. A four-year college with undergraduate offerings that include business, networking, Christian ministry, communications, pastoral ministries, and a number of other subjects, Grace ultimately has a focus on biblically integrated education. On the Grace campus, the primary focus is on the Bible, with the humanities and sciences serving a secondary role. Bachelor-level students must pursue a double major in Biblical studies along with the field of their choice. The campus, located south of downtown Omaha just a few blocks from the Old Market area, covers six city blocks. During the past five years, Grace invested more than $11 million in campus renovation, remodeling, and upgrading, bringing the school to a new level. Four dormitories, modern classrooms, a campus library, and numerous other offerings make Grace an up-to-date facility.

### METROPOLITAN COMMUNITY COLLEGE
**Various campuses around Omaha**
**(402) 457-2400**
**www.mccneb.edu**
With seven campuses spread all over Omaha, Metropolitan Community College has a strong presence in the city. Its two-year programs offer degrees and certificates in more than 100 areas, including business, computers, culinary arts and management, horticulture, industrial technologies, and nursing and health.

Its culinary arts program is one of its fastest growing and most popular and has its own state-of-the-art building in North Omaha. The program offers a popular restaurant that operates during the school year where students produce gourmet cuisine for a fraction of most of Omaha's other fine dining experiences.

Metro is supported with taxpayer money from Douglas county and a number of other surrounding counties; it began in 1974 when the Nebraska State Legislature consolidated a number of smaller community colleges. Class size at metro is small—around 15 students—and total enrollment is close to 50,000. Visit the Metro website for a full list of campus locations and programs offered at each site.

## NEBRASKA WESLEYAN UNIVERSITY
**Campuses in Lincoln and Omaha**
**(402) 827-3555**
Liberal arts with a Christian bent is the goal of Nebraska Wesleyan University and its been doing it right since its founding in 1887. It's considered one of the strongest schools of its kind in the Midwest, and its more than 1,600 undergraduates can choose from more than 50 majors, 40 minors, and nearly 20 pre-professional programs. Loads of student organizations, a number of Greek chapters, and buzzing study abroad and service learning programs make Wesleyan a popular choice.

## SOUTHEAST COMMUNITY COLLEGE
**www.southeast.edu**
Southeast Community College has four campuses in and around Lincoln: two in the city proper, one in Beatrice, and one in Milford. Its two-year programs serve students in 15 Nebraska counties and offer more than 50

programs of study. Most of its programs are technical, and include trades like auto mechanic, welding, and HVAC. Academic transfer programs are gaining popularity at Southeast: Students begin with a course of study at the two-year institution and transfer to a four-year college.

## Public Schools

### OMAHA PUBLIC SCHOOLS
**3215 Cuming St., Omaha**
**(402) 557-2222**
**www.ops.org**
With close to 50,000 students of all ages, the Omaha Public Schools are the largest school system in Nebraska and have a focus on diversity. The system is divided into 11 wards as part of the Douglas-Sarpy County Learning Community, which the Nebraska Legislature created to make sure underprivileged kids in the Omaha area get the same opportunities and education. The group distributes property tax dollars to help poor districts and also created a diversity plan for the district. The first council took office in 2010.

OPS test scores are above the national average for large school districts, and more than 60 percent of OPS graduates go on to college or other post-secondary schools. OPS has Nebraska's largest special education program for students with disabilities, and a number of magnet schools offer special instruction in math, performing arts, languages, communications, economics, technology, university preparation, science, engineering, and international studies. The programs are so popular that students who are selected consider it a special opportunity. Gifted and talented students can enroll in advanced curriculum on all the core subjects as well as a series of special topics. OPS athletic programs produced a number of professional athletes and Olympic gold medalists.

## LINCOLN PUBLIC SCHOOLS
**5901 O St., Lincoln**
**(402) 436-1000**
**www.lps.org**
The state's second largest school district, Lincoln Public Schools has been growing quickly over the past few years in number of students, academic offerings, and school standards. LPS high schools offer a number of singular programs, including an International Baccalaureate Program; a number of school-to-career programs; alternative classrooms; and programs specially focused on science, humanities, information technology, and other entrepreneurship opportunities.

Younger students can take advantage of all-day kindergarten, and LPS also has an English language learner program as well as a gifted program and a special education program.

The district has a strong focus on both the core subjects and the humanities; a strong athletic program and after school activities round out LPS offerings.

## Private Schools

### BROWNELL TALBOT
**400 N. Happy Hollow Blvd., Omaha**
**(402) 556-3772**
**www.brownell.edu**
Brownell Talbot is Nebraska's only independently run private school. Located in historic Dundee in midtown Omaha, the school enrolls students beginning in pre-school all the way through grade 12. The school has been operating in the city for close to 150 years; the independent nature of the school lets it set its own curriculum, much of which is college preparatory. A board of trustees

governs the school and the parents of its students pay a premium for their kids to attend.

The school recently did a survey of its parents to find out why they sent their children to Brownell, and the overwhelming answer was for college preparatory class work. Other reasons included being able to participate in a number of different activities, knowing students in all grade levels, and developing a strong work ethic as a student. Half of Brownell instructors have advanced degrees and more than half have been teachers for ten years or more.

### OMAHA CATHOLIC ARCHDIOCESE
**100 N. 62nd St., Omaha**
**(402) 558-3100**
**http://schools.archomaha.org**
More than 20,000 students in Omaha attend Catholic Schools. Omaha's Catholic Schools, managed by the Omaha Catholic Archdiocese, include 58 elementary schools and 18 secondary schools. The schools have high records of standardized test scores and the heart of their curriculum is based on religion. Catholic school students have high graduation rates as well as college attendance rates after graduation. More than 1,500 teachers work at the schools; nearly half of them have advanced degrees.

## Child Care & Preschools

### BEANSTALK CHILD CARE AND ACADEMY
**6518 N. 46th Ave., Omaha**
**(402) 932-5909**
**www.beanstalkcc.com**
Located in the heart of North Omaha, Beanstalk Child Care and Academy offers a family-oriented environment with care available 24 hours a day, transportation to schools and an open minded, multi-ethnic

environment. Flexible payment options make Beanstalk a good choice for people of all socioeconomic means.

**CHILDREN'S DISCOVERY CHILD CARE CENTER AND PRESCHOOL**
14210 Arbor St., Omaha
(402) 333-5032
http://cdcomaha.net

The teachers at Children's Discovery Center are all trained in early childhood development, making this a popular destination for parents. Teachers are also all certified in CPR and first aid, ensuring a safe environment. Programs are designed for specific age groups of children, beginning with infants and going through school-aged children. Focus areas include development of social skills, play, art, science, reading, and music. Exercise, crafts, and quiet time are built into the schedule, too. School-age kids take field trips during the summer months. A large outdoor playground is always open when weather permits. The center offers breakfast, lunch, and a snack daily, as well as food for infants—the center will provide food or the parent can bring food from home.

**CHILD'S PLAY CHILD CARE CENTER**
820 Mayfield Ave., Omaha
(402) 556-4028

Child's play has been operating in Omaha for more than 20 years and has consistently been one of the city's top child care and pre-school centers in the city. A large outdoor play area, transportation to area schools, year-round programs, and field trips on a regular basis make the center popular, and its programs cater to kids from 18 months to 12 years old.

Kids at Child's Play are divided into different areas by age: Toddlers have a discovery room for kids 2½ to 3½, the rainbow room for kids 3½ to 4½, the crayon room for kids age 4½ to 6, and school age for kids 6 to 12. The center serves breakfast, lunch, and an afternoon snack daily. Activities in each area strive to meet the needs of different aged children.

## HEALTH & WELLNESS

### Health Departments

The **Douglas County Health Department** is responsible for the health and safety of those living in Omaha, while the **Lancaster County Health Department** is responsible for Lincoln. Both organizations run similar programs and have extensive websites full of information. Staff runs programs concerning environmental safety, healthy life choices, safe food, wellness for children and adults, disease control, and much more. Comprehensive websites offer a wealth of information, including information on seasonal vaccines, health and wellness tips for the holiday months and summer safety, health and wellness education, and information on food safety rankings at restaurants throughout the respective cities.

**DOUGLAS COUNTY HEALTH DEPARTMENT**
Omaha/Douglas Civic Center
1819 Farnam St., Omaha
(402) 444-7471
www.douglascountyhealth.com

**LANCASTER COUNTY HEALTH DEPARTMENT**
3140 N St, Lincoln
(402) 441-8000
http://lincoln.ne.gov/city/health

## Hospitals

**BERGAN MERCY MEDICAL CENTER**
**7500 Mercy Rd., Omaha**
**(402) 398-6060**
The emphasis at Bergan includes maternity, orthopedics, cardiovascular services, oncology, surgery, emergency and hospice, and senior health care. In 2007, Bergan began a more than $100 million expansion project that includes a new birthing center, a cancer center, a diagnostic center, and additional parking. The project will lead to 84 new beds for medical and surgical use and a larger neonatal intensive care unit.

**BRYAN LGH HEALTH SYSTEM**
**www.bryanlgh.com**
Bryan LGH Health Systems serves Lincoln residents with two locations, one on each side of the city. Bryan offers a comprehensive list of health care services, state of the art facilities, more than 4,000 staff members, and several clinics around town. The hospital is known for its programs in cardiology, orthopedics, trauma, neuroscience, mental health, women's health, and oncology. **Bryan LGH Medical Center West:** 2300 S. 16th St., Lincoln, (402) 475-1011; **Bryan LGH Medical Center East:** 1600 S. 48th St., Lincoln, (402) 489-0200.

**CREIGHTON UNIVERSITY MEDICAL CENTER**
**601 N. 30th St., Omaha**
**(402) 449-4000**
**http://Creightonhospital.com**
Centrally located and close to downtown, the Creighton University Medical Center was founded in 1870 by the sisters of mercy. A newly opened center for digestive disorders opened in spring 2010. The hospital also offers a wide variety of basic services with an academic bent, and Creighton University medical students work in all the hospital's programs.

## Alegent Health System

**Alegent** is easily the largest health care system in the Omaha area, and it's ranked among the nation's top 100 health care systems by *Modern Healthcare* magazine. It currently has about $315 million dedicated to renovation and expansion projects throughout the five hospitals it runs in the Omaha metro area; most will conclude sometime in 2011. Aside from the five hospitals, Alegent also runs the Lasting Hope Recovery Center and the wellness centers at Lakeside and Immanuel.

It's website, www.alegent.com, has extensive information on all five hospitals. The website also lists addresses and phone numbers for Alegent's clinics and quick care facilities, which blanket Omaha and the surrounding communities. Some clinics are located inside Hy-Vee supermarkets in Omaha. The website also offers a handy calculation tool that lets patients figure out the cost of just about every common procedure.

**IMMANUEL MEDICAL CENTER**
**6901 N. 72nd St., Omaha**
**(402) 572-2121**
Immanuel is located in Northwest Omaha and serves the area's growing population. An $88 million renovation project scheduled to end in 2011 will expand an existing

diagnostic center and bring a new cancer center facility to the hospital. All of the hospital's rooms will be private, the emergency department will be larger, and a new treatment center for mental health patients will be the main treatment facility in the city. About a fourth of that budget will go toward a new brain and spine injury center.

## JENNIE EDMUNDSON HOSPITAL
933 E. Pierce St., Council Bluffs, IA
(712) 396-6000

A nondenominational group of women called the Faith Band started the hospital in 1886 as a five-room cottage in Council Bluffs. Today, the hospital serves eastern Council Bluffs as well as the surrounding areas. Recent renovations include a state-of-the-art cardiac catheterization lab and a 3,500 square foot expansion.

## LAKESIDE HOSPITAL
16901 Lakeside Hills Ct., Omaha
(402) 717-8000

Serving the exploding population of far West Omaha, Lakeside will conclude a $52 million renovation in 2011 that will bring more operating rooms and privatize all hospital rooms. The hospital will also broaden its maternity services, adding more labor and postpartum rooms along with an additional newborn ICU area. Lakeside also has a cancer center, a breast health center, and many in- and outpatient services.

## MERCY HOSPITAL
2800 Mercy Dr., Council Bluffs, IA
(712) 328-5000

Founded in the late 1880s, Mercy Hospital is across the river from Downtown Omaha in Council Bluffs, Iowa. It's a basic service hospital.

## METHODIST HEALTH SYSTEM
www.bestcare.org

Methodist Health System includes facilities throughout Nebraska and Western Iowa; the three hospitals include one specifically for women. Its website, bestcare.org, includes information on the hospitals and Methodist physicians' clinics, as well as the Carepricer tool, which allows patients to get an estimate on treatment costs.

## METHODIST HOSPITAL AND CHILDREN'S HOSPITAL
8303 Dodge St., Omaha
(402) 354-4000

Located on the busy corner of 84th and Dodge Streets, Methodist Hospital is a long-time Omaha landmark. The hospital offers a full range of educational, medical, and surgical services. Its long history in the city includes a number of health care innovations: It was the first hospital in Omaha to offer lithotripsy treatment for kidney stones, and it was also the first to have an outpatient surgery center. Children's Hospital shares the Methodist Hospital campus. It focuses on pediatric services of all kinds, including more than 30 pediatric clinics that each have a specialty. A newborn intensive care unit has close to 50 beds and offers comprehensive heart services for infants.

## METHODIST WOMEN'S HOSPITAL
707 N. 190th Plaza, Omaha
(402) 815-4000

Opened in 2010, Methodist Women's Hospital is the first health care center in the city dedicated almost entirely to women's health. Gynecologic services, pregnancy care, bone health, menopause services, and a host of other outpatient services are at the heart of the center's work. The Methodist

Physicians Clinic Women's Center is located near the hospital and offers counseling, sexual health services, physical therapy, and skin renewal. Though the hospital focuses mostly on women, it also offers services for men, though inpatient services are only offered to women. Men can receive emergency services, a variety of outpatient treatments, and procedures and outpatient lab services.

## MIDLANDS COMMUNITY HOSPITAL
**11111 S. 84th St., Papillion**
**(402) 593-3000**
Midlands specializes in sleep and breathing disorders, cardiovascular disorders, and other general inpatient and emergency treatment. A recently completed expansion expanded the emergency room and ICU areas, made the patient rooms private, and created a new office building for practicing physicians.

## ST. ELIZABETH REGIONAL MEDICAL CENTER
**555 S. 70th St., Lincoln**
**(402) 219-8000**
St. Elizabeth's is Lincoln's first hospital. Nearly 300 beds and an environment that encourages spirituality and healing has helped it continue to be one of the city's two main venues for health care. St. Elizabeth's has a network of family practice and internal medicine clinics, including three stand alone urgent care centers and two physical therapy clinics. Home care and hospice services, a nationally recognized burn center, a cardiovascular rehabilitation center, radiology and angiography services, and a wellness center are all on the docket at St. E's. The hospital is currently undergoing a three-year expansion plan that includes a full remodel and expansion in the West tower.

## UNIVERSITY OF NEBRASKA MEDICAL CENTER
**4350 Dewey Ave., Omaha**
**(800) 922-0000**
Recent renovations have further improved the offerings of Midtown Omaha's University of Nebraska Medical Center, which in the late 1990s merged with what used to be Clarkson Hospital. The hospital is the teaching center for the University of Nebraska; current expansion projects include the Bellevue Medical Center, which opened in early 2010, and the Clinical Cancer Center, part of a west Omaha medical center.

The Med Center is one of the most groundbreaking research hospitals in Omaha, and was the first in the Midwest to offer Intensity Modulated Therapy, which improves radiation targeting of cancerous tumors without harming nearby tissue. It's also groundbreaking in terms of prostate cancer treatment using ultrasound technology. It runs a once-a-month clinic for diagnosis and treatment of cancer and other tumors. In 2009, the hospital opened a special wing and treatment program for patients who have epilepsy, Alzheimer's, Parkinson's, and dementia.

Other Med Center facilities on the central Omaha campus include a clinical cancer center, a diabetes center, an outpatient center, the Lied Transplant Center, and the Nebraska Orthopaedic Hospital.

## VETERAN'S HOSPITAL
**4101 Woolworth Ave., Omaha**
**(402) 346-8800**
Omaha's VA Hospital offers care and service to hundreds of thousands of veterans each year in Nebraska, Western Iowa, Kansas, and Missouri. A community-based outpatient clinic in Lincoln offers services there, while

the Omaha center offers specialty care, in- and outpatient services, and primary care. For more information, visit Nebraska.va.gov.

## Urgent Care

### MIDWEST MINOR MEDICAL
www.midwestminormedical.com
Open seven days a week for emergency service, Midwest Minor Medical has three locations around Omaha: two centrally located and one in West Omaha. It was the city's first urgent care center and has been operating for close to 30 years. The centers treat minor injuries and illnesses and perform worker's compensation care, routine medical services, and regulatory treatments for businesses. MMM staffs full-time, professional doctors and is a more cost-effective option when compared with an emergency room visit. MMM accepts most insurance programs, and for those who do not have insurance, the clinic offers a 20 percent "quick pay" discount. **Locations:** 8610 W. Dodge Rd., Omaha, (402) 827-6511; 5310 S. 84th St., Omaha (402) 827-6510; 13518 W. Center Rd., Omaha (402) 827-6502.

### URGENT CARE OF OMAHA
http://uccomaha.com
With three locations in Omaha and hours every day of the week, Urgent Care of Omaha is another option for quick care in the city. The company has future plans to open more clinics in the area in the next few years. Urgent Care will take patients of all ages, including infants, children, teens, adults, and seniors. The clinic accepts most insurance plans, as well as worker's compensation cases, Medicare, and Medicaid. Urgent care will also perform pre-employment physicals, DOT physicals, drug screens, tetanus shots, and other treatment of work-related injuries.

**Locations:** 3830 N. 167th Ct., Omaha, (402) 965-4000; 8814 Maple St., Omaha, (402) 343-0095; 17650 Wright St., Omaha, (402) 334-2300.

## Alternative Medicine

**Heartland Healing** (www.heartlandhealing .com) is the best resource to alternative medicine, natural healing, natural therapies, and healing arts in both Lincoln and Omaha. The comprehensive website lists a plethora of businesses focusing in a wide range of services, including but not limited to aromatherapy, zero balancing, chakra cleaning, nutrition assistance, stress management techniques, hypnosis, homeopathy, hypnotherapy, chronic fatigue syndrome, intuitive healing, and a variety of other alternative healing therapies. Look for these in the listings in the online practitioner database.

They publish a free bi-monthly magazine available in more than 250 locations around Omaha and Lincoln. It includes stories about holistic centers in the region but is also a resource for the *Healing Arts Directory*, which lets businesses publish a free listing about their services. Heartland Healing also has a partnership with the *Omaha Reader* newspaper, and each week it publishes articles about the healing arts in Nebraska.

## Chiropractors

### BODY IN MOTION
4638 Dodge St., Omaha
(402) 341-2216
http://omahaspine.com
A two-time winner of a Best of Omaha award, Body in Motion treats a number of disorders using Chiropractic techniques, low level laser therapy, pain neutralization technique, rocktape, drop technique, and

Graston Technique. (Their website has details on most of the lesser-known treatments.) The techniques are for the relief of a variety of disorders, including back and neck pain, carpel tunnel syndrome, headaches, stress, sports injuries, and a variety of other aches, pains, and ailments.

## MOSIER/TIMPERLEY CHIROPRACTIC CLINIC
**4645 Normal Blvd., Lincoln**
**(402) 483-6633**
**www.mtchiro.net**
One of the area's oldest and largest chiropractic centers, Mosier/Temperley's practitioners have more than 100 years of combined experience in the field. The treatment begins with an adjustment and then continues from there, with treatment specific to the patient's disorder and needs. The office also offers nutrition consultation, braces and exercise balls, custom orthotics, laser therapy, and numerous treatments for sports and brain injury.

### Oriental Medicine/Acupuncture

## HEART AND HEALTH SOLUTIONS
**2120 S. 56th St., Lincoln**
**(402) 488-6100**
Lincoln's Heart and Health Solutions specializes in acupuncture; they offer full medical acupuncture options for their patients. Medical acupuncture is performed by a doctor trained and licensed in Western medicine that has also been trained in acupuncture. Heart and Health's approach may help patients with digestive disorders, gastritis, spastic colon and other digestive disorders; respiratory disorders; headache and other neurologic disorders; female problems; and problems related to tension, stress, and emotional conditions. Because the practitioners

at HHS are board certified MDs, the office visit to the clinic may be covered by insurance as would other specialist doctors.

## OMAHA HEALING ARTS CENTER
**1216 Howard St., Omaha**
**(402) 345-5078**
**www.omahahealingarts.com**
When you walk in the door of the Om Center, in Omaha's Old Market, you feel calm. The center—which has played host to numerous visits from Tibetan Monks—has an air of serenity about it, from the warm wood floor to the scented candles to the knowledgeable, friendly staff. The Om Center offers a number of holistic health treatments, including massage therapy, acupuncture, yoga, Ayurvedic medicine of India, chiropractic care, psychotherapy and hydrotherapy, private meditation classes, and saunas. A tea bar, import shop, and a regularly changing schedule of classes and events round out the Om Center's wide array of offerings.

### Fitness Centers & Spas

## HYP YOGA WEIGHT LOSS & HEALTH CENTER
**13512 W. Center Rd., Omaha**
**(402) 933-7401**
**www.hyweightloss.com**
A melding of hypnosis and yoga with a focus on weight loss goals, Hyp-Yoga was invented by three Omaha women and has become a national phenomenon, featured in *Self Magazine, Ladies Home Journal,* and *Woman's Day.* Great for beginners to yoga, the program is a gentle introduction to the activity and includes a session of hypnosis at the end of each class that taps into the subconscious to change behaviors in the conscious mind—emotional eating is one of the main things the class tackles.

A Hyp-Yoga class comes with a manual and DVD that lets students continue the workout on their own schedule. If weight loss isn't a goal, the class can also be used to achieve other changes, including stress release, living presently, increasing energy, improving sleeping, and quitting smoking, among many other issues.

## PINNACLE CLUB
2027 Dodge St., Omaha
(402) 342-2582
www.pinnacleclubomaha.com
Located in downtown Omaha, the Pinnacle Club is popular with downtown Omaha residents. Corporate discounts, lots of parking, cleanliness, and a knowledgeable staff help Pinnacle maintain its popularity. Facilities include a 25-yard lap pool, sauna and Jacuzzi, an indoor track, group exercise classes, a variety of equipment and a weight circuit, and a number of other pieces of exercise equipment. Though the club has a Dodge Street address, it is on the lower level of a building and is not visible from street level.

## PRAIRIE LIFE FITNESS CENTER
www.prairielife.com
With a number of locations around Lincoln and Omaha, Prairie Life is an Nebraska-owned and -operated fitness club that has nine locations in four Midwestern states. More than 30,000 members exercise at this high-end fitness center, and the club offers programs, activities, and classes for all age and ability levels. The first center opened in Lincoln in 1985 (Former Nebraska Congressman Bob Kerrey was one of the two founders) and the second club opened in Omaha five years later. Offerings include aerobics, indoor and outdoor swimming, weight lifting, indoor jogging, an array of exercise classes, a nursery and child care facility, and lots of programs for youth.

# MEDIA

## Newspapers

### DAILY NEBRASKAN
12th and R Streets, Lincoln
(402) 472-2588
www.dailynebraskan.com
The *Daily Nebraskan* is the independent student newspaper of the University of Nebraska–Lincoln and is published every school day during the regular school year and weekly during the summer. It's staffed completely by UNL students and has a paid staff of advisers as well as a publications board comprised of journalism professionals from the college and community.

### LINCOLN JOURNAL STAR
926 P St., Lincoln
(402) 475-4200
www.journalstar.com
The capital city's daily newspaper, the *Journal Star* came into being when the two major dailies—the *Lincoln Journal* and the *Lincoln Star*—merged in 1995. The morning paper is now owned by Lee Enterprises, and it's the most read paper in the city. Its circulation now is close to 80,000 and it circulates in a number of surrounding southeast Nebraska towns.

### MIDLANDS BUSINESS JOURNAL
1324 S. 119th St., Omaha
(402) 330-1760
www.mbj.com
Since 1975 the *Midlands Business Journal* has been operating weekly to report on local businesses and owners. Twice monthly, they publish the *Lincoln Business Journal,* and the

newspaper's annual "Forty under Forty" is one of its most popular issues.

### THE OMAHA READER
**2314 M St., Omaha**
**(402) 341-7323**
**www.thereader.com**
Omaha's largest and longest running independent newsweekly, the *Reader* covers local news, arts, music, theater, and happenings. The free newsweekly is widely available throughout Omaha and on a limited basis in Lincoln.

### THE OMAHA STAR
**2216 N. 24th St., Omaha**
**(402) 346-2121**
**www.omahastarinc.com**
Founded in 1938, the *Omaha Star* is the area's only African American newspaper. It's been publishing for more than 70 years and has a circulation of about 30,000. Mildred Brown founded the newspaper in 1938, and she's the first African American woman to found a newspaper in the state's—possibly the nation's—history. Brown died in 1989 and her niece, Marguerita Washington, took over the paper, which is now available at a number of locations throughout North and central Omaha.

### OMAHA WORLD-HERALD
**14th and Douglas Streets, Omaha**
**(402) 444-1000**
**www.omaha.com**
The *World-Herald* is the state's largest paper and the area's most relied-upon daily source of news. Founded in 1885 by Gilbert M. Hitchcock, the paper circulates through most of the state of Nebraska and a large portion of southwest Iowa. Throughout the life of the newspaper, it's remained locally

owned and it's been employee-owned since 1979; it's the largest employee-owned paper in the United States. The newspaper's headquarters are in downtown Omaha, as is its state-of-the-art printing facility, which includes three presses that print five editions every day. The paper features five sections daily: main news, midlands news, living, sports, and money. On Thursday, it prints a special entertainment section, Go, and the Friday edition features an especially popular local food review.

## Local Magazines

### FAMILY SPECTRUM MAGAZINE
**www.familyspectrum.com**
*Family Spectrum* goes home with every student in the Omaha Public Schools. The publication focuses on stories affecting Omaha families and parents, and has an active blog, a partnership with KGBI radio, and an online version of the magazine available for download. It recently became available for home delivery; subscription options are available on its website.

### FOOD & SPIRITS MAGAZINE
**www.fsmomaha.com**
A monthly publication focused on food, dining, and wine, *Food & Spirits* invites local writers to contribute interviews, question and answer pieces, reviews of restaurants, and previews of places yet to open. The free publication is distributed widely through Omaha, and also includes an active blog attached to its website.

### L MAGAZINE
**926 P St., Lincoln**
**(402) 473-7113**
Lincoln's premier social magazine is managed by the *Lincoln Journal Star* and comes

out on a monthly basis. It focuses on fund-raising activities and features popular articles on local society, restaurants, and an extensive events calendar of charity and fundraising events.

## *METRO* MAGAZINE
**www.spiritofomaha.com**
*Metro Magazine* is a free lifestyle, fashion, and event-centric magazine focused on dining, entertainment, and happenings around Omaha. The magazine regularly profiles local "movers and shakers" and has a number of society pages featuring charity events near the back. Its website focuses on articles from the magazine and also includes an extensive events calendar.

## OMAHA PUBLICATIONS
**5921 S. 118th Circle, Omaha**
**(402) 884-2000**
**omahapublications.com**
Though *Omaha Magazine* is the flagship publication of Omaha Publications, it also publishes a number of other local, free magazines that are widely circulated around the city, including *B2B, Her, The Encounter,* and *Physician's Bulletin.* All the magazines are widely available, and each has a focus that ties in with its title. *Omaha Magazine* is circulated through more than 100,000 Omaha households, and comes out six times a year. It's also available for purchase at grocery stores around town.

## Radio Stations

### *FM Stations*
**KMLV 88.1**
Contemporary Christian music
**KYFG 88.9**
Spirit Catholic radio

**89.7 KIWR**
College/alternative
**90.7 KVNO**
Classical
**91.5 KIOS**
Omaha Public Radio, NPR affiliate, jazz
**92.3 KEZO**
Rock
**92.7 K224**
Christian
**93.3 KTWI**
Classic country
**93.7 KBUL**
Mav radio
**94.1 KQCH**
Top 40
**96.1 KQBW**
Classic rock
**97.3 KBLR**
Country
**97.7 KBBX**
Spanish
**98.5 KQKQ**
Rock
**99.9 KGOR**
Classic rock
**100.7 KGBI**
Contemporary Christian
**101.9 KOOO**
Adult contemporary
**102.7 KVSS**
Catholic radio
**103.7 KXKT**
Country
**104.5 KSRZ**
80s, 90s, and today
**105.5 KFMT**
Classic rock
**105.9 KKCD**
Classic rock
**106.9 KOPW**
Hip hop

**KCUV FM 91.1**
NPR
**KZUM FM 89.3**
Local independent radio

### *AM Stations*
KFAB AM 1110
KKAR AM 1290
KOZN AM 1620
KXSP AM 590

### Television Stations

KMTV CBS Ch. 3
WOWT NBC Ch. 6
KETV ABC Ch. 7
KYNE PBS Ch. 26
NET Television
KPTM Fox Ch. 42
KFXL Fox Ch. 4 (Lincoln)
KLKN ABC Ch. 8
KOLN CBS Ch. 10
KUON PBS Ch. 12

# INDEX

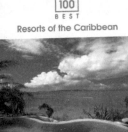

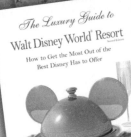

# INSIDERS' GUIDE ®

**The acclaimed travel series that has sold more than 2 million copies!**

## Discover: Your Travel Destination.
## Your Home. Your Home-to-Be.

**To order call 800-243-0495
or visit www.Insiders.com**